The 15 Steps To Profitable YouTube Marketing

The World's Leading Guide To Building Money-Making YouTube Ad Campaigns

By Daniel Rose

The 15 Steps

YouTube: The World's Most Powerful Money-Making, Brand-Building Marketing Platform 5

How I Went From Broke Loser To Running A Multi-Million Dollar Company By Using YouTube Marketing 13

Step 1: Learn The Ten Most Common Mistakes That Could Cause You To Lose Money With YouTube Marketing 24

Step 2: Create A Brilliant Idea For Your YouTube Marketing Campaign 57

Step 3: Create Your First Content Video, And Set A Regular Upload Schedule 87

Step 4: Learn The Universal "Master Formula" For Creating Killer YouTube Ad Scripts 119

Step 5: Film And Edit Your First Batch Of Ads 169

Step 6: Create A Website Designed To Convert Your YouTube Traffic Into Cash 197

Step 7: Set Up Your Google Ads Account, And Create Your Remarketing Campaigns 235

Step 8: Learn The Targeting Ladder, And Start Your First InStream Cold Traffic Campaign 267

Step 9: Start Your First Video Discovery Cold Traffic Campaign ..295

Step 10: Learn The Ten Pillars Of Great Ad Management 322

Step 11: Take Your Creative To The Next Level With Advanced Ad Formulas 373

Step 12: Expand Your Campaigns With My 13 Advanced Google Ads Strategies 397

Step 13: Learn The Top Ten Ways To Take Your YouTube Sales Website To The Next Level 431

Step 14: Build A Valuable, Long-Lasting Brand With The Four Pillars Of Modern Branding 465

Step 15: Find The Perfect People To Help You Scale Up Your Campaigns 495

How We Can Work Together 527

THE END? 537

YouTube: The World's Most Powerful Money-Making, Brand-Building Marketing Platform

Nine Years Ago, on This Day...

A sick feeling of fear surged through my body as I stared at my bank account balance on the screen. I stopped breathing momentarily. My heart started beating faster in panic. I was *overdrawn — again.*

Staring at the multi-thousand dollar negative balance in my checking account, I thought about how Christmas was less than a month away — and I still hadn't bought my daughter anything yet. How could I possibly tell my four-year-old that I couldn't afford to buy her any presents this year?

How was I going to pay our rent at the end of the month?

I lowered my head onto my computer desk in defeat, ready to give up.

My Present Day Reality

Fast forward nine years later, and this moment barely seems real to me.

After building a company which made hundreds of millions of dollars in revenue — and then selling it — I now live a lifestyle of freedom and abundance.

I wake up when I want, I buy what I want, and I only work on projects that I enjoy. I drive the car I've always dreamed of driving – and I've enjoyed many of the vacations I've always wanted to take.

I have an investment portfolio that ensures my family and I will never experience the fear of going broke again.

And to top it all off, I share an amazing home with the woman of my dreams.

What changed everything for me?

In two words: *YouTube Marketing.*

How Learning YouTube Marketing Skills Will Change Your Life

I believe that YouTube is the single most powerful money-making and brand-building platform in the world. And I'd like to congratulate you on being smart enough to recognize how important it is — and for making the investment in this book.

You've made a great decision to give yourself an "edge" in YouTube advertising. One day I believe you'll look back on reading this book as one of the best decisions you've ever made.

If you're reading this, you already know that YouTube advertising represents a huge money-making opportunity. But in the next few chapters, I'll show you why YouTube is the BIGGEST opportunity for business owners like us — and why you need to go "all in" investing your time and money into YouTube ads.

But obviously, you can't just start blowing thousands on YouTube ads without knowing what you're doing. This just leads to losses, tragedy, and failure. Unfortunately, I've seen it happen to far too many business owners.

That's why you need to dedicate yourself to mastering the all-important skill of creating money-generating, brand-building YouTube ad campaigns.

I personally wasted hundreds of thousands of dollars on unprofitable YouTube campaigns in my early years. And if you start advertising on YouTube without knowing what you're doing, you are going to lose a lot of money — *fast.*

But losing money will actually be the LEAST of your problems…

If you advertise on YouTube without knowing what you're doing, you'll end up wasting hundreds of hours creating weak ads and managing money-losing campaigns. And if you repeatedly fail to create profitable YouTube campaigns, it could fatally damage your confidence — and permanently kill your entrepreneurial dreams.

But by investing in your YouTube advertising skills through this book, you've given yourself a HUGE advantage.

After reading just a few chapters, you'll **immediately feel a surge of confidence** knowing that you have a leg up on the masses of uneducated advertisers. You'll know that *you can do this* — and you'll start thinking big about the success you can create.

Once you've mastered YouTube advertising, you'll be able to create profitable ad campaigns quickly, simply, and inexpensively. You can then reinvest your profits into scaling your campaigns up. Over time, you can parlay a small initial investment into a massive return. Just like I did myself, and just like hundreds of other entrepreneurs have done.

And if you have a business that's overly dependent on Facebook/Instagram, or any other single advertising platform, you'll be able to quickly build a second revenue source. And having two significant sources of revenue could save your ass if you ever get suspended or experience problems with your main ad platform. Even if the worst never happens, you'll have more profits, more stability in your business, and you'll be building more long-term equity value for your business.

YouTube advertising might even be your path to one day selling your company for millions of dollars. Many other people have done it, and there's no reason why you can't as well.

But here's the single most important reason why every business owner needs to dedicate themselves to YouTube advertising…

YouTube isn't just *one* of the biggest advertising platforms today — it represents THE FUTURE of online marketing. I guarantee you that ten years from now, not only will YouTube still be around — it will grow exponentially bigger. It will be far more important as an advertising platform than it is today.

While Facebook, Instagram, Google Search, and other ad platforms are also big opportunities, most successful business owners agree that YouTube is the biggest opportunity of them all.

This not only because YouTube has a virtual monopoly on long form video sharing today. It's also because future improvements in technology are going to make YouTube a far better marketing tool in the near future.

Right now, most people are streaming YouTube on their phones in a low resolution. Think about what will happen to YouTube when phones get better...when cellular bandwidth improves...and when the data centers and infrastructure that serve YouTube's videos improve.

It's obvious that technology will rapidly improve the video watching experience and increase consumption of YouTube videos. And this means more advertising opportunities for people like us.

But here's an even more important reason why YouTube represents the future of marketing...

YouTube advertising is managed through the world's most technologically advanced advertising platform – Google Ads.

Right now, it offers powerful targeting and optimization tools which are far beyond what any other platform has. This back-end ad management technology will improve exponentially every year, just like video serving technology does. And this makes YouTube a MUCH BIGGER opportunity than you'd think just by looking at the side of it that consumers see.

These are just a few of the reasons why YouTube represents the future of marketing – I'll discuss many more later in this book. But here's the bottom line:

You need to jump on the YouTube money train before you are left behind. Once you do, you can surf the wave of YouTube's exponential user growth and ever-improving ad technology to carry your business to success.

How You'll Master YouTube Marketing By Following A Series Of Simple Steps

So how am I going to take you from where you are now, to running money-printing, brand-building ad campaigns?

First, I am going to remove your limiting beliefs. These are "common sense" things that most people think are true about YouTube advertising, which are actually destroying your chances of success.

The first step — BEFORE you learn what to do with YouTube advertising — is to learn what NOT to do. Once you know the potentially fatal mistakes to avoid, and you've uninstalled the "common sense" beliefs that could sabotage you, you'll be primed to start your journey to YouTube advertising mastery.

Once I've removed your limiting beliefs, I am going to walk you through the exact 15 step process that I used to build the business and the life of my dreams with YouTube marketing.

Most marketing books dump a bunch of knowledge on you, and then expect YOU to figure out how to implement what you learned, and what order to implement the new techniques in.

That's a recipe for failure. This book will be the exact opposite.

That's because I've learned from working with many clients that breaking the process of mastering YouTube advertising down into a series of simple steps has a MUCH higher success rate.

This is for three simple reasons…

First, you can use this book to start making money with YouTube BEFORE you've fully mastered YouTube advertising — and before you've even fully finished reading the book! With just the basic skills I teach in the first few chapters, you can start running small-scale campaigns. Not only will these campaigns make you money, they'll also build your confidence and get you excited to do more.

Breaking the process down into simple steps will also make learning YouTube marketing much easier. You won't ever feel overwhelmed or confused, even if you're totally new to online advertising.

And finally, you'll be implementing the techniques you learn in THE RIGHT ORDER. And this makes a huge difference!

For example, if you first learn about advanced ad targeting options, but you don't know how to create a basic video ad, there will be months where your targeting skills atrophy and are not used. By the time you finally learn how to create an ad and start running it, you may have forgotten what you learned about targeting.

That's why this book won't just teach you YouTube marketing skills. It will also show you exactly the right order to learn the skills in. This series of steps to learn YouTube marketing has been honed based on my experience teaching many different clients.

I've designed this book to be useful to YouTube advertisers of all skill levels — whether you're an entrepreneur who knows nothing about YouTube advertising right now, or if you're an experienced YouTube marketing executive managing a multi-million dollar ad budget.

If you are totally new to YouTube advertising, you should read this book thoroughly from cover to cover. I recommend implementing the steps in exactly the order I describe. Don't skip anything, and make sure you IMPLEMENT the action steps I give you at the end of each chapter before moving on to the next chapter.

If you're an experienced advertiser, you can feel free to quickly skim through the chapters which cover basics you already know, or things that don't apply to you. For example, if you're already committed to a business, you can skim through Step #2, which is about how to choose a profitable business niche for YouTube advertising.

I'm not a novelist or a sensitive artisté, and I won't get offended if you quickly skim through the parts of the book that don't apply to you. I just want to get you making money with YouTube advertising as quickly and simply as possible.

How To Get The Most Out Of This Book

Since I sold SixPackAbs.com, I've consulted with many different entrepreneurs and established companies. I've also spoken about YouTube advertising at many different business events. And I've found that the clients who get the most out of what I teach all have one thing in common:

THEY IMPLEMENT WHAT THEY LEARN RIGHT AWAY, WHILE IT'S FRESH IN THEIR MINDS!

That's why I've included Action Steps at the end of each chapter. They aren't suggestions, or things you should "think" about doing. They're what you NEED to focus on first, before implementing anything from the next chapters.

It's perfectly OK to read this book through normally your first time through to get an understanding of how my YouTube marketing method works. But after you do that, you should re-read one chapter at a time, and implement ALL of the action steps I give you at the end before moving onto the next chapter.

I'll make the process of creating profitable YouTube ads as simple as possible, but you'll need to commit to learning the skills and doing the work to get results from this book.

And I promise you, it will all be worth it. You can use these skills to make immediate profits, to build a business you can sell, and to make your dream lifestyle happen.

That's exactly what hundreds of other people like you have done with YouTube marketing, and it's what I've done myself.

After selling my company, I'm now living a lifestyle of wealth, freedom, security, and happiness that I never thought I'd experience.

But it wasn't always this way. In fact, I think you'll be shocked to discover exactly how I started advertising on YouTube nine years ago...

How I Went From Broke Loser To Running A Multi-Million Dollar Company By Using YouTube Marketing

PLUS: The Seven YouTube Marketing Lessons You Can Take Away From My Experience

---

Nine years ago, I was broke, depressed, and directionless.

I was living in a dingy, cheap studio apartment. It was all I could afford. I had no car, and my only way of getting around was a beat up old bicycle.

I'd just been laid off. The company that I worked for went out of business, and I was struggling to generate income doing affiliate marketing (selling products online for a commission for other businesses.)

It was boring, grinding, purposeless work — but I was desperate to generate money any way I could to support my family.

Strangely enough, the moment everything started to change for me was when a friend introduced me to...his personal trainer.

This guy was an expert in fitness, but he didn't know the first thing about running a business or marketing on YouTube.

Over the next few months, we became better friends and I got in much better shape using his advice. I gained muscle, lost fat, and began feeling more energetic and less depressed. I got better results with his unique approach to working out than anything I'd ever tried before.

And eventually the thought hit me that...*other people would tremendously benefit from what my trainer taught me if I could just put my trainer's knowledge online.*

KEY LESSON #1: If you get tremendous value from a product or service but it's poorly marketed and only available locally, it could represent a huge opportunity for YouTube advertising!

For a few months, it was just idle talk.

What led us to get serious about it? Of all things, a salsa dancing party.

I personally despise salsa dancing, and my trainer did as well.

So, while everyone else danced, we sat around drinking vodka and watching YouTube videos on our phones.

And that's when we found something that seemed laughable at first — but which led to the realization that changed everything.

After searching around for videos on many different fitness topics, we noticed that videos about getting six pack abs were getting ABSURD amounts of views. And the videos about getting abs on YouTube back in 2009 were absolutely HORRIBLE quality!

For example, a video of a girl drawing six pack abs on herself with a marker had over ten million views.

A grainy video of an overweight guy doing a terrible ab workout on his couch had over fifteen million views.

My trainer had chiseled abs himself, and I knew firsthand his ab workouts were excellent. And I thought...*we can make something far better than any of the ab workouts on YouTube right now and help millions of people.*

_KEY LESSON #2__: If you see poor quality videos about a certain product or service getting huge amounts of views on YouTube, this is a sign it could be a great business opportunity for you!_

So right then and there, we decided to make this the focus of our company.

I was broke, so I couldn't afford to pay my trainer anything to make videos for me. But he agreed to come on board when I promised him a significant equity stake in the company.

_KEY LESSON #3__: Even if you're not interested in being on camera yourself, there are many people who are truly extraordinary on camera who need skilled marketers like us. And even if you're dead broke right now, you can often get skilled on-camera talent to partner with you by giving them an equity stake (minority ownership) of your company._

We spent the next few months creating a course which taught men how to eat and exercise to get six pack abs. We called it "Six Pack Shortcuts," because our program was the fastest way for men to lose their belly fat and get six pack abs.

To get exposure and market our program, we made a few workout videos and uploaded them to YouTube, Facebook, and a few other platforms.

And we were shocked when after a month, one of our videos had gotten over ten thousand views!

Those were INSANE numbers for us back when we first started our business. We never thought that many people would ever watch our videos. And we also discovered that almost all of our meager sales — a few hundred dollars a week — were coming from this one YouTube video.

So, we decided to go "all in" on YouTube. We focused everything we could on it for the first few years of our business.

KEY LESSON #4: If a video about a certain product or service you offer takes off on YouTube, go ALL IN and put as much of your focus on growing your YouTube sales as you can until you have a big team. Be smart enough to recognize how huge the opportunity could be!

But that was just the beginning. The magic REALLY started to happen when I started advertising our YouTube videos...

The first ad I made was embarrassingly bad. It was nothing but a grainy screen capture video of myself flipping through a PowerPoint presentation, with some music in the background.

There was nobody on camera, and there wasn't even a voice reading the words. My PowerPoint slides were basic, ugly, and had multiple typos in them.

I started running the ad without high expectations...but shockingly enough, the ad actually started bringing in a small amount of sales and profit the very first week!

Today, I know that this was because the MESSAGE in our ad connected with customers...and customers will overlook poor video production if you can get your message dialed in well enough.

KEY LESSON #5: The most important part of building a profitable ad campaign is your MARKETING MESSAGE — promising the right benefit to the right person, and being able to prove that you can deliver. Marketers who craft a great message can make even the most basic of video ads profitable.

Even though I was only making a few hundred dollars a week in profit from my campaigns, it was enough for me to see the potential. I knew that if the data showed our ads were profitable on a very small scale, it was very likely they'd still be profitable if I increased our campaign budgets.

But there was just one problem.

With our tiny budget, Google didn't give us 30 days to pay like they do for large advertisers. They required that I pay them immediately for the ads I ran. And I didn't have enough money in my bank account to spend more.

I asked my trainer if he'd be willing to invest some money for more equity, but he was even broker than I was. He'd also just defaulted on a huge amount of real estate debt, so he couldn't get any credit.

So, I took a calculated risk — a risk that seemed shockingly reckless to most non-marketers.

I decided to finance our ad spend by taking out personal credit card debt. But my income was tiny and my credit was bad.

Because of this, I couldn't get approved for a high limit.

So, I filled out a bunch of credit card applications, where I exaggerated (lied) about my income. And I got approved for three personal credit cards, with limits of around $5,000.

Armed with my new cards, I scaled my campaigns up...and the profits continued to roll in!

_KEY LESSON #6__: If you can make your campaigns profitable on a small scale, they'll probably continue to be profitable if you scale up. That means if you increase your spend ten times as much on advertising, you'll make ten times as much profit! That's why I was confident enough to put my ad spend on credit cards and risk personal bankruptcy._

I don't recommend ever using personal credit cards to finance a business if you can avoid it . But I DO recommend aggressively "doubling down" on your initial investment in YouTube ads if you see encouraging initial results.

I started off spending just $10/day on YouTube advertising. Over the next few months that became $50/day...then $100...then eventually $1,000/day. And my trainer and I were making an incredible ROI. Plus, we were acquiring tons of paying customers for our monthly membership program.

Because the ads were so profitable, I was able to scale up our campaigns shockingly fast. Within a few months, I was spending over $20,000 a day on ads, AND making a multiple of this back in profits. And our advertising spend, and our sales just kept growing from here.

But this wasn't the only benefit of our advertising...

In addition to making huge direct profits, our YouTube views and subscriber base exploded in growth. Before I started my campaigns, we would usually get a few thousand views per video, and a few dozen new subscribers a day.

After I started advertising at scale, it became common for us to gain *thousands* of subscribers every day, and to get *millions* of views on each video. Not just for the commercials I was buying views for, but for my trainer's unadvertised content videos too.

Our little company we were running out of my apartment now had millions of people around the world watching our channel. Six Pack Shortcuts was becoming an internationally recognized brand — and my trainer was fast becoming a social media celebrity. Soon, investors were approaching us to ask if we'd be interested in selling a piece of our company.

KEY LESSON #7: When you use the RIGHT kind of YouTube marketing, you can make a measurable, direct, and immediate profit from your ads. AND you can massively build your YouTube channel's subscribers and views at the same time! You'll also be building a valuable brand, which is the key to an enduring business. It's also the key to one day being able to sell your company for a big payout.

I refer to this new style of marketing as "Social Response Marketing," because it's designed to make you a direct response profit while building your social engagement.

And the rest, as they say...is history.

I started hiring more employees to support our exploding YouTube sales. We eventually moved the company into a bigger apartment, then a real office, then eventually a much bigger and nicer office.

Eventually my first trainer decided he wanted to travel the world, and he left the business. He was sorely missed, and for a few months our business declined as I struggled to find a new spokesman. But I eventually found three great new trainers to create a new Six Pack Shortcuts product with, and our company started growing again.

A few months later, I hired a 54 year old trainer to take advantage of a huge market opportunity I saw helping men over 40 improve their health. I eventually hired two more older trainers, a younger trainer who focused on intermittent fasting, a female trainer, and many other assistant trainers and nutritionists to help us break into new markets.

Over the next few years, I continued scaling our YouTube campaigns up as aggressively as we could. And while we focused intensively on YouTube in the beginning, we eventually started advertising heavily on the Google Display Network, Google Search, Facebook, Instagram, and other ad networks.

By this time, it was hard for me to believe how far the little company I'd started in my apartment had come. We had a small army of people working for us in our office. And we were making more in profit every month than I used to make in a year!

After almost nine years of running the company, I negotiated a deal with an investor group to sell SixPackAbs.com, along with the other brands and assets of my companies. It was a long and difficult negotiation. But once the deal was done, it felt amazing to receive the payout and to have total freedom again after so many years of hard work.

I took a few months off to travel and spend time with my family. I thought about retiring and simply living off the earnings from my investment portfolio, since I had enough to live comfortably without having to work for the rest of my life.

But after a few months of relaxing, I knew there was something more meaningful that I had to do.

Learning how to create profitable, brand-building YouTube marketing changed my life. It was the critical skill that took me from being a broke loser to being a millionaire. And I knew it had the power to change many other struggling business owners' lives as well.

I knew there was much more I had to accomplish — and a more impactful business that I had the potential to build.

And that's why I'm writing this to you today. I want you to learn from my experiences, so you can use your YouTube marketing skills to achieve your dreams.

And it all begins in the next chapter…

Over the years, I've made a huge number of MISTAKES with YouTube advertising which have cost me millions of dollars in lost profits. These mistakes usually came from adopting beliefs which seemed to be "common sense," but which were actually sabotaging my success.

In the next chapter, I'm going to break down exactly what the ten most common — and most deadly — mistakes I've seen clients make with YouTube marketing are.

This next chapter could save you millions over your career — and it will prime your brain to learn my step-by-step method to creating YouTube profits.

So pay close attention. And when you're reflecting back on this in a few years from your yacht or private jet, you'll be glad you did!

Step 1: Learn The Ten Most Common Mistakes That Could Cause You To Lose Money With YouTube Marketing

Why are so few people making big profits from YouTube advertising, even though it's a huge opportunity? It's usually because they're making one of ten very common mistakes.

This chapter will teach you exactly what the mistakes are and how you can avoid them. Read this chapter carefully, because avoiding these mistakes could save you millions of dollars over your career.

I've met many people who have seen my ads on the internet and who are familiar with the growth of Six Pack Shortcuts / SixPackAbs.com. To most of them, it seems like my last business was smooth sailing straight to the top with steadily increasing profits week after week.

Unfortunately, that wasn't the case. I'll be the first to admit that I've made my share of stupid mistakes advertising on YouTube — *especially* in my early years.

These mistakes have literally cost me millions of dollars and caused me some serious stress. For example, I once lost over twenty thousand dollars in a single day — simply because I accidentally clicked on the wrong targeting setting in Google Ads.

Fortunately, I've learned from the school of hard knocks what the most important things to avoid doing are if you want to create successful YouTube campaigns. And my clients have tremendously benefited from that knowledge.

I've consulted with many different clients, from solo entrepreneurs to large corporate brands. And I've found that there are some very common mistakes that many of them are making which hold them back from making their YouTube campaigns profitable. Many of my biggest early improvements to these clients' accounts simply came from correcting these mistakes.

My goal is for you is to learn the mistakes to avoid from reading this chapter — not the hard way, through losing money and damaging your brand. You'll cut years off your learning curve and get to the promised land of profitable advertising much faster.

Mistake #1 — Listening To Social Media Experts

I'm going to piss a lot of people off with this one — but it's true, and it needs to be said.

The vast majority of "social media experts" out there are total frauds. And listening to advice from these so-called "experts" is not only worthless, it can severely damage your business — ESPECIALLY when it comes to YouTube marketing.

And this is painfully obvious if you do a little basic research rather than just taking the "gurus" on faith.

The easiest way to tell if an "expert" knows what he's talking about is to simply check out the public YouTube subscriber and view counts on the channels he's built.

Anyone who knows what they're doing with YouTube ads — or even just with making organic content — will have a highly subscribed, highly viewed channel to show for it.

If the "expert" has less than ten thousand subscribers — or less than a million views on their channel — you can safely dismiss their YouTube marketing advice. Anyone who is truly an expert will be able to build a MUCH bigger channel than this.

Of course, they may have large followings on other platforms and they may in fact be bona fide experts on other platforms.

But if an "expert" doesn't even have ten thousand subscribers on YouTube, they're unlikely to be able to teach you YouTube marketing. Even if their content was mediocre, they could get more than ten thousand subscribers just by buying a small amount of well-managed advertising.

Of course, YouTube subscriber count isn't the ONLY thing you should be looking at to decide if an expert is legit. But by simply looking at subscriber and view counts on an expert's channel, you can quickly eliminate 95% of the junk advice out there.

Now, here's one caveat: when evaluating a social media expert, make sure you look for the channels they've built for ALL of their businesses — not only for their social media training business.

For example, I'm writing this book a few months after my exit from my last company. At the time of this writing, I have very few YouTube subscribers and views on my new channel myself.

However, I have a track record of building channels with over five million subscribers with SixPackAbs.com — and I also have testimonials from many clients who I've helped build large channels as well. And if you find others with a track record of building big channels outside their marketing advice business, I'd recommend you listen to their advice too!

Having a highly subscribed channel is important, but the end goal of YouTube marketing isn't just to build a channel. It's to make profits and build a brand. So, you need to make sure that any experts you listen to have a track record of doing those things in addition to having subscribers.

You might think it's impossible to tell how much someone is making from YouTube marketing, or to assess how much their brand is worth. But there is actually a surprisingly easy way to estimate it.

If you see multiple different ads from an advertiser with millions of views, chances are that they are a real YouTube Marketing expert.

That's because most advertisers don't have a trust fund of money to buy money-losing advertising with. Virtually everyone advertising on a large scale can do so only because their advertising is profitable. If you are spending one dollar and making two back, you can get millions of views from advertising and essentially get paid to do so. But if you are spending a dollar and making ninety cents back, buying millions of views becomes impossible.

View counts are not publicly visible on all YouTube ads, but you can see them for Video Discovery ads (not the skippable ads, but the ads you click on next to or below the video you're watching). Many advertisers also just publicly post their most highly viewed commercials to their channel.

So, if you have the opportunity to get advice from someone who has a commercial with millions of views, make sure you listen closely! I know I do myself.

And if you hear advice from someone whose ads only receive a few hundred views — or even worse, someone who's buying no advertising at all — make sure you tune them out.

Finally, you should make sure that any YouTube advertising experts you listen to have a track record of building a valuable brand. Of course, it's great to make immediate profits and get lots of subscribers — but in my opinion, the ultimate level of success with YouTube advertising is building a brand you can sell, or a lifestyle business you love that lasts for decades.

The easiest way to tell if someone has done this is to see if they've sold a company based on YouTube advertising in the past. Company sales are usually public knowledge, and they're nearly impossible to fake.

Another way to tell is if someone has built iconic, nationally recognized brand names that have become the clear leaders in their industries, and embedded in our culture.

One example of this is the Harmon Brothers ad agency.

They're the ones who created the Squatty Potty mega-hit ad — the one with the unicorn that poops ice cream that received over thirty million views. Before this ad, Squatty Potty was an obscure toilet stool company that nobody had heard of. Now, they have a company they could easily sell for millions if they wanted to.

Harmon Brothers has done this over and over again with many different brands — Purple, ClickFunnels, Chatbooks, Orabrush, and more. So, it's safe to say they know what they're talking about when it comes to this YouTube marketing thing.

That's why running a campaign with them costs half a million dollars at the minimum, and multiple millions for most of their clients. I got this quote from them years ago, and it's probably much more expensive now.

It's also why when Jeff Harmon (one of the founders of Harmon Brothers) gave a rare talk at an Internet Marketing event, I made sure I was in the front row taking notes.

So, there ARE legit YouTube marketing experts out there. They are just hard to find, expensive to hire, and rare. And they are usually running a multi-million dollar company — not teaching YouTube marketing.

Now that you know quick and effective ways to recognize fraudulent social media advertising gurus, you'll know how to protect yourself against potentially dangerous advice. And when you do have the chance to learn from someone with a proven track record of success on YouTube, you'll be smart enough to take the opportunity to learn everything you can from them.

Mistake #2 — Spreading Your Resources Too Thin, And Not Understanding The Power Of Focus

If you are a huge corporation, you should absolutely be advertising on every major platform — YouTube, Google Search, Facebook, Instagram, Twitter...maybe even TV and radio.

But if you are an entrepreneur running a company making less than a million dollars a year in revenue, advertising on every platform is a HUGE mistake.

If you think about it from your perspective as a business owner, it doesn't seem to make sense. But if you flip the script and think about it from your CUSTOMER'S perspective, it makes a ton of sense.

When you're browsing YouTube as a viewer and potential customer, and you're looking for a channel to teach you something, what do you do?

Do you look for the BEST channel on the topic you're interested in? Or would the 3rd best, or 9th best be just as good?

Of course, when we're the customer we want to follow the BEST channel. We might also watch some videos from the 2nd or 3rd best, but the best channel we find will get the lion's share of our attention.

The same thing goes for how we assess ads. We usually buy from what we perceive to be the BEST company, and also-ran companies usually get their ads skipped.

But how do customers determine which channel or which advertiser is the best?

Like most people, I used to believe that people logically assessed a few different channels and made a rational decision based on which one was best for their needs. Later, I believed it they would follow the channel or buy from the advertiser that was the most entertaining.

Both of these ideas are mostly wrong. But I didn't realize it until I met my friend Adam Lyons about seven years ago.

Adam is one of the top experts in psychology in the world, as well as one of the world's top dating coaches. He taught me something that was critical to our growth in the early years of my last business — and which you need to internalize as well.

Adam taught me that scientific studies have proved that while humans believe we make decisions independently, we actually base our opinions mostly on the opinions of people around us. For example, if women believe that other women find a man attractive, she'll be more likely to be attracted to him herself — and vice versa.

On YouTube, customers will assume the most popular channel is by default the best channel. They will also assume by default that the brand whose ads they see the most frequently is the best brand.

That is, UNLESS there is a major reason why they can see it's not right for them. Almost always, the channels with the most subscribers and the advertisers who they see most frequently will win. It's just human nature to always assume that what's most popular is also the best, UNLESS we can see a major, obvious reason why it's not right for us.

And YouTube's organic and advertising algorithms basically put this aspect of human nature on steroids.

As humans, we're all biologically wired to follow the crowd and believe the most popular channel is the best channel.

YouTube's algorithm for recommending related videos strongly reinforces this, because almost all the recommendations it serves up are from the most popular channels.

And YouTube's advertising algorithm — and their advertising policies — take this to the next level.

Later in this book, you'll learn why AUTOMATION is the future of advertising — and why companies that know how to use automated bidding and ad targeting will win. When you have them dialed in, these "Conversion Optimizer" campaigns can seem like magic — bringing in thousands a day in sales with little work required to maintain them.

But these Ad Automation algorithms work MUCH better if you are running a large campaign. They don't work nearly as well for small campaigns. These algorithms feed off of data, and the bigger your ad campaign is, the better the automation works.

This creates a strong "winner take all" effect with YouTube advertising. The highest spending advertiser in a certain market will be taking home many times the sales and profit than the also-ran advertisers.

Not only this, but if you are one of the largest advertisers in your market, Google (YouTube's parent company) will give you much better customer service than if you are an also-ran.

You'll get your own rep who helps you grow your campaigns, and you'll also have an easier time fixing ad policy problems that frustrate smaller advertisers.

This is why most YouTube channels and YouTube marketing campaigns fail. When you're going up against a more popular competitor who has a bigger advertising budget, it's nearly impossible to win no matter what you do.

Now, I know this might sound discouraging if you are just starting off and are nowhere near the most popular channel in your market.

For example, let's say you're starting a fitness channel. How can you become the most popular, most advertised trainer on social media when other businesses already are spending millions on ads — and when they have millions of followers on every platform?

The brutal truth is that you can't. It's impossible.

You should give up on this losing strategy. Instead, use the same approach that I successfully used in the early days of the Six Pack Shortcuts channel.

When my trainer and I first started our channel, I recognized that we would never be able to compete by following the conventional approach of uploading videos on all fitness topics to all social media platforms. In the beginning, the company was just me, my trainer, and our laptops. Our funds were very limited. And admittedly, our work ethic was not the best.

So, we made two decisions which later proved to be very important:

First, we focused ONLY on YouTube in the early days of our business. While we had a page on Facebook, Twitter, etc., almost no attention went into those platforms — and we focused intensively on YouTube.

Second, we didn't upload videos on every fitness topic like most channels do. We focused very narrowly on teaching men to get six pack abs in the early days of our channel, and made most of our videos on that topic only.

We also made our product — and our advertising — heavily focused on getting six pack abs, and exclusively for men. It was extremely difficult to get my trainer to agree to focus our business down to such a narrow niche. But in hindsight, I'm very glad I fought for this.

By focusing on teaching men to get six pack abs, we totally changed customers' perspectives on us. Within a few months, we were able to get about 9,000 subscribers — which made us THE MOST POPULAR channel in our new, ultra-narrow category.

There were ZERO other YouTube advertisers selling a product teaching men how to get six pack abs back then. So, we were the highest spending advertiser in our category — right after spending our first dollar!

This is how you use the human nature and YouTube's algorithms that reinforce human nature to your advantage. You focus on ONE single social media platform — and you focus on a narrowly defined market niche. This gives you a realistic chance of becoming the most subscribed channel and the highest spending advertiser in your category within a year.

This seems counterintuitive to business owners. We naturally want to appeal to the widest possible audience, and it seems like we're limiting ourselves if we narrow ourselves down to a small niche on one single social media platform at first.

But in fact, this is not a valid concern at all. And here's why...

Once you've dominated a small niche, it's FAR easier to then take over a bigger, adjacent part of your industry.

For example, Mark Zuckerberg started by building Facebook into the most popular social network at Harvard. Then he expanded out, and Facebook became the most popular social network at Ivy League schools. Then they became the most popular social network at all colleges. Finally, Facebook dethroned MySpace and became the most popular social network for everyone.

THIS is how smart entrepreneurs take over industries, and dethrone entrenched competitors. They follow the Mark Zuckerberg blueprint of first taking over a tiny niche, then a bigger adjacent niche, and repeating this process until they dominate a massive industry.

Here's how I used this strategy for Six Pack Shortcuts...

Once we had ten times the subscribers and many times more advertising spend than any other six pack abs channel, we then set our sights on becoming the leader in men's fitness channels generally.

Once we became the leader in men's fitness, we expanded into other adjacent categories — fitness for 40+ men, intermittent fasting, the ketogenic diet, detoxification, and women's fitness.

If we had tried to do all this from Day 1, we would have failed miserably. But by establishing our "beachhead" in the tiny niche of teaching men to get six pack abs, we were later able to take over huge swathes of the YouTube fitness market.

So remember this:

Do not squander your time and money by sprinkling a little bit of resources everywhere, like rain over the ocean.

Focus intensively on YouTube, and focus your channel intensively on a niche you can dominate — and later use your category leadership to take over adjacent, bigger categories.

Mistake #3 — Having A "Quick Buck" Mentality — Not A Channel-Building And Re-Marketing Strategy

The single most common mistake I see new YouTube advertisers making is creating a few ads, spending a few thousand bucks advertising them on an empty channel, and then concluding that YouTube advertising "doesn't work" when they don't make an immediate profit.

Then they give up on YouTube. This is a tragedy, because YouTube advertising obviously DOES work, and IS working for thousands of different businesses.

They just failed at it because they followed a bad strategy.

And here's why this "quick buck" strategy doesn't work...

Buying habits on the internet have changed drastically from what they were 10-20 years ago. As consumers, we're more skeptical of advertising than we have ever been before. We've all been burned before, and we all want to know for sure that an advertised product is legit before buying it.

More than 90% of customers will not buy from the first ad they see. Typically, people will watch 5-10 different ads before buying. They'll also check out the organic (unadvertised, content-oriented) videos on your channel to verify your business is popular and trustworthy.

Think about your own behavior as a customer. Do you frequently see an ad on YouTube for a company you've never heard of, then whip your credit card out right away? Or do you usually only buy after seeing multiple ads, checking out other videos, checking out reviews, etc.?

On first glance, this reality of customer behavior seems discouraging.

But it's actually GREAT NEWS for those of us who understand it!

Why is this great news?

Because many YouTube advertisers will just focus on making ads, and will only make a minimal amount of crappy organic content videos for their channel. But now that you know the importance of an organic YouTube presence for advertising campaigns, you can differentiate yourself and make yourself more trustworthy to customers.

A great example of this is the Orabrush YouTube channel.

Watching the channels of most dental hygiene brands is more painful than having your teeth pulled — if there are any unadvertised content videos at all. Orabrush differentiates themselves by creating funny, educational content videos in an otherwise dull market.

Anyone who sees an Orabrush ad but is still a little skeptical can just check out their channel — where they'll see videos that are entertaining, but which also reinforce their sales message. They'll also see this weird little tongue scraper has a shockingly engaged community, and thousands of people in the comments talking about how great their product is.

If you can build a highly engaged channel like Orabrush, you'll have a huge advantage over other advertisers. ESPECIALLY if you're in a boring product category like dental hygiene where most advertisers have small subscriber bases and poor quality content.

The second reason why the skepticism of consumers works to our advantage is that you're going to learn advanced, ninja level "remarketing" strategies later in this book. For those of you who don't know, **remarketing is advertising targeted to people who have already visited your website, watched your YouTube videos, or subscribed to your email list.**

This means that once you've identified a great prospect, you can show them ads five...ten...or even twenty different times.

And not just the same ad over and over again. You can design a SEQUENCE of ads that will start with giving your potential customers value, and which gradually and naturally leads them into buying later in the sequence. And I'm going to give you three of my best strategies for doing this later in the book.

Most marketers don't put nearly enough effort into their remarketing campaigns because they underestimate how important they are. They repetitively show the same stale ads to the customer over and over again — if they are doing any remarketing at all. They don't know how to design a sequential campaign so customers see ads in the right order. And they don't know how to use the advanced "combination targeting" remarketing strategies that you're about to learn.

By putting together killer remarketing campaigns — and by having engaging organic videos on your channel — you'll differentiate yourself from other advertisers and set yourself up for success.

You won't come off like most marketers who seem like they're just looking for a quick financial "one night stand" with the customer. You'll be showing your customers — and the YouTube algorithms — that you genuinely want to help your customers, and that you want to have a long-term relationship with them. The YouTube algorithms and your customers will both reward you for this.

Mistake #4: Being Afraid To Spend Money On Advertising, And Thinking You Can Build A Business Based On Unadvertised Organic Videos Alone

There certainly have been some businesses that have been built on YouTube with zero advertising whatsoever. And this has led a lot of people to believe all they need to do to get rich on YouTube is put out great content, and you'll start getting subscribers and sales without needing to figure out this whole marketing thing.

After all, PewDiePie and other mega-stars did it...so why can't you do it too?

But there's a BIG PROBLEM with this line of thinking…

While there are many prominent examples of people who make tons of money on YouTube without buying a cent's worth of advertising, you are not seeing the huge graveyard of people who failed with this approach.

That's why I say that trying to make money from YouTube without advertising is like trying to get rich by buying lottery tickets. **Like playing the lottery, it is POSSIBLE to make money with this approach — and some people do. But it's not a good strategy because your odds of success are very low.**

But if you love making YouTube content and helping your viewers, there is some GOOD NEWS…

Having great organic content on your YouTube channel will give you a big advantage when you buy advertising. And when you add advertising to your YouTube strategy — even in small amounts to start with — it will massively improve your chances of success.

Here's some more good news: you now have a complete guide to creating great YouTube ads in your hands. You'll be able to create your first YouTube ads quickly and simply — even before you finish the entire book.

Once you know how to advertise, you can quickly create profits without having to wait years for your channel to organically grow. And these profits can fund making even better content for your subscribers.

The more you advertise; the more people will subscribe to your channel. YouTube has designed their advertising system this way. Their goal is for advertisers to develop a YouTube community in addition to making sales. And that's why I — and many other advertisers — love writing YouTube big checks for ads.

The simple truth is that ONLY making organic content for your channel, and ONLY making ads are both bad strategies. They might work — but the odds are not in your favor.

But you can stack the deck to your advantage by having BOTH good organic content and good ads.

It is absolutely worth the effort to learn how to do both. And in the long run, it's FAR less effort than struggling to make a one-dimensional YouTube strategy work.

Mistake #5 — Thinking That Being Good On Camera Is A Matter Of Talent Rather Than A Matter Of Practice

Many people never get started with YouTube because they think they don't have the talent to be on camera. Or they'll make a few videos, and then quit because their on-camera skills are nowhere near those of professional YouTubers.

But the truth is, being great on camera isn't a matter of talent.

Being great on camera is almost entirely a matter of practice — just like any other skill.

One great example of this is Joe Rogan. Joe is the host of the popular Joe Rogan Experience podcast, and he's also the color commentator for the Ultimate Fighting Championship.

He's one of the most popular creators on YouTube, and on many other platforms as well.

If you listen to Joe's podcasts or watch one of his UFC broadcasts today, you'd think he was born with some kind of amazing talent. On his podcast, he always knows the right thing to say to keep it interesting — when to say something funny, when to say something insightful, and when to challenge the guest. As a UFC commentator, he makes the broadcast interesting while also adding in valuable martial arts insights. And he does all this seemingly with no effort.

However, this wasn't the result of talent. It was the result of years of practice.

If you want to prove this to yourself, go listen to one of Joe's early podcasts or listen to one of his first UFC broadcasts.

They were both truly awful. Most of his early podcasts were boring, pointless, and unfunny. His early UFC commentating was so bad, it was an embarrassment to fans of the sport.

Online trolls loved mocking him in the early days, and making fun of his numerous on-camera screwups.

But since that time he's done THOUSANDS of podcasts and hundreds of UFC shows. He steadily improved with practice each year. And that's why he seems like a polished talent machine today.

The truth is, being great on video is just like any other skill.

You wouldn't expect to have a "talent" for computer programming, and you wouldn't get discouraged if you couldn't code a great app with no learning or practice. And being good on camera works the same way.

So if on-camera talent is just a matter of practice, why are so few people developing these valuable skills?

The reason why it's is that by posting videos of ourselves, we are opening ourselves up to online criticism.

People might judge us and laugh at us!

It seems silly when I put it like that, but being socially rejected is one of our deepest and most primal human fears. It's powerful even though it doesn't make any logical sense.

I know it's tough, and I struggled myself with receiving negative feedback on my early videos before ultimately achieving success. But the first key to overcoming this will be to visualize how these comments will seem to you five years down the road.

How important will it seem if some troll laughed at your early videos when you are financially free, with a thriving business and YouTube channel?

Probably about as important as those early haters seem to Joe Rogan right now. By imagining your future perspective on these comments, it'll help to get you through the early pain period of being unpracticed.

In my early YouTube days, one hater made a video mocking the way I did an exercise that racked up over 700,000 views. You can check it out here:

15StepsBonuses.com/HaterVideo

I have to admit, this bothered me a lot at the time. But today it's easy to laugh at it, and to link to it from my book so others can have a laugh too.

This is how you'll see your haters just a few years down the road. When you've built a great business and are living the life of your dreams, nothing they say will bother you anymore. And you are closer to that point than you think!

The second key to overcoming camera anxiety is **to give yourself permission to make bad videos.** Look at everything you upload in your first month as being purely for practice. If every video you put out sucks, that's totally fine!

It's not reasonable to expect to be able to make good videos with zero practice. But you'll learn quickly, and once you have some practice the quality of your videos will dramatically improve. And the only way to get there is to first make those practice videos — just like Steph Curry only became great at basketball by taking many practice shots.

If you are not willing to make any crappy videos, you will never make any videos and you will never get the practice you need to improve.

If you're REALLY anxious about people judging your unpolished practice videos, this is what a few of my clients have done to successfully overcome this...

Upload your first few video as PRIVATE so nobody can see them. Do this as many times as you need until you feel like you've practiced enough to release something publicly.

I guarantee you that you'll see a significant improvement in just a few videos — and by the time you've made 10 videos you'll see a HUGE improvement.

You don't need to spend thousands of hours or years to become good on camera. While becoming superstar on-camera talent like Joe Rogan takes years of work, you can become good enough on camera to build a million dollar business with just a few months of focused practice.

And once you're practiced, people will watch your videos and say "Wow, she's so talented. She's so lucky to be born with that gift!"

Mistake #6 — Thinking You Must Be On Camera Yourself To Build A Successful YouTube Business

I strongly believe that anyone can become great on camera with practice. But before you decide to make yourself the on-camera face of your business, you should ask yourself these three questions:

- Do you dislike being on camera?

- Are there other things in the business that you could be doing that are more valuable than being on camera? Examples of things that are more valuable than being on camera include writing ad copy, managing your campaigns in Google Ads, and making your products.

- Can you partner with or hire someone who will be significantly better on camera than you?

If your answer to any of these questions was "yes!" then I have some good news for you...

You can build a profitable YouTube brand without ever needing to be on camera yourself.

I've done it, and hundreds of other business owners like me have as well.

Before I hired my first trainer, I had planned to create a fitness channel where I was the on-camera talent. I love being on camera, I'm in decent shape, and I knew enough about fitness to teach the average person.

But in hindsight, I'm really glad that I didn't do it.

My first trainer was in FAR better shape than me back in 2010 when we started on our channel. He also knew much more about fitness than I did.

And I knew much more about marketing and advertising — and I enjoyed these aspects of the business much more than he did.

In hindsight, we never would have gotten five million subscribers and built a successful business if we hadn't made the decision to each specialize at what we were best at.

And I'm not the only one who's done this. **Many YouTube based businesses which seem to be based around a single on-camera talent actually have a behind the scenes partner who is handling the marketing aspects of the company.**

And here's some more good news for those of you who'd rather not be on camera...

Back when I was broke, I was able to get great on-camera talent without having to pay a dime in salary. I did this by partnering with my trainer, and showing him how owning a percentage of the company would be valuable down the line.

I'll show you how I did it later in this book — and how you can do the same thing to partner with great on-camera talent.

Mistake #7 — Thinking You Need Expensive, Complex Production To Get Started On YouTube

If you already have a large business, it is definitely worthwhile to invest in an expensive filming setup. Having a great camera, lighting setup, mics, etc. can make your videos 5-10% better. And when you're running a multi-million dollar business, 5-10% more sales is a lot.

But if you are just getting started, you DO NOT need to have an expensive setup. In fact, there are many examples of entrepreneurs who built million-dollar ad campaigns with nothing more than a smartphone and a selfie stick.

When I first started making YouTube ads, we had nothing but a consumer grade Sony Handycam I bought for $400 and some construction lights I picked up at Home Depot.

Check out the first few uploads on the SixPackAbs.com channel, and you'll see the video production is embarrassingly bad. You could make a far better video today using a cheap cell phone.

Yet, these videos got millions of views, and tremendous positive feedback from our viewers. And we made millions of dollars from low budget ads like this in our early years.

How can it be possible for videos that look this crappy to be so profitable?

There are two reasons:

First, although YouTube is video medium, it's totally different from TV. The expectation for YouTubers is not that you're a corporation broadcasting to them — it's that you're a person, and in some ways that you're like a friend to the viewer.

Just like you will watch a cell phone video from a real life friend, many people will gladly watch this type of video from their YouTube "friends." That's because they are interested in YOU — not in your video production skills.

In fact, low-quality videos can sometimes work BETTER than highly produced videos as ads. That's because most video ads are highly produced and come from big corporations.

Having a more personal, friend-like video can make you stand out. And it can induce people to watch your ad without skipping.

The second reason why low production value videos can work is that for any marketing campaign, **your marketing message is much more important than the bells and whistles of your video production.** People buy solutions from people they think can solve their problems. If you can convince someone you have the solution to their problem, they'll put up with poor production.

It's easy to understand why if you put yourself in the customer's shoes...

Imagine if there was a car salesman offering you your dream car at a great price. You like him, you trust him, and he's providing the best solution to your problem of needing a new car.

Would you turn down your dream car if the salesman was wearing a cheap suit and had a basic-looking office? Of course not! You need the car, he has the best solution to your problem, and you trust him to treat you right.

Your potential customers think the same way. They're focused on solving the problems in their life, not on your production value. If you can promise them the solutions they're looking for — and back your promises up with proof — this is what they care about most.

While you can start cheap, you SHOULD reinvest your profits in improving your video setup over time. For example, if you're making $500,000 in sales a year from your YouTube-based business, it's clearly worthwhile to invest $5,000 in a good camera along with a good lighting and sound setup. You can expect to improve your sales conversion by 5-10% with better production, so it's clearly worth the investment once money is coming in.

Later in this book, I'm going to give you the ideal filming setups for an extremely small budget, a small budget, a medium budget, and a big budget. So, no matter what your starting budget is, you'll know exactly how to get started and what equipment to buy.

Mistake #8 — Not Testing Your Ad Creative — Or Testing Your Ad Creative The Wrong Way

Since I run a YouTube advertising agency, I've seen dozens of different clients' Google Ads accounts. And by far, the most common mistake I see beginner advertisers making is *not testing their ads.*

Amateur marketers will say "I think this ad is great! Plus, my friends Joe and Susie said it was great too! There's no way this isn't going to work!"

But what the amateurs don't understand is that advertising doesn't work like that. **It's totally impossible to predict in advance which ones of your ads will work the best.**

In fact, even the best marketers in the world will routinely guess wrong when asked to choose which ad is better. And 99% of the businesses who advertise on YouTube without testing ads ultimately fail with their campaigns.

That's why you need to perform **split-testing** on your campaigns.

To split-test, you'll first identify what your most profitable ads are right now. These ads are called your **controls.** You then test new ads against these controls, and try and find an ad that outperforms them.

Let's imagine that you create an ad which brings you $1.20 in sales for every $1 you spend.

Amateurs would be happy with that, and just run the ad as long as they can.

But veteran marketers know that this is just the starting point.

They'll do a split test to improve their sales conversion by 30%...then another to improve it by 50%...then another to get a 10% bump.

They can continue this indefinitely, increasing the profitability of their ads until the advertiser is swimming in a vault of money like Scrooge McDuck.

If you've been doing online marketing for a while, you're probably very familiar with split testing. But here's something that even most veteran marketers don't know…

The vast majority of advertisers who are doing split testing on their YouTube ads **are split testing their ads the WRONG way!**

Unfortunately, I've seen many clients who actually made their advertising WORSE over time through unscientific split testing until I intervened.

In Step 7, I'll walk you through exactly how to split test your ads and your YouTube sales funnel. I'll show you how many ads to test, for how long, and exactly what data to look at to be mathematically certain your tests are improving your campaigns. I'll also give you my Three Level Split Testing system – the unique ad testing method which has been responsible for much of my success with YouTube marketing in the past.

Using the Three Level Split Testing system is going to give you a HUGE advantage over other advertisers. It's the invisible, behind-the-scenes factor driving the success of my campaigns, and many of my clients' campaigns as well. And you're just a few pages away from learning it yourself!

Mistake #9 — Not Realizing You Can Improve Your Marketing Over Time

I recently set up a new YouTube ad campaign for a client.

They had an incredibly engaged YouTube channel with millions of subscribers who loved their content. But they were totally new to online advertising.

We spent a few weeks making the creative, and then we ran a small test campaign, spending $10,000 on ads in our first month. After taking into account the cost of their product, they made about $8,800 in gross profit back from these ads.

And they were VERY disappointed! The way they saw it, they had just lost $1200. In fact, they were about to stop our campaigns and give up on YouTube advertising altogether.

Fortunately, I was able to convince them not to do that.

I told them that these were actually GREAT initial test results, because by using split testing it was extremely likely that we could improve our profitability in the next few months.

They were skeptical, but they decided to give this whole "split testing" thing a try.

Over the next few months, we were able to make significant improvements to our ads by creating five new ads a month and testing them against our previous best ads. We also got a few major website split test "wins." We beat their control sales video by adding a new intro, and we got another major bump in sales conversion when we added a video to their shopping cart.

Within a few months, we improved their campaigns to the point where they were making an 18% profit on their ads to acquire new customers.

Not too bad! But this actually wasn't even the best part...

They were acquiring customers at an 18% profit, but many of those customers came back to buy from them again without requiring any advertising cost.

We were also able to massively grow their remarketing lists (the audience of people who visited the client's website, subscribed to their email list, or bought their product.) And campaigns targeted to these remarketing lists returned $2.11 for every dollar we spent! They were much more profitable than our campaigns to cold prospects, since they were already familiar with the client's business.

Their email list also grew...their YouTube subscribers took off...and their phone sales team started producing much more with the influx of new customers to call.

Today, they're making hundreds of thousands of dollars a month in direct profit from their YouTube advertising. YouTube advertising has also helped them tremendously to grow their channel and to increase the value of their brand.

And it's crazy to think they were about to give up on YouTube because of the apparent $1200 loss in the first month!

There are literally THOUSANDS of advertisers who give up on high potential campaigns every year because they see small losses in the first month.

And this is a shame, because any marketing veteran knows that advertising campaigns almost never make a direct profit in the first few weeks. But they CAN make a big profit after a few months. By this time, split testing will have improved sales conversion and the effects of repeat purchases start to be seen.

I've launched dozens of YouTube ad campaigns in many different industries. Over time, I've learned to recognize when something has potential — and when something doesn't.

Here are the rules of thumb I give my clients...

If you make less than 60% of your initial investment back from your test campaign, you should reconsider your approach. It doesn't mean you should give up on YouTube advertising altogether, but it does mean you should make significant changes to your ads, your sales funnel or eCommerce store, or your checkout and upsell process before spending more money.

If you make 60-100% of your initial investment back, this indicates an offer that you can almost certainly make profitable with split testing.

You should keep spending conservatively and test new ads, new targeting options, and improvements to your website until your campaigns make it to the promised land of profits. If you are a skilled YouTube marketer, most of the new campaigns you create will fall in this category.

Online advertising campaigns almost NEVER make a direct profit in their first few weeks of testing. But occasionally they do.

If you are making a direct profit from your ad campaigns right off the bat with no split testing whatsoever, this indicates you have a massive hit on your hands.

You should immediately double down and focus everything you have on fully maximizing this huge opportunity you've been given. You should increase your campaign budgets, spend time making more ads, try different targeting options, and focus intensely on improving your website.

With these rules of thumb to guide you — combined with the advanced split testing strategies you're about to learn in later chapters — you will have a HUGE advantage over other advertisers. While they foolishly turn off potentially profitable campaigns, you will patiently split test and improve your customer value over time until your campaigns are raking in cash.

Mistake #10 — Thinking That You Can Create Great Advertising Campaigns Without Training

Nobody would ever think they could just "wing it" and program a great app if they've never received any training in computer programming.

Nobody would ever try to prepare financial statements for a large, complex business without accounting training.

And yet, there are MANY people who suffer from the delusion that they can create profitable advertising campaigns with no training, or with half-assed training.

This is because most people have seen many ads as consumers. And they believe that all they need to do to make great ads is to make something that they'd like and respond to as a customer.

Even worse, many people believe they can create great marketing campaigns by getting opinions from other amateurs — people who have never created a successful YouTube advertising campaign themselves.

But think about this for a minute. If it was really as simple as thinking about what you'd like as a customer or polling your friends, EVERYONE would be running million-dollar ad campaigns.

Since this isn't the case — and campaigns that make millions in profit every year are very rare — we know that this popular, amateurish approach doesn't work.

The truth is, advertising is a skill just like any other. Nobody is born intuitively knowing it. Just like anything else, the only way to learn is by learning from experts who have done it before.

So, pat yourself on the back for investing in your YouTube marketing education through this book. By spending the time to learn from someone experienced, you'll be giving yourself a huge advantage over the crowds of ignorant amateurs.

And not just with creating your ads or running your campaigns.

In the next chapter, you'll learn my proven method for identifying the most profitable YouTube advertising opportunities.

Once you know this, you'll have an advantage going into a market — before you even make your first sale or create your first ad!

So, keep reading — we're just about to get into the good stuff.

Step 2: Create A Brilliant Idea For Your YouTube Marketing Campaign

Creating a successful YouTube marketing campaign starts with your idea for what to sell. If you start with a great idea, building a profitable ad campaign will be easy. But if you start with a mediocre idea, it will be nearly impossible to make your ad campaigns profitable.

That's why you need a proven, scientific system for identifying great YouTube marketing ideas. And that's exactly what you'll get in this chapter.

If you haven't yet started your business, this chapter will show you how to come up with a killer idea for a YouTube based business. And if you already have an established business, this chapter will show you how to come up with an ingenious concept for your next marketing campaign.

"Sell what you love, and the money will follow."

This is the most dangerous and the most destructive myth in business. And it's a guaranteed recipe for failure with YouTube marketing.

We'd all like to believe that if we're passionate enough about something, we can make money from selling it. But a decade of experience with my own companies, and consulting with many different clients, has shown me this simply isn't true.

For example, one of my first coaching clients when I started Social Response Marketing was a friend who I'd known for years. She wanted to start a classical ballet dance studio, and she thought YouTube marketing would be the perfect way to get clients.

She absolutely loved ballet — it was her life's passion. She was an incredible ballet teacher, and an amazing dancer herself. So, it seemed clear to her that starting a ballet business was her calling.

But after talking with her about her business idea, I began to see a lot of problems with it...

First of all, the market in our city was already very saturated in world-famous contemporary ballet teachers teaching classes at incredibly cheap rates. The costs of having a physical studio were also very high — likely leading to low profits and limited funds available for advertising.

Compounding the problem further, she wanted to start the studio in a very poor neighborhood where there was little demand for ballet, and where few people could afford dance lessons.

But the worst aspect of her business idea was that many of her dance videos relied on copyrighted music she did not own the rights to. Because YouTube is able to detect copyrighted music in videos, I knew this would create big problems for her when she started advertising. In fact, it would be tough to even create organic, unadvertised content videos because her dances relied so heavily on copyrighted music.

I hesitated to tell her about these problems at first, because she was so excited to start the studio. But ultimately, I knew I had to let her know the reasons why I thought she should reconsider this idea if she wanted to use YouTube as her main marketing platform.

I told her about the problems with her business idea as gently as I could. And I told her I'd work with her to come up with a new business idea, or adjust her dance concept to something that would have a higher chance of making significant profits.

She listened, but told me she was set on starting a dance studio and nothing I said could convince her otherwise. I told her that she should work with a different agency if she was set on this idea, because I didn't feel right taking tens of thousands of dollars from her when I believed it was likely the business would ultimately fail.

She decided to hire another marketing coach and to move forward with the idea, and I wished her the best of luck.

Two and a half years later, she ultimately had to close her studio down. Tragically, she had to quit dance and to go back to working a corporate job after depleting her life savings. The business didn't make enough profit to pay her bills — and she was not able to get any online advertising to work for her. Not only was her profit margin too low to make YouTube advertising profitable, but she also struggled to show how great her dance classes were on video when no copyrighted music was allowed.

This happens to all too many entrepreneurs — and I want to make sure something like this doesn't happen to you.

Stories like this are incredibly sad, and there are far too many of them. **But on the other hand, I also know many people who successfully built a very profitable business from YouTube in a matter of months.**

They didn't work any harder and they weren't any smarter than my ballet dancer friend. **They just had a better system for choosing ideas for their marketing campaigns.** And since they started with a fundamentally better idea, it was much easier to make their campaigns profitable.

So that's why in this chapter, I'm going to walk you through the process I use with my clients to identify great ideas for YouTube marketing campaigns. If you use this process, you'll have a huge advantage over other YouTube advertisers — and you'll be dramatically improving your chances of building a large-scale profitable campaign.

If you already have a business, this chapter will help you choose which one of your products to sell on YouTube, or which new product to launch on YouTube. And if you haven't yet started a business, this chapter will help you come up with your business concept and first marketing campaign.

The Other Side Of The Coin: It's Not Just About Profitability On Paper

Now, before I show you how to assess the profit potential of a YouTube marketing campaign idea...you should know that **your individual passions and strengths DO matter.** They should be taken into account along with profit potential — but in a very specific way.

If you love a certain product or service, you'll be far more motivated to work on your business. It'll be easier to put in the extra time to make sure your marketing campaign is a great one.

And your personal strengths can be just as important to take into account. If a business relies on something you aren't good at right now, it's going to be harder...but if it aligns with your natural strengths it'll be far easier to succeed.

So how exactly do you take both profit potential, your passion for the idea, and your personal strengths into account?

It's simple: you first assess the profit potential of 5-10 different ideas, and eliminate those which don't have a high potential for profit.

Once you've narrowed it down to 2-3 high profit potential ideas, you choose the one which is most aligned with your personal interests and strengths.

The Six Factor Profitability Test

Coming up with great marketing campaign idea is not a matter of luck or inspiration. **Creating great marketing campaign concepts is a skill, and it can easily be done over and over again by someone who has a good system for creating marketing ideas.**

That's why I created the **Six Factor Profitability Test.** It's a sophisticated, proven way to create winning ideas for new YouTube ad campaigns.

To use the Six Factor Profitability test, you simply ask yourself these six questions:

- **Is there substantial user engagement in this category on YouTube?**
- **Are there other high spending advertisers in the category?**
- **Can you create a product significantly different from the existing competition?**
- **What is the average gross profit margin?**
- **What is the potential for repeat business?**
- **What is the likelihood of compliance problems with this product with Google Ads or YouTube?**

If you don't know what some of this stuff means, don't worry. I'm about to explain it all in simple terms.

To see if an idea has potential to become a great YouTube marketing campaign, you will look at each factor and rate the business on a scale of 1-10. It's a subjective assessment, and it's not exact. However, I will give you examples to guide your ratings — and although it's not exact, this test has proven to be shockingly reliable when I've used it to help clients find the perfect idea for their offer.

A business can still have high profit potential if it scores low in one category. You should look for a high TOTAL score when using the Six Factor Profitability Test to identify which ideas have the most potential.

I've personally used the Six Factor Profitability Test to create seven different YouTube ad campaigns that have made more than a million dollars in profit for my own companies. I've also used it to create many more winning ideas for my clients. So, you should know that this process is something I've extensively tested, and it's thoroughly proven to work.

A high score on the Six Factor Profitability Test doesn't guarantee your campaign will make millions. The way you execute on your idea matters a lot too.

However, the Six Factor Profitability Test will TREMENDOUSLY improve your odds of success versus just "following your passions," or some other similarly foolish method of creating ad campaign ideas. It stacks the deck in your favor and gives you a significant edge over other advertisers right out of the gate.

So, let's dive into the six factors...

Factor 1: How Much YouTube User Engagement Is There In The Product Category?

If your product has a rabid following of people watching videos about it on YouTube, your marketing campaign is more likely to succeed. If nobody is watching videos about your idea on YouTube right now, it's less likely to work.

That's because videos closely related to your product or service are usually the most profitable videos to advertise on.

Not only can you advertise directly on videos related to your product or service, but you can advertise to people who have watched videos about your product category in the past. If this audience is large and engaged, it'll be easier to make your campaign profitable.

If people are liking, commenting, and sharing videos on a certain topic like crazy, it also indicates they're passionate about the product category. And that means they're likely to spend a lot of money getting something they love rather than just buying the cheapest option.

Examples of "10" ideas in this category:

- **Teaching men to get six pack abs** — seeing shockingly high views and user engagement on videos teaching men how to get abs was a huge part of why I decided to create Six Pack Shortcuts as my first YouTube marketing campaign. In hindsight, being in a hyper-engaged product category was a critical part of our success.

  Cosmetics — Makeup and skin care tutorials have INCREDIBLE views and engagement on YouTube. Cosmetics videos get billions of views every year, giving cosmetics marketers a prime place to advertise.

Examples of "10" business ideas in this category:

- **Insurance** — Insurance is a huge industry, but watching videos about insurance is incredibly boring.

  Because there are very few people watching videos about insurance on YouTube, it's a big disadvantage for insurance advertisers. However, many insurance companies have still made YouTube advertising work for them because they aligned multiple other factors in their favor.

- **Treatments For Embarrassing Health Conditions** — Treatments for conditions like erectile dysfunction, yeast infections, herpes, toenail fungus, etc. are all huge industries. But the fact is, very few people are watching videos on these topics on YouTube — and NOBODY is sharing these videos with their friends.

  This is a significant disadvantage. But again, some advertisers in these categories are able to succeed by aligning many of the other factors in their favor.

To assess your business's profit potential for the YouTube User Engagement, estimate where it falls on the continuum from "no views or engagement whatsoever" to "billions of views and a rabid following."

For example, I would rate the entrepreneurship category as a seven. It has a substantial following on YouTube with a few big channels, but nowhere near as big as something like men's fitness. While entrepreneurship isn't the most engaged video category on YouTube, it's much closer to cosmetics than it is to toenail fungus cure.

VERY IMPORTANT NOTE: For this factor, you'll be assessing the CATEGORY your product is in, not the idea itself. You don't want to speculate on how much engagement your idea MIGHT get, since it doesn't yet exist.

Instead, you want to assess the market environment you're going into. If it's full of passionate and dedicated fans, selling your product on YouTube will be much easier.

Factor 2: How Many Successful Advertisers Are There In Your Product Category?

This one might surprise you.

Most people think that if NOBODY is advertising a certain type of product right now, that's a good thing. They'll be the first one to bring this amazing widget to YouTube!

However, it doesn't really work like that.

If there are no high volume advertisers in your category, it's probably because nobody can make this product category profitable. If there are lots of businesses heavily spending on ads in the category, that shows that there's tremendous demand for what they're selling.

Of course, you also have to differentiate your product from the competition (which we'll address in the next factor.) But as long as you can do that, heavy advertiser competition in your category is most definitely a GOOD thing. **And all else being equal, it's better to start YouTube marketing campaigns in product categories with many other high spending advertisers.**

Examples of "10" ideas for this factor:

- **Entrepreneurship** — If you've watched any videos about business or entrepreneurship on YouTube, chances are you've been bombarded with ads from Tai Lopez, Billy Gene, Keala Kanae, myself, and many other entrepreneurship and business teachers. There are many different advertisers in this category who have millions of views on their ads. This shows that there are many different businesses who are making a profit in our market.

- **Cosmetics** — Not only do cosmetics have a huge, highly engaged following on YouTube, there are also many different high volume advertisers in the category.

  With the female Google account that I use for market research, I've seen many ads which have millions of views. After watching cosmetics videos, this account is constantly bombarded by makeup ads. I've also observed this in my girlfriend's YouTube account, and in other women's YouTube accounts as well.

Examples of "10" ideas for this factor:

- **Books** — While I buy and read many books, I have not seen ANY successful advertising campaigns for books on YouTube. If you're an avid book reader, you might also notice that you see very few ads for books.

  The only exception to this is educational books given away for free or for the price of shipping that are in a highly advertised category — categories like entrepreneurship or fitness. Giving away a book for free can work in certain categories, because the value of customers in certain industries is so high that it's worth losing money to acquire them.

- **Dance lessons** — As I pointed out to my friend and ex-client, there are very, very few people advertising dance lessons on YouTube. I have never seen one in my main male profile. And I've never any in my female market research profile either. There is simply too little profit to be made in this market, and too many challenges to overcome with copyrighted music. It's not that people haven't tried. Many people have tried, and all of them have failed.

Again, remember you're assessing how heavily the CATEGORY is advertised – not your specific idea.

Factor 3: How Differentiated Is Your SPECIFIC IDEA From Your Competitors?

Being in a niche with many different people profitably advertising is a good thing — IF you can differentiate your product from the other players in your industry.

Especially in very competitive niches, it's important that your product is not perceived as a "me-too" product. If your product is too similar to established brands, the customer's tendency will be to buy from the older, more established company rather than the upstart.

You need a VERY compelling reason why the customer is going to buy from you. Making your product 10% better than the competition is NOT going to cut it.

Differentiation is important for a few reasons:

- **Your customers are already buying from your bigger, more established competitors.** If there is not a strong reason to do business with you too, it's much easier for them to just continue their existing buying habits.

- **The attention span of the people you're trying to reach on YouTube is very limited.** If you can't convey why your product is better in a sentence or two, your potential customers won't stick around to hear more.

  They're busy, and buying a slightly better widget isn't a big priority for them.

- **When you're in a great category AND you're highly differentiated from your "competitors," then you aren't really competing with them at all.** In fact, there will be great opportunities for collaboration between people in the same category who have highly differentiated products.

It's important to note that with this factor, you are not evaluating the category your product is in, like in the last two factors. **You are evaluating your specific idea, and how differentiated it is compared to the other brands in your category.**

Examples of "10" ideas for this factor:

- **Teaching entrepreneurs YouTube marketing —** There are many different advertisers teaching people how to start a business, make money online, and achieve financial freedom. But except for myself, there are no large scale advertisers teaching them how to do it with YouTube marketing. There are large scale advertisers teaching how to start a CHANNEL so you can make money from selling advertising — but none teaching how you can make money buying advertising.

  And that's one of the reasons why I decided to start this business.

- **Supplements, cosmetics, or skin care products that are a unique blend of ingredients** — If you can formulate your own products in these industries, you have a great opportunity to create the type of differentiation we're looking for. And even if there are many other people selling similar products, they'll buy yours as well if there is an easy to understand, compelling reason why they should.

  For example, there are hundreds of different greens supplements out there, and dozens of them advertised on YouTube. We differentiated Green Detox, the greens supplement I created with my fitness business, by marketing it as the only greens supplement made with no cereal grasses. Because we could easily explain and substantiate why our ingredients were better, the product was a hit.

Examples of "10" ideas for this factor:

- **Supplements, cosmetics, or skin care products that are commodities** — I personally am a huge believer in Vitamin D. Studies show many people are deficient in it and get huge benefits from supplementing — and I personally experienced incredible benefits when I started taking Vitamin D.

  However, I would NEVER attempt to sell Vitamin D on YouTube because it's a commodity. Since there's no way to differentiate my product from the competition's Vitamin D, profits will be low. There's simply not a strong enough reason for people to switch brands when every product has identical ingredients.

  The same thing can be said for any supplement, skin care product, or cosmetic product that only has one ingredient, or which is made from a common formula.

- **Coffee** — Unfortunately, I know this from experience from someone who has tried to sell coffee on YouTube before. I discovered a coffee made by a small company which I believed was the best I'd ever tasted when consumed black. I'm a huge believer in the health benefits of drinking cold brew black coffee, so I thought we had a huge winner on our hands with this new campaign.

  Unfortunately, customers didn't see it that way. While they loved the taste, they didn't love it enough to pay three times more than they would for established gourmet coffee brands (which was the bare minimum we required to make a profit after paying for advertising.)

  The same thing can be said for any other one ingredient commodity foods. They're simply not differentiated enough to build profitable advertising campaigns around.

Is your idea highly differentiated, like YouTube marketing training? Or is it closer to being a commodity, like Vitamin D and coffee? Make an honest evaluation based on the criteria above and give your ideas a score in this category.

Factor 4: What Is Your Product's Gross Profit Margin?

Forgive me while I get all math-y on you for a minute. We're going to dive into some accounting nerdery. But this is important stuff – so pay attention.

Your gross profit margin is the price your customer pays for your product, minus the money it takes you to make and deliver that product. Unlike your "net profit margin," this number does not factor in the fixed costs of your business, such as your computer, your video camera, or your employees.

For example, if I sell my widget for $100 but it costs me $20 to make it and ship it to you, my gross profit margin is 80% — a pretty solid number.

A healthy gross profit margin is incredibly important for a successful business. Most entrepreneurs drastically underestimate the importance of gross margin. They think their product is so amazing that they can make up for their low gross profit margin by selling more units.

Usually it doesn't work out. In fact, they usually end up selling FEWER units than advertisers with high gross profit margins, while also making less on each sale. That's because with a low gross profit margin, they can't afford to buy much advertising. Because they can only afford a tiny advertising budget, they never make many sales.

I cannot stress this point enough. **DO NOT underestimate the importance of a healthy gross profit margin — it is often the difference between success and failure in business, and in YouTube advertising.**

Examples of "10" ideas for this factor:

- **Apps, audiobooks, video courses, coaching, and consulting** — These types of products and services can be delivered for virtually zero cost. It will require a significant amount of your time to create information products, or to perform consulting services. But they have a gross margin of almost 100%, which is a HUGE advantage when buying advertising.

  Information products like audiobooks and video courses also have the advantage of not requiring your time on an ongoing basis. While this isn't the case with consulting, consulting does have the advantage of enabling you to create quick profits with little up front work required.

- **Supplements, cosmetics, and skin care products** — The gross profit margin on many of these products is incredible. It's common in these industries to buy a product wholesale for $5 and to resell it for $50.

  This isn't quite as good as nearly cost-less information products and consulting. However, physical products do have many other advantages such as being easier for the customer to understand, and making it possible for a customer to buy the same product over and over again. And that's why so many profitable YouTube advertising campaigns have been built in this category.

Examples of "10" ideas in this category:

- **Food** — The profit margins on food products are brutal. I know this because four years back, I found an amazing service in my city that delivered healthy meals.

  I absolutely loved it, and I thought that it could be a great advertising opportunity.

  But once I talked with the owner of the business, I had to reconsider.

  We found out that these meals – like most food products – have gross profit margins of under 10%. That means for every $10 in revenue you make, you only keep $1 in gross profit. *And that's before paying for all the other costs of your business, like your equipment and employees!* After accounting for these costs, most businesses selling food are only making a 1-3% net profit margin. That's horrific!

  It is nearly impossible to build a successful YouTube advertising campaign with these meager profit margins — regardless of how good your product or marketing skills are.

- **Furniture** — The profit margins in furniture as almost as brutally low as the profit margins in food. It simply costs too much to make and ship the products relative to what customers are going to pay. Especially for low priced furniture, there is just no way you can provide a significantly better product than IKEA and other discount furniture sellers.

  High end furniture and household items are somewhat better, but still are not ideal. You may be able to make a 20-40% gross profit margin on high end furniture, but it will still be challenging to compete against advertisers in other categories with higher margins.

Factor 5 — Potential For Repeat Business

Convincing someone who's never bought from you before to buy your products is hard. And it's very expensive.

Because of this, most profit in business is made from what's called the "back-end" — from selling your customer more products or services after they've already bought something from you.

If your business is the type of business that people will buy from over and over again, this is a big advantage. You'll be able to spend more aggressively to acquire a customer than other businesses — and this is the type of idea you want to aim for.

Examples of "10" ideas for this factor:

- **Consumable products, such as supplements, cosmetics, skin care products, and food** — Consumable products are great for business owners because your customer needs to buy them repeatedly to keep getting the benefits. This means that once you get a customer, they'll probably buy from you for years if they're happy with the product.

- **Software as a service (SaaS)** — This is software that's hosted on your company's servers, and which users subscribe to on a monthly or quarterly basis. An example of a SaaS product is ClickFunnels — you pay a monthly fee, and they give you access to their software to build sales funnels.

  SaaS products are great because they lend themselves to a subscription model. You just have to convince someone to try your software for a month. If they're happy with it, you can continue to bill them for years.

  Not only this, but many SaaS companies provide opportunities to upgrade their product with additional features later. And once someone is committed to your main product, selling them upgrades is far easier.

Examples of "10" ideas in this category:

- **Dating advice for single people** — Advice on how to find a girlfriend or boyfriend has an inherent problem. If your advice works, then the customer's problem is solved and they don't have any need to keep buying products and services from you. If your advice doesn't work, your customer is pissed off and still doesn't continue buying from you.

  However, I know from consulting with clients in the dating industry that it is possible to build a successful dating advice business. There are high profit margins, and a lot of demand for the advice. And the most clever entrepreneurs in this niche have figured out how to keep selling these people services when they're no longer single.

- For example, my friend Adam Lyons that I previously mentioned is one of the top dating coaches in the world. But he also owns a company called Psychology Hacker, which uses many of the same social influence principles as his dating advice business to help his customers make more money and build a better lifestyle for themselves. This way, once his advice works and his customers find a girlfriend, they can still keep doing business with him.

  If you are clever, you may be able to figure out a way to engineer repeat business into your idea like this — even if it doesn't naturally lend itself to repeat business.

- **Real estate agent and mortgage services** — I had a great experience working with my realtor and mortgage broker. But I probably won't utilize their services again for five years or more – if I ever do at all. Buying a house is just inherently the type of thing you don't need to do every month.

  However, there are some other advantages to these types of services. They have high profit margins, and they're easy to differentiate from other players in the industry. But the smartest real estate agents and mortgage brokers will figure out a way to engineer repeat business even though their industry doesn't lend itself to it.

For example, my mortgage broker sends me a monthly email newsletter with updates on mortgage rates. He also sends a card and a small gift every year on my birthday. By staying in touch for multiple years, he maximizes the chances of repeat business down the road. And if I do buy a new house or get a new mortgage 5-10 years from now, I'll probably end up doing business with him again.

Factor 6 — What Is The Likelihood Of Policy Compliance Problems With This Product On Google Ads?

Even if every other factor is in your favor, it won't do you any good if you're not allowed to advertise it. Since Google owns YouTube, this means complying with all the policies for Google Ads and avoiding any ideas they might consider to be a grey area.

This can be more complex and difficult than a lot of new advertisers think, especially in product categories Google considers to be "high risk."

Some categories are totally prohibited, such as porn, firearms, explosives, or tobacco. It's very clear and obvious Google doesn't allow these products though, so advertisers in these categories usually know what they're getting into.

However, many advertisers enter "grey zone" categories with a high potential for Ad Policy compliance problems without knowing what they're getting into. Advertising in a category with potential for problems will be a disadvantage, and you should not enter a category like this unless many other factors are in your favor.

Examples of "10" ideas for this factor:

- **Clothing (except for risqué clothing)** — The nature of clothing is that it doesn't require aggressive marketing claims — it's sold based on the way it looks.

  There also isn't really any way clothing can be dangerous to the user. Because of this, clothing advertisers encounter very few compliance problems with Google Ads.

The only exception to this would be risqué clothing categories, such as bikinis and lingerie. Ads with models wearing these products are sometimes disapproved for violating Google's "nudity" policy. It is still possible to build a successful business in these categories, but you'll have an additional significant challenge to deal with compared to most of the clothing industry.

Apps, software, computer hardware, and electronic devices — As a technology company, Google is inherently friendly towards technology advertisers. Technology products also have the advantage of not requiring aggressive marketing claims, and not posing any danger to users. As long as you are not installing malware or doing something similarly evil, you should not encounter any problems.

Examples of "10" ideas in this category:

- **Firearms related products** — While firearms are explicitly prohibited from Google Ads, holsters, firearms training courses and other related products are not.

  Nevertheless, Google is so unfriendly towards anything having to do with firearms that I would advise against trying to sell anything that's even remotely gun-related on Google Ads.

  Gun advertisers are a huge legal and political risk for Google. Because of this, anything even remotely related to firearms tends to have massive compliance problems.

For example, a friend of mine once worked at a T-shirt company whose logo had a musket in it. They had huge compliance headaches with Google Ads all the time. Despite the fact that their product was completely safe to customers and required no marketing claims, the musket in their logo alone was enough to cause them constant Policy headaches.

- **Supplements intended to treat a health condition —** If your product is intended to treat a specific condition, such as tinnitus, arthritis, or high blood pressure, you will have a tougher time advertising it on Google Ads.

    Google Ads compliance for all supplements is pretty tough, but it's the toughest for supplements intended to treat a specific condition. Most businesses selling products like this are not allowed to access remarketing, one of the most powerful targeting features in Google Ads.

- I've sold supplements like this before, and I know this type of product poses significant Policy compliance challenges. But if there are many other factors in your favor, you can still make this type of business work.

The "Gut Feeling" Tie-Breaker Test

So now you know what each of the Six Factors is, and how to score your idea on each Factor.

Here's how to turn those scores into a winning ad campaign idea...

First, come up with 7-10 different ideas for ad campaigns. The more ideas you can brainstorm the better!

You score them on each factor on a scale of 1-10.

You add them up the scores on each factor, and see which ideas got the total highest score.

Then you eliminate ALL of your ideas outside of your top three. This will ensure that you're pursuing one of your highest profit potential ideas, while still giving you a few options to choose from.

At this point, think about your remaining campaign ideas.

Which one is most aligned with your strengths?

Which one do you feel most EXCITED to work on?

Don't assign your ideas a score for these things. Just try and imagine how you would feel if this ad campaign consumed most of your time for the next few years.

Is the thought of that depressing and de-motivating despite the profit potential? Or does it fire you up and fill you with excitement?

Is this idea in alignment with your natural strengths? Or does it require you to do things you don't have a natural affinity for?

This is the time to listen to your gut, and to get in touch with how you feel on a deep level about the idea. Not the profit potential — we've already assessed that. You need to see how you feel about this idea on an emotional — some would even say a spiritual — level.

You're justified in taking a few days to get in touch with your feelings, to ensure you're working on the idea you're most excited about.

Once you know in your gut which one of the three you're most aligned with and excited about, commit to that business idea.

By using this process, you'll be able to create an idea that you're excited to work on and which matches your natural strengths — AND which has big profit potential.

It's the best way that I've found to balance the logical and the emotional factors that go into creating a successful business or marketing campaign.

The Two Ways To Use The Six Factor Profitability Test

There are two ways that you can use the Six Factor Profitability Test.

If you already have an existing business, you can use the Six Factor Profitability Test to create ideas for new products, new brands, and new YouTube ad campaigns.

If you're using it this way, you should restrict yourself to ideas that are related to your business. This way you can take advantage of your existing audience, and you can sell them your other products on the back end.

For example, in my fitness business, we'd only consider ideas for workout courses, nutrition courses, supplements, healthy foods, workout clothing, fitness equipment, fitness apps, gym memberships, and other products related to fitness.

Of course, there is always an option to start a new business.

But if you start a new business, you won't have the advantage of your existing audience and product line. So usually this does not make sense.

The second way to use this process is to create ideas for a totally new business that will primarily drive sales through YouTube marketing.

In this case, you don't have to restrict yourself to any particular category since you have no existing business. If you don't yet have a business, this is how you should use the Six Factor Profitability Test.

How I Used The Six Factor Profitability Test To Create Social Response Marketing

I'm going to peel back the curtain a little bit, and show you how I created the idea for this book and my current business with the Six Factor Profitability Test:

After I sold SixPackAbs.com, I took a few months off and spent some time thinking about the next company I was going to start. While I had a large enough portfolio to retire comfortably, I wasn't satisfied with what I'd achieved and I knew that I wasn't going to stay retired forever.

So, I spent a lot of time browsing YouTube, looking into different potential products, talking with other business owners, and simply thinking about ideas for new businesses I was interested in starting. Here's the list I came up with:

- A Brazilian Jiu Jitsu gym
- A video course teaching online dating advice
- A cold brew coffee delivery company
- A CBD oil company
- A book and video course teaching people how to profit from Libra, the cryptocurrency Facebook and an alliance of many other companies are attempting to create
- A book and video course teaching entrepreneurs how to hire and manage employees
- A book and video course teaching people how to sell their company and retire early
- A company selling nootropic supplements
- A book and video course teaching people YouTube marketing
- A political podcast, monetized with books, premium memberships, and merchandise

I used the same simple worksheet I've been using for years to score the ideas for the Six Factor Profitability test. Here's what it looked like:

SIX FACTOR PROFITABILITY ANALYSIS

Confidential - For Internal Use By ███████████ Only

Your 10 Business Ideas:	YouTube Engagement	Successful Advertisers	Differentiation From Competition	Gross Profit Margin	Repeat Biz Potential	Compliance Problems	TOTAL SCORE:	
1. Jiu Jitsu Gym	6	1	4	3	8	4	26	
2. Online Dating Advice	4	2	9	10	2	2	29	
3. Cold Brew Coffee Delivery	2	1	3	2	8	10	26	
4. CBD Oil	5	1	3	6	10	1	26	
5. Libra Video Course	6	1	5	10	7	1	30	
6. Hiring + Management Advice	2	2	8	10	8	7	37	✓
7. Early Retirement Advice	4	2	8	10	4	6	34	
8. Nootropic Supplements	5	6	9	8	10	3	41	✓
9. YouTube Marketing Advice	6	7	10	10	8	6	47	✓
10. Political Podcast	9	2	9	5	5	1	31	

My top three scoring ideas were:

- Hiring & Management Advice
- Nootropic Supplements
- YouTube Marketing Advice

I eliminated all of the other ideas from consideration, since the Six Factor Profitability Test showed me that my top three ideas had more potential.

Once I narrowed my choices down to three ideas — all of which had high profit potential — I spent a few days getting in touch with how I *felt* about working on these businesses.

While Hiring & Management Advice had high profit potential, it didn't excite me very much. I managed a company with over 100 employees with SixPackAbs.com, and I'm very experienced and knowledgeable about managing employees.

But it just didn't seem very fun to me.

Nootropic Supplements seemed significantly better. Since I've spent years selling supplements previously, it was aligned well with my strengths. I'm also a passionate user of nootropics myself and the idea of being able to formulate my own product really excited me.

However, I wasn't too excited about some of the headaches I knew were part of the supplement business. I'd have to sink a significant amount of money in inventory, deal with FDA compliance, and hire a large team of employees.

This made sense for me 5-10 years ago when the huge potential of the supplement business outweighed the lifestyle factors. But now that I had a large enough portfolio to cover all my expenses out of my investment income, lifestyle was more important to me than scale.

YouTube Marketing was the idea most aligned with my strengths, since I've spent the last ten years intensively focusing on it. It's also the part of my last business I enjoyed the most. To me, figuring out the psychology of the customer and creating a marketing campaign around my insights is exciting. I love seeing my ideas come together into completed videos, and seeing my own ads on YouTube when I'm browsing is still a rush to me to this day.

I also really love the process of scaling my campaigns with Google Ads. To me, it's like the ultimate strategy based video game. And rather than getting points or a congratulatory screen at the end, you get real money for winning the YouTube marketing game.

YouTube marketing has also made me a much better person.

It took me from barely being able to afford rent on a studio apartment to being financially free. And beyond that, my success with YouTube marketing gave me confidence in all areas of life, and the belief that I could achieve big goals if I set my mind to it.

Helping other entrepreneurs to change their life in the same way seemed like a higher calling that would really motivate me.

And after a decade of being behind the scenes I was really excited about going on camera again and getting to speak directly to motivated business owners like you.

After getting in touch with my feelings about each of the ideas, the decision was clear. My next product and ad campaign would be for products teaching YouTube marketing advice.

In this case, my top scoring idea and what I was most passionate about were the same. But I would have chosen YouTube Marketing advice even if it was the lowest scoring out of my top three.

You should do the same when using the Six Factor Profitability Test. All of your top three ideas have will have high profit potential, so at this point you should "go with your gut" to choose between them.

Frequently Asked Questions About The Six Factor Profitability Test

Do I really need to come up with ten different ideas for the product offer I'll be advertising? It seems like a lot.

Yes. You need to take this process seriously — it will have a tremendous impact on how successful your campaigns are.

Starting a business based on the first idea that pops into your head, and then wasting years of your life working on a low potential idea is a mistake I don't want you to make.

You should come up with **at least** ten different ideas if you are starting a new business. We are talking about the way you'll be spending the next 2-10 years of your life, so it's worth spending a few days doing research and brainstorming ideas for such a massive decision.

In fact, you are justified in spending a few months on this process if it ultimately helps you come up with a better business concept.

If you have an existing business and are brainstorming ideas for a new product or advertising campaign, it can sometimes make sense to have a quicker brainstorming process, and to start with just the bare minimum of ten ideas. But you should make sure that you have a minimum of ten ideas, even if you're doing this for an existing business whose product category is already defined.

Of course, you could always come up with a few good ideas, then load the rest of it up with crappy ideas you're not seriously considering. But you're only cheating yourself by doing this.

To maximize your chances of a brilliant, home run idea, it's critical to brainstorm as many potentially viable ideas as possible so you have an abundance of good options.

What's the minimum score I should aim for?

As a general rule of thumb, if NONE of your ideas score over a 30 you should keep brainstorming.

However, some people tend to have a higher skewed rating scale across all the categories than others...and some tend to give everything lower ratings. Unless your ideas are scoring extremely low (below 30), your top three ideas are probably the best you'll be able to come up with unless you half-assed the brainstorming process.

I'm already committed to an existing product offer and advertising campaign. How can I use this test?

If you already have an existing profitable advertising campaign, you definitely should not abandon it. Not even if you can come up with an idea that scores higher, which you're also more excited to work on.

However, you SHOULD use this process to brainstorm your NEXT advertising campaign.

Unless you're unhappy with your current business, most of the time it will make sense to use the test to brainstorm products already in your business's product category. This way you can take advantage of your existing audience and product line, and sell your new customers all your other products.

Your Action Steps From This Chapter:

If you're already committed to a specific product to sell in your marketing campaign, you don't have any immediate action steps from this chapter.

Just make sure to re-read this chapter and use the Six Factor Profitability Test when you're creating your next offer that you'll market on YouTube.

If you have not yet committed to a specific product offering for your marketing campaign, here's what I want you to do:

1. Go to <u>15StepsBonuses.com/SixFactor</u> to download your copy of the worksheet. You'll get the exact worksheet I've used myself to create many different multi-million dollar ad campaigns in multiple different industries.

2. Print the worksheet out. Spend some time brainstorming at least ten ideas, and fill them into the left columns. Use multiple worksheets if you have more than ten strong ideas.

3. Score each idea on the six factors as objectively and accurately as you can.

4. Highlight your top three ideas.

5. Spend some time thinking about how you FEEL about each of the ideas. How aligned are they with what you're good at? How excited are you to work on the ideas? How aligned are these ideas with your life's purpose?

6. Choose the idea you FEEL the best about from among your top three highest profit potential ideas.

Step 3: Create Your First Content Video, And Set A Regular Upload Schedule

Your content videos are the unadvertised videos you make on your channel that viewers want to watch. These videos should teach the viewer something, but also entertain them and give them an opportunity to connect with you.

Remember, the formula for making money with YouTube advertising is great content + great marketing. So before creating your first ad, you need to create a small amount of unadvertised video content. This will increase the conversion on your ads, and also allow you to experience engagement and brand-building effects from your advertising.

You can skim this chapter and skip the action steps if you already have an established YouTube channel. Come back to this chapter once you've implemented the remainder of the book to learn how to improve your content.

If you have not yet uploaded any videos, this chapter is going to change your life!

Why Upload REGULARITY Is More Important Than Upload QUALITY

We've established that the best way to make money on YouTube isn't uploading ads with no content videos behind them — and that it also isn't to make content videos with no advertising.

It's to synergistically use BOTH advertising and video content together.

Your ads quickly bring large amounts of viewers to your channel, and make you an immediate direct response profit.

Your content videos (sometimes called "organic videos") support your ads, and increase your profits by building trust and showing potential customers you're the real deal. They also get people to subscribe and engage with your channel, which builds the long-term value of your brand. So, having great content videos is important — no matter what industry you're in or what product you're selling.

But HOW do you make great content videos to support your advertising?

REGULARITY: The Master Key To Creating A Successful YouTube Channel

Of course, there are many things that go into creating great YouTube content that gets people to buy from you. And we're going to dive more into the details later in this chapter.

But there is one single MASTER KEY to making great YouTube content that you absolutely must know about first. If you get this right, you are virtually guaranteed to get all of the other details right over time.

And this master key to getting people to love your content videos is **UPLOAD REGULARITY.**

This means that you have a set upload schedule that you talk about in your videos, and that you stick to religiously. It can be once every two weeks, once a week, twice a week...or even every day. Uploading more often will help — but it's less important than ALWAYS sticking to your set upload schedule no matter what.

Could the key to building a massive YouTube channel with millions of subscribers really be that simple? I know it's hard to believe, but in the next few pages I'll prove it to you.

Why Regularity Is The Master Key

To understand why regularity is the Master Key to building a successful YouTube channel, **you need to understand how powerful HABITS are — and how they control the vast majority of all human behavior.**

To get a deep understanding of why this is, I highly recommend reading *The Power Of Habit* by Charles Duhigg.

Here's the link to buy the book on Amazon:

15StepsBonuses.com/PowerOfHabit

If you haven't read it, I'll summarize the most important part here. And I'll show you how it applies to becoming popular on YouTube.

We all believe that our behavior is controlled by our decisions.

In reality, though, the majority of our behavior is controlled by our habits.

A 2006 study by a Duke University researcher showed that **40 percent of the average person's daily actions were caused by habits — not decisions.** Another study said that **50 percent of our actions were caused by habits.** A third study showed a whopping **95 percent of our daily actions were caused by habits!**

As Duhigg says in the book, *"Most of the choices we make each day may feel like the products of well-considered decision making, but they're not. They're habits."*

Now, obviously we do all have some willpower. We do have the ability to make some decisions actively.

But people VERY RARELY use willpower to change their YouTube viewing habits. We'll mostly save our limited willpower to improve the important things in our lives. Things like our job performance, our relationship with our spouse, being a good parent, and the other things that affect our lives significantly.

Psychologists have found that our behavior-controlling habits work in a three part loop. And this loop perfectly describes most people's YouTube viewing habits.

- First, there is the **cue** — what triggers the habit. The person has some downtime where they're not doing anything else, and they're a little bored and lonely. This usually occurs at the same time each day.

- The **routine** is the behavior they automatically engage in once triggered. They pull up the YouTube app and watch videos from the channels they're in the routine of watching.

- The **reward** is what the user gets from completing the routine. For watching our YouTube videos, there are two layers to this reward.

First, your viewer's logical brain feels good because they took the time to educate themselves about you and your product category.

They didn't just watch Netflix or cat videos like every other schmuck. They now know a little bit more about dog training, fashion, investing, lawn care, cars, or whatever you're making videos about.

Our viewer's EMOTIONAL brain also gets rewarded from watching our videos. This is the second, deeper layer of the psychological reward our videos are giving them.

Most people who are trying to better themselves in one way or another feel a little lonely. They don't know anyone who's trying to better themselves in the way that they are, and this makes them feel like they don't fit in. In many ways YouTube channels like ours can substitute for this lack of real life connection.

For example, when I was in high school, I was a shy, awkward nerd. I wanted to learn how to become more attractive to girls — but none of my friends were interested in this, or even believed it was possible. So, I turned to online discussion forums (this before YouTube) for virtual "friends" who I could relate to in this area of my life.

When I was in college, I set a goal to build muscle, to lose my flabby gut, and to get in shape. None of my beer-drinking friends really cared about these goals. So, I started watching YouTube videos where my virtual "friends" educated me about fitness, and affirmed that what I was doing was normal.

Today, I'm grateful to have an amazing network of friends who run successful businesses. But there are still times where I feel bored and where I need someone to relate to.

So, I've gotten into the habit of watching Graham Stephen's videos every Monday, Wednesday, and Friday night. The reward I get from this habit is learning about personal finance, real estate, and business — and also the connection of shared goals that I can't get from most of my real life family and friends.

Now, I happen to be the type of person who consumes huge amounts of information. But this principle applies to physical products as well.

For example, millions of car enthusiasts are in the habit of watching sports car channels. They tune in to learn about cars, and also to feel a sense of connection with someone that shares their interest.

My girlfriend is in the habit of watching videos from Jackie Aina, a makeup YouTuber. Her reward for this habit is learning more about makeup, and feeling a sense of connection with someone who's like her in many ways her real-life friends are not.

Most YouTube viewing is habit-driven like this.

And that itself is a big reason why you need to upload regularly — it gets people in the routine of regularly watching your videos.

But there's actually an even more important reason...

How YouTube's Algorithms Reinforce The Power Of Habits

Most YouTube views come from habituated subscribers regularly watching the same channels over and over again.

But of course, people will also sometimes discover videos from new channels to watch.

These are usually the videos recommended to them in the "Up Next" columns next to the videos they're already watching, or the suggested videos that play automatically after their video finishes.

How does YouTube determine which videos will show up in these recommendations?

The most important factor is the **engagement your videos get in the first 48 hours after being uploaded.**

And this is why getting subscribers who are habituated to IMMEDIATELY watching your videos when they're uploaded is important.

Your subscribers will be notified when you post a new video and are likely to watch it right away. There is no other way to get views, likes, comments, shares, etc. on your video within the first 48 hours, unless you're sending large amounts of people to YouTube from outside the site.

If you have a large base of habituated subscribers, you'll get a lot of engagement in the first 48 hours. This leads to YouTube recommending your video to more people. And this leads to you getting more subscribers, more engagement on the video...etc.

It's a self-reinforcing cycle after that — but you need your habituated subscribers to start everything off.

Our Own Habits: The Most Important Reason Why Regularity Is The Master Key

We entrepreneurs like to think of ourselves as smarter and more disciplined than the unwashed masses who passively consume YouTube videos. But the reality is that we're the same.

Most of our behavior is driven by habits too. **The difference between successful people and everyone else is that successful people just have better habits.**

And this is the most important reason why I believe regularity is the Master Key to creating highly engaged YouTube content that supports your ad campaigns.

Because the quality of the content you're creating matters — a lot. But the way to become great at creating content for your YouTube channel is to get in the habit of regularly uploading videos on a set interval, and sticking to your habit for the long term.

Many people obsess about the quality of their first few videos, resulting in a sparse and irregular upload schedule. The result of this is that they never really develop a strong habit for making videos. Because they're not getting in consistent practice, they never really get good at it. And they're never able to improve the quality of their content over time because of their lack of practice.

And you can see this for yourself just by looking at videos from top YouTube advertisers who have a big organic following.

My first Six Pack Shortcuts content videos were truly awful by my standards today. The content was rambling and unorganized, the sound was awful, the lighting was poor, and the editing sucked. Yet, once we got in the habit of uploading regularly, we rapidly improved our ability to make content.

Another example of this is my consulting client The Attractive Man, the biggest men's dating advice channel on YouTube.

Watch their earliest videos, and you'll see both the content and production is poor by their standards today. But you can see a rapid, steady trend of improvement over time.

They've now got the best men's dating advice content videos on all of YouTube, and I highly recommend checking them out if you're a single guy.

The Big Takeaway From All This

If you want to become great at creating YouTube content, you have to let go of your desire to produce great content right off the bat. **And you have to dedicate yourself to the religion of regularity.**

You're going to pick a realistic upload frequency based on what I'm about to tell you in the next section. **And once your upload frequency is established, you will never deviate from that frequency — no matter what.**

Under no circumstances will you allow your subscribers to become de-habituated from watching your videos.

Even more importantly, you will never break the habit of uploading new content in your set frequency, since that's the only way to improve your ability to create content over time.

Like a fitness enthusiast who regularly goes to the gym in a set schedule no matter what, **you will regularly upload videos on a set schedule no matter what.**

If you have nothing to upload and you can't think of any good ideas, you are going to pull out your phone and create a crappy video.

If your house and all your devices are destroyed by a tornado, you will borrow a phone from someone else and update your subscribers on what happened.

Under no circumstances will you EVER break your set upload frequency.

I guarantee your viewers will appreciate hearing from you. And keep in mind you can always go back and delete the video later if your other content really is that much better.

But you might surprise yourself — many YouTubers have actually created great videos when they were under the gun and making something quick to avoid missing an upload.

It might seem daunting right now, but I'm going to show you how regularly making YouTube content can be FAR easier and less time consuming than you think.

Batching & Queueing: How To Upload With Perfect Regularity While Still Having A Life

When you're running a business there's a ton of things you have to do. So how can you stick to a perfectly regular upload schedule while still having time for everything else in your business — and your life?

From many years of making YouTube content, I've learned that the keys to doing this are **batching** and **queueing.**

Rather than create videos one by one when you need them, you create a "batch" of 10-20 outlines that you film all in one big full day shoot. This has a few advantages…

You'll be able to dedicate a large block of time to writing outlines, and once you get in the rhythm, they'll flow from you easier. You also won't have to set up your camera, lights, etc. for each individual video.

And once you're in the flow of filming, you'll be better on camera, and you'll finish each video quicker…

If you're hiring someone to film your videos, they can film them all in one day rather than having to drive back and forth for each individual video. If you're renting a location or traveling somewhere, you get a ton of videos out of it rather than just one.

Once you have your batch filmed, you can then dedicate a focused block of time to editing them all. Or you can hire an editor to do the same.

And when they're edited, you can upload them all to YouTube and release them individually on your regular upload schedule.

This means that you'll never be "under the gun" and in a situation where you're under pressure to quickly create a video to maintain your upload schedule. Even if some catastrophe happens and you can't film for weeks, you'll still maintain upload regularity if you have enough videos in the queue.

Batching and queueing also enable to you maintain perfect regularity without having to be a slave to your channel. You can take a month's vacation or work on another project for a month without letting your subscribers down.

And when you have a large queue of videos, you can still make videos "on the fly" to respond to current events, or just when a new idea strikes you. If you make one-off videos like this, you can upload them right away and just bump everything else in your queue back.

When you see YouTubers uploading videos with machine-like regularity, this is how they're doing it. It's far more efficient and way less stressful than filming and editing each video as you need it.

And you can now upload with machine-like regularity too by using batching and queueing.

How To Determine The Right Upload Frequency

So how often should you upload videos?

The absolute bare minimum upload frequency to maintain habituated viewers is once a month. If you're just starting off and you doubt your ability to create regular videos, then start here.

Once a month may work as a permanent upload schedule for you if you're in a product category with extremely low YouTube engagement. If you're selling toothpaste, a yeast infection treatment, or funeral home services, once a month will be fine.

You'll have some content to let viewers know you're legit. And you'll have enough views and enough subscribers to show Google Ads you're legit. For these types of low engagement product categories that's all you need.

For most businesses, your long term goal should be to upload more often. You can start with a once a month frequency, and then move to twice a month as soon as possible.

If you can maintain a frequency of once per week while still making decent content, that's even better for building viewer habits — and your own habits. Upload your videos on the same day every week so the viewer gets in the habit of watching your videos on that day.

If you're in a highly engaged YouTube category, you'll benefit from uploading even more often than this. Some examples of highly engaged categories include technology, fashion, fitness, dating advice, car tuning, makeup, and entrepreneurship.

If you're in a highly engaged category and you can upload good content regularly 2 or 3 days a week, it will significantly help you.

The holy grail of regularity — the ultimate habit building frequency — is to upload a new video every single day.

However, it is very difficult to maintain this heavy of an upload schedule while still keeping your quality up, and still having time to focus on all the other important areas of your business.

This type of frequency is ideal for full time YouTubers who mainly make money from selling ads on their channel, or companies that have a large team of people creating content.

For the vast majority of entrepreneurs and small business owners, the most I recommend uploading is three times per week.

Even three times a week can be challenging, and will require a team of people to film, edit, and upload your videos.

When I was running SixPackAbs.com, we uploaded videos twice per week to each of our two channels for a total of four per week. This tremendously helped our sales and brand value, and it was absolutely worth it. But making four quality videos per week required a team of four trainers, two video editors, and a social media manager to upload and set up the videos.

For most businesses, something like this should be your eventual goal. But you can always start off with a lower frequency and crank it up later once you have a bigger team.

To summarize, if you're just getting started on YouTube, commit to an upload frequency of once per month. Once you have a large queue of videos to upload built up, and you're confident you can stick to a higher frequency, step it up to once every two weeks or once per week.

And if you're in a highly engaged category and you have a team to edit and upload your videos, upload even more frequently than this.

It's OK to start off at a low frequency — you can always increase it later. **But make sure that you stick to the commitment you've made to your viewers to upload at your chosen interval no matter what.**

How To Brainstorm Ideas For Content Videos

Now that you've been thoroughly indoctrinated into the cult of regularity, it's time to talk about WHAT you should be uploading.

How do you come up with ideas for videos that people will want to watch, and which will drive sales of your product?

The best place to start is making videos about the **benefits** your customers are interested in. And this requires that you have a deep understanding of one of the most fundamental and most important distinctions in marketing — **features vs. benefits.**

Features are factual aspects of your product or service.

For example, some features of my Audi S5 include its 349 horsepower turbo-charged engine, its Quattro all-wheel drive, and its Bang & Olufsen sound system.

Benefits are the RESULTS your customer gets from your product or service. The benefits of my S5 include great acceleration, exceptional handling in bad weather, a relaxing luxury car ride when you want it, and the ability to impress women on dates.

The distinction is critical because as marketers we usually want to focus on the features of our product. But what customers are most interested in is the benefits.

So, benefits are the best place to start when making your videos.

Sub-Benefits: The Best Place To Start When Brainstorming YouTube Videos

Every market has an overall "big benefit" that your customer wants as their ultimate goal. In the weight loss market, the big benefit is to lose fat. In the cosmetics and fashion market, the big benefit is to look better. You get the idea.

But in every market, there are also many "sub-benefits" that customers are looking for that are part of achieving their overall big picture goal. And these sub-benefits are a great place to start when looking for video ideas.

For example, for Six Pack Shortcuts, the big benefit our customers were looking for was to get a lean, muscular physique with six pack abs. But they were also interested in other smaller benefits that were part of their ultimate goal.

We spent some time brainstorming these sub-benefits our potential customers were interested in, and we came up with this list:

- How to lose love handles
- How to lose chest fat
- How to build your biceps
- How to build chest muscle
- How to improve ab definition
- How to get a smaller waist
- How to get broader shoulders
- How to improve athletic performance

We made videos on all of these topics in the early days of our channel. Many of them eventually got millions of views, and I believe these videos helped our advertising tremendously.

These became some of our most viewed videos, and most of them are still up on the channel if you want to check them out yourself.

So, to come up with ideas for the first content videos for your channel, I recommend you follow the same process.

Of course, there are many videos on YouTube about any given sub-benefit. And it's OK if you're making a video about a sub-benefit that's been done hundreds of times before, like how to build chest muscle.

The key is that you show your viewers how to get the benefit in a new and unique way. For example, we taught viewers that rotational fly exercises were a better way to build your chest than traditional pushing exercises like bench press. And in other videos, we showed a unique type of fly/press hybrid exercise that gave the chest-building benefits of flys without the danger of a muscle tear usually associated with them.

And you do this with your sub-benefits as well. Even if there are thousands of videos about how to get that sub-benefit, people will watch yours if you show them how to get the benefit in a unique way that's never been done before.

Big Benefit + A Killer Feature — Another Great Way To Generate Video Ideas

Another great formula to generate ideas is showing viewers how to get the big benefit in your market using a killer feature that you know many of them are interested in.

For example, in the weight loss market, the big benefit is to lose weight. But there are an infinite variety of killer features you can combine with this benefit to generate video ideas.

Here are some examples:

- How to lose weight with a vegan diet
- How to lose weight with the ketogenic diet
- How to lose weight with the paleo diet
- How to lose weight with intermittent fasting
- How to lose weight while maintaining muscle mass

- How to lose weight when you're on your period
- How to lose weight if you have kids
- How to lose weight quickly for a wedding

Think about how you could apply this formula to your Big Benefit, and combine it with features you know will get your customers' attention.

Title Mirroring — Another Great Way To Generate Ideas

Title Mirroring is another easy way to come up with ideas that you know people in your market are interested in.

What you want to do is to look at the titles of the most popular videos in your category — and then make videos with a very similar title on the same topic.

An easy way to do this is to look at the channel of one of the most subscribed channels in your category, and to sort them by "most popular." You can then see the most viewed videos from that channel at the top — and you can make videos on similar topics.

For example, Matthew Hussey has one of the most popular channels in the women's dating advice category. If I were marketing a product in that category, the first thing I'd do is go to his channel, and see the most viewed videos.

One of the most viewed videos is titled "How To Text Guys — 4 Messages He'll Love." It's got over seventeen million views!

I'd then advise my client to make a video like this. It should have a title that's very similar, but not exactly the same. "How To Text Men — 3 Messages That Men Love" would be fine.

Now, here's the key to this strategy…

While you can make a very similarly titled video, you SHOULD NOT copy the content in the video itself. If you copy the content, it'll just be perceived as a copycat video by viewers, and you won't get a good response. You'll also make the creator of the original video pissed off at you, and you'll be establishing a reputation as a shitty person and a plagiarist.

It's perfectly OK to make videos on the same topic, and to have a similar title. **But you need to need to make all the content in the video unique.**

For example, in the "How To Text Guys" example, you need to provide DIFFERENT text messages than Matthew did in the original video. Not just slightly different, but truly new ideas.

If you do this right, it can be a great formula that could generate hundreds of video ideas for you.

Here's another benefit to this strategy — your videos are more likely to show up in the "Up Next" recommendations near the original video if it has a similar title. So not only is this a great way to generate proven ideas, but it may send organic traffic to your channel from the similar video as well.

The Ultimate Goal: Getting A Feel For What Your Audience Wants

There's nothing wrong with creating all of your videos according to one of the formulas above during your first year or two on YouTube. **But your eventual goal should be to develop a "feel" for what your audience is interested in watching.**

After uploading many videos, the best YouTubers have a sense for what people are interested in and what they're not interested in. And developing this type of intuition should be your long term goal.

Once you've developed this, you'll literally have limitless video ideas. And this is a great position to be in.

Because the best way to get great topics for videos is to brainstorm a huge amount of ideas, and to only use the very best ones. If you religiously stick to a regular upload schedule, you will develop this limitless idea generating capacity faster than you think.

How To Create Your Video Outlines

For the first few videos you create, I don't recommend using a teleprompter.

Teleprompters are a great tool to use in certain videos once you have a little on-camera experience. But sounding natural when reading a teleprompter takes time. You or your spokesperson can develop this skill later once you've mastered the basics.

Rather than a teleprompter script, you should just make a simple **outline** of your video to go off of when you film.

Your outline will be essentially a list of the main points you want to talk about in the video. When people make videos without outlines, they frequently get to be rambling and disorganized. Having an outline will give your video structure and direction — while also keeping your tone more natural and conversational than a script.

If your goal is to build a business with YouTube advertising, you should focus on making videos that educate your viewers about how to get the Big Benefit they want. It will also help if you can make your videos entertaining, and if you can personally connect with the viewers in these videos.

But the main thing that you want to accomplish in these videos — and the first thing to focus on learning — is helping your viewers to get their Big Benefit.

When you're starting off, it'll be much easier to create these video outlines if you have a proven formula to work off.

So, here's the formula I've personally used to outline many different content videos that have gotten tens of millions of views.

The Four Part Content Formula

First, you briefly tell your viewer **what** the video is going to be about. You hook their attention in, and let them know this video is going to be about something they're very interested in.

Then, you tell you viewer **why** it's important they learn about this topic. This increases their commitment to the video, and hooks their attention in more deeply. For some videos, this can be brief when it's obvious why they need to learn about it.

For other topics where it's not so obvious, this part will be a little longer.

After the *why*, you tell your viewer exactly **how** they can get the benefits you're talking about. This is the meat and potatoes of the video's content, and the bulk of the time in your video should be spent on this.

At the end of the video, you tell the viewer to take **action.** You show them a specific, concrete step they can take now to move towards their goal.

This is the Four Part Content Formula you can use to create your first outlines. Just remember:

WHAT — WHY — HOW — ACTION

These outlines don't have to be fancy. A rough bullet point list of the major points you want to hit in the video works just fine.

So, what does it look like when you create an outline with the Four Part Content Formula? Here are a few examples from different product categories that use the formula.

Example Outline #1: Women's Swimwear

- **Topic**
  - How to conceal stretch marks

- **What**
  - In this video, I'm going to show you the best ways to minimize the visibility of your stretch marks in a swimsuit.

- **Why**
  - If you don't know how to do this, you are going to be self-conscious about your stretch marks when you wear swimwear.

  - But if you do know how to do this, you'll know how to look great regardless of any stretch marks you have. And you'll have the confidence to have fun when you're wearing your swimwear.

- **How**
  - Find a one-piece that conceals stretch marks, but which also looks sexy

    - Show example suit #1
    - Show example suit #2

  - Use waterproof cosmetics to minimize the appearance of minor stretch marks

    - Show cosmetics spokeswoman personally uses

- o Learn to love your stretch marks. Realize that almost all women have them, and they probably appear much more significant to you than they do to everyone else

  - ▪ Tell a story of how spokeswoman learned to be less self-conscious about her stretch marks

- o Show the process in action and the difference it makes

  - ▪ Spokeswoman shows her stretch marks in a regular swimsuit, with self-conscious body language

  - ▪ Spokeswoman shows her stretch marks in a swimsuit that conceals the most severe ones, with cosmetics to assist cover-up, with confident body language

- **Action**
  - o Watch my video on body image to learn how to love your body more

  - o Check out these pieces on my site which are perfect for women who have stretch marks

---

Obviously, I'm not an expert on women's swimwear. So, I can't tell you exactly which one-pieces conceal stretch marks and look sexy, or which cosmetics are best for concealing stretch marks.

But you get the idea for what your outline should look like. And if you are an expert on this type of content, you should have no trouble filling in the specific examples.

Note that this outline is just a very rough outline of the major points I want the spokeswoman to hit. This isn't a script — it's just the skeleton of the video to give it structure and keep it on track.

You can say the points in the "What" and "Why" sections nearly verbatim, and usually these sections will be brief.

This will help you build momentum, and ensure that the critical first part of your video is well planned.

Each point in the "How" section might take a few minutes to flesh out.

For example, you might spend ten minutes showing great one piece swimsuits with just that bullet point to guide you. The "how" content will be the bulk of your video, and keeping your outline to rough bullet points will make sure the bulk of your content sounds natural and unscripted.

In the "Action" part of the video, you show them a concrete, specific step they can take to start benefiting from what they've learned.

This is very important. Even if people loved your video, they may be confused about exactly how to implement what you taught if you don't give them specific action steps. The more action you get can your viewers to take, the better results they'll get – and the more they'll love your channel.

Here's another example of what an outline could look like from another market.

Example #2: Men's Dating Advice Market

- **Topic**

- How to create a great online dating profile

- **What**
  - In this video, I'm going to show you how to create a great online dating profile that attracts quality women

- **Why**
  - It's important that you learn about this, because if you don't know how to make a great profile, you'll struggle to get women to respond to your messages online. You'll spend a lot of time and effort, and be frustrated by the results

  - On the other hand, once you know to create a great profile, everything becomes easier for you.

    You'll get more responses to your messages, women will start messaging you, and ultimately, you'll get more dates and have a better chance of finding the right woman.

- **How**
  - Have professionally taken and edited photos

    - Walk them through how to hire a photographer inexpensively to do this

  - Mention the things which may attract more women in your profile, but frame them as things you are grateful for to avoid coming off as bragging

    - Example: you could say "I'm grateful to own my own company" or "I'm grateful to have such an amazing group of friends"

- o Maintain profiles on multiple dating sites and apps to improve your odds

  - ▪ Discuss the best sites and apps to focus on

- **Action**
  - o Hire a photographer on Craigslist to do a photo shoot for you

  - o Write new online dating profiles on the sites and apps we discussed based on what you learned in this video.

The Four Part Content Formula can be applied to any market, and it's a great way to generate quality video outlines fast.

How To Film Your Videos

Once you've got your outlines, it's finally time to film!

I cover how to film and edit videos in-depth in Step 5. If you want to get started with a sophisticated filming and editing setup right away, you can skip to that chapter and use one of my recommended packages.

But if you're just getting started and working with a small budget, I recommend keeping things super simple to start with. Here are the bare bones basics you can use to make your very first videos:

- Film your videos with a high end smartphone, or with whatever camera you have right now.

- Buy a three-point lighting kit from Amazon. Here's the one I recommend for people with a limited budget:

15StepsBonuses.com/BeginnerLighting

- Search on YouTube for "three-point lighting tutorial" to learn how to set up your lights.

- Buy a basic smartphone lavalier mic. Here's the inexpensive one I recommend:

  15StepsBonuses.com/PhoneMic

- Edit your videos using iMovie if you have a Mac or Windows Movie Maker if you're on a PC. Search on YouTube for "How To Edit Videos With iMovie/Windows Movie Maker" to learn the basics.

Keep in mind that your viewers are watching your videos because you're showing them how to get the big benefit they want. They're not watching because of your production skills.

So, it's perfectly fine to keep things extremely simple like this when you're first starting off.

If you have a larger budget, you can also buy one of the better setups in Step 5 from the start. Or you can simply hire someone with their own equipment to film and edit these videos for you.

Any of these options can work, but the important point is to get started as soon as possible on a regular upload schedule and to spend minimal time on the production of your first few content videos.

Don't wait until you have the perfect filming setup. **Film your videos NOW, and figure out how to perfect your setup later.**

And don't worry — you're going to learn much more about video production in Step 5. You won't need to use a simple setup like this forever.

Upload And Set Up Your Videos On YouTube

Once you've filmed and edited your videos, it's time to upload!

Whenever you upload a video, you should always include a video description. While not many people will read the description, it can be important for YouTube to help people discover the video through its "Up Next" recommendations.

Again, I recommend keeping things super simple to start off.

In the first sentence of your description, include a link to your website and why the person should go there. This way people who just glance at the beginning of your description are more likely to go to your site.

It should look like this:

Learn more about YouTube marketing at
https://SocialResponseMarketing.com

Make sure to include "http://" or "https://" in your link. YouTube needs this to make your URL into a hyperlink, so a person can go to your website by clicking it rather than having to type it into their browser.

Below this first line, include a brief paragraph or two talking about what your video is about. You can write this quickly, and you don't need to spend a ton of time on it.

If you're making a long video, it can also help to add timestamps so people can skip to key content they're looking for. YouTube will make these clickable so the video player will skip to this point in the video when the user taps or clicks on them.

We'd use this feature a lot when uploading long workout videos. We would timestamp each individual exercise within the workout, so that people who wanted to learn that exercise or review it could skip directly to that part.

If you are uploading a batch of videos, you'll also want to make sure the videos you don't want to immediately release are set to "Private." This will prevent them from all showing up on your channel at the same time. When you're ready to release the video later, you just need to go in and change it to a "public" video, and it'll appear on your channel and in your subscribers' feeds.

And that's it...your video is live!

Monitor Engagement — This Will Be Important For Your Ads Later

When you upload your first videos, don't be surprised if very, very few people watch them.

That's normal, because there's usually no way for people to discover videos from a new channel. The only way new channels immediately take off is if you're buying advertising, or you're sending people from an external source (like a big Facebook page or email list.)

The views, shares, likes, etc. on your content videos will drastically increase once you begin advertising so people can discover your channel.

Now even though the engagement on your channel will be low when you're first starting off, it's still important to pay attention to. It's a critical source of information for when you start making ads later.

You'll probably be surprised by which videos get more views and engagement, and which videos get less. And it will help you refine your understanding of what the market wants. And in Step 4, you're going to learn how to use that information to make great ads.

Your Action Steps From This Chapter:

1. Brainstorm 20 different ideas for YouTube videos based on one of the three formulas you've learned: **The Sub-Benefit Formula, The Big Benefit + Killer Feature Formula,** and **The Title Mirroring Formula**

2. Pick the ten ideas from your list you think your potential customers will be most interested in.

3. Create short, rough outlines for each of the ten videos using the **Four Part Content Formula (What, Why, How, Action.)**

4. Buy your filming setup if you don't have one. You can either use the bare bones setup I showed earlier in this chapter, or you can skip to Chapter 5 and buy one of the better setups. Alternatively, you can hire someone to film and edit everything for you if you have a larger budget.

5. Film your first ten videos in one batch

6. Edit your first ten videos

7. Upload your videos to YouTube, and set them up with a basic description

8. Set all your videos to "Private" except the one you want to release immediately. Put the remainder in your queue, and release them on your set upload schedule.

Step 4: Learn The Universal "Master Formula" For Creating Killer YouTube Ad Scripts

Many people believe that writing a great ad scripts is just a matter of "being creative" and getting lucky. But nothing could be further from the truth!

The truth is that most successful YouTube ads are made by applying a proven marketing formula. By learning and applying the proven formulas that successful YouTube advertisers use, you can massively increase the profitability of your YouTube campaigns.

Why Proven Formulas Beat Creativity

In this chapter, I'm going to teach you how to write great scripts for your YouTube commercials — or what's commonly referred to as your ad "creative."

But the first thing you need to learn about your ad "creative" is that being "creative" is only a minor part of the process.

It helps and can add style points, but it won't be the main factor that determines whether your YouTube advertising is profitable.

The main thing that differentiates YouTube marketing millionaires from broke "wantrepreneurs" is **whether they know and apply proven marketing formulas in their YouTube ads.**

Because YouTube ads appear to be so different from each other, many people do not realize that most successful YouTube ads are created from a small number of proven formulas. In fact, a huge number of ads are created using a single **"Master Formula"** — which you're about to learn in this chapter.

When you're first starting off, I recommend scripting all of your ads using the Master Formula to keep things simple. Later in this book, you'll learn more advanced, nuanced ad scripting formulas you can use to take your creative to the next level.

Ad Scripting: The Single Biggest Key To Success With YouTube Advertising

There's a reason why you want to stick to proven scripting formulas for YouTube ads you intend on spending your hard-earned money on.

That's because the marketing message in your ad script will be the single most important factor in whether your campaign succeeds.

The way you manage your ad campaigns matters, and your video production and editing matters as well. But you can get away with just doing the basics in other areas and still make profits if you have great ad scripts.

Remember: if you can identify benefits your potential customers want, promise those benefits, and prove you can deliver, people will respond to your ads.

It's also fairly easy to hire someone who can do a great job filming and editing your videos. For a higher salary, you can even hire someone who can do a decent job managing your Google Ads account.

But it's extremely difficult to hire someone to script great YouTube ads. Since it's significantly different from most forms of marketing copy, there just aren't that many people who have successful experience doing it.

So, your ability to create great ad scripts is an incredibly important skill — and it's worth investing some time and money in learning this skill.

Why You Need To Script Your Ads

There are occasionally advertisers like Tai Lopez who can create successful ads going off the cuff without a teleprompter script. But this approach usually fails.

The vast majority of successful ads on YouTube are scripted and read off a teleprompter. And until you've made your first million with YouTube advertising, all of your ads should be scripted too.

The reason for this is that **every second counts** in a YouTube ad. You cannot afford to waste any time on rambling. You cannot let your viewer's attention slip for an instant. The skip button is always right in front of them, and if you lose their attention even for even one second, they will be gone.

To avoid losing their attention you need a polished ad message — and this can only be accomplished by scripting.

If you don't have a teleprompter or someone to operate it for you, don't worry. In the next chapter I'm going to show you how you can get a pro-quality teleprompter for under $200.

And I'll also show you an app you can use which listens to your voice and automatically moves the script as you speak — so you can use a teleprompter even if you're filming by yourself.

Most people sound a little unnatural their first few times reading a teleprompter. But it's a skill you'll develop quickly, and within a few hours of practice you'll be sounding natural and unscripted.

You should also keep in mind that you don't have to be the one on camera for your commercials. I've built many successful campaigns just by writing a great ad script, then hiring an actor off Craigslist to deliver the script for me.

The Master Formula For Great YouTube Ads

The vast majority of successful YouTube ads are written with a single common, basic formula. I recommend using this Master Formula to script your first batch of ads, before moving on to more advanced and complex formulas.

There are five elements to the Master Formula:

- **The Skip Stopper**
- **The Believable Promise**
- **The First Call To Action**
- **The Conditioning Content**
- **The Final Call To Action**

We'll go through each element here, and I'll show you how to master them all.

The Skip Stopper: Grab Your Viewer's Attention In A Relevant Way

This is the most critical element of the Master Formula. Even experienced copywriters usually struggle to create great Skip Stoppers, since it's something that totally unique to YouTube advertising.

The single biggest difference between YouTube advertising and other types of online video advertising is that most YouTube ads are skippable after just five seconds. That's because the vast majority of the YouTube ad inventory is now in the InStream (skippable) ad format.

This means your YouTube ad will usually show up in the viewer's video player before the video they wanted to watch.

After five seconds, they'll be given the option to skip your ad.

According to a study of 1,015 adults by the research firm ORC International, **ninety percent of YouTube InStream ads are immediately skipped.** This means that unless you learn how to make your ad more interesting than 90% of other ads within the first five seconds, chances are nobody will ever see the rest of it.

That's why your Skip Stopper is so critical. If most people are skipping your ad, Google will charge you more for every view for people who do watch it. If your view rate gets low enough, Google won't even run your ad at all. But if you can get a great Skip Stopper, you'll pay less per completed view, and you'll have an easier time scaling your campaigns up.

Of course, there is also a non-skippable ad format on YouTube — Video Discovery ads. In this type of ad, the user clicks on your video's thumbnail to start your ad playing rather than having a skippable ad show up in their video player.

But Skip Stoppers are important even for Video Discovery ads. Even though the user doesn't have the option to skip explicitly in front of them, they have still been trained to evaluate ads quickly based on the first few seconds.

That's because most of the ads they see on YouTube are InStream, and this influences their behavior even when they click on your Video Discovery ads.

Now, don't get mad at your viewers for skipping ads so flippantly. When you think about it, they really have no choice.

We all see dozens of different ads every day and there's no way we can spend our time or attention on all of them. So, we evaluate whether an ad is something that's worth our time extremely quickly — especially on YouTube.

Because of this tendency of YouTube users, the first 5-10 seconds of your ad are absolutely CRUCIAL.

One of the biggest mistakes I see new advertisers making is being far too lazy and lackadaisical about the first ten seconds of their ad. This results in the first ten seconds of their ads being full of "throat clearing," or verbally warming up before the really interesting part of their ad starts.

They foolishly waste this crucial time on things like introducing themselves, or showing their animated logo.

To the viewer, this type of thing just seems like boring, meaningless pablum. It triggers their reflex to skip the ad.

The result of this is that by the time the good part of their ad comes, 90% of the audience is already gone.

If this happens to you, it doesn't matter if the rest of your commercial is brilliant. It doesn't matter if you have the world's highest converting sales video. The many hours you've spent on developing these assets will be wasted, and your campaign will lose money.

As you cry yourself to sleep in the homeless shelter each night, you'll say to yourself, "If only I had listened to Dan's advice and made better Skip Stoppers!"

Obviously, I'm exaggerating to add some humor to this dire warning. But Skip Stoppers are critically important, and without a good one, nothing else in your ad will matter.

That's why you need to take Skip Stoppers seriously. You absolutely cannot just make an ad that starts with the first thing that pops into your head. You cannot "warm up" and take 20-30 seconds to catch their attention, like you could on a sales video, a website, or a Facebook ad.

And if you want to build profitable YouTube advertising campaigns, **you need a proven process for creating high performing Skip Stoppers.**

Here's how all of the top YouTube advertisers do it:

First, top YouTube advertisers will usually employ multiple highly paid, highly skilled copywriters. These are guys who have spent years studying how to write killer copy, and studying great YouTube ads.

These guys will usually spend HOURS brainstorming ideas for commercials. They'll spend at least HALF of their time on brainstorming the Skip Stoppers, since the Skip Stopper is as important as every other part of the ad combined.

After generating dozens of ideas, they'll give each other feedback on them and tweak the ideas based on this feedback.

Then they'll choose the cream of the crop — the best 20-30% of ideas — to actually make into ads.

When the video is scripted, a huge amount of wordsmithing will go into the first ten seconds of the script. Hours and hours will be spent perfecting it.

And once the video is filmed, there are multiple rounds of revisions to perfect the Skip Stopper until the copywriters are confident it will perform.

This is how I've created many great Skip Stoppers, and this is the process that other big YouTube advertisers use to create great Skip Stoppers too.

I tell you that so that you know **you aren't going to create a great Skip Stopper by "getting lucky"** or by having a lightning bolt of inspired creativity hit you. You are only going to consistently create great Skip Stoppers if you educate yourself about how to do it, and if you have a process for creating these ideas.

Having a team of elite copywriters to brainstorm ideas with is definitely an advantage. **But you can still have a great process for creating Skip Stoppers even if you're a solo entrepreneur.** I personally brainstormed and scripted many different winning ads simultaneously before I had a large team, and many other marketers have done the same.

How To Create A Great Skip Stopper

First, you need to grab the viewer's attention. It's not enough to just be mildly interesting or more attention-getting than the average ad.

To make it likely your ad will not be skipped, your Skip Stopper must be in the top 10% of most attention-getting ads that your viewer sees on YouTube.

Here's what it looks like when most people watch YouTube ads:

A viewer pulls up a video she really wants to watch...and then an *annoying ad* comes up before the video she wanted. Ewww!

Her finger starts hovering over the "Skip" button on her phone before the ad even starts playing.

The ad starts playing, and almost always it fails to arrest her attention immediately. After all, she's TRYING to ignore the ad. She already watches far too much advertising, and she doesn't want to pay attention to skippable ads unless there's a compelling reason to.

She just wants to watch the video that she clicked on. Your ad is just blocking her from the video she wants.

But every now and then, an ad comes up that's different. Something that grabs her attention, so she HAS TO keep watching to find out more.

Some people will end up buying if they start the ad, and some people won't. But if the rest of the marketing message is good, the advertiser now has a solid chance to turn that attention into cash.

ALERT!!! URGENT WARNING!!! AVOID ALL OUTRAGEOUS SKIP STOPPERS!!!

Because you need to be more attention-getting than 90% of ads to get a high view rate, you might think that a great way to create Skip Stoppers is to load up the front of your ad with explosions, sirens, special effects, yelling, and other outrageous stuff.

But this is actually a huge mistake!

It's not enough to just catch a viewer's attention with your Skip Stopper. You have to catch their attention in a way that's not annoying, and which is RELEVANT to the Big Promise you're eventually going to make.

This is for two reasons.

First of all, my testing shows that outrageous stuff like explosions, yelling, etc. in the beginning of the ad will actually DECREASE your view rate and ENCOURAGE people to skip.

If you think about your own behavior as a YouTube viewer, it's not hard to see why. If you get a first impression that an ad is annoying, it doesn't matter if it's loud and outrageous...your first impulse will be to turn the annoyance off by hitting the skip button.

But there's an even more important reason why annoying, outrageous Skip Stoppers are ineffective...

SEX! Now That I've Got Your Attention...

Imagine that you're a teenage boy starting his first year of college.

You're browsing YouTube like you usually do, and an ad comes up before the video you want to watch. You're about to hit the skip button like you always do...but then you see them.

Beautiful young women in string bikinis walk across the screen.

You're transfixed! You stare drooling at the screen, your thoughts of hitting the skip button instantly forgotten.

Then the camera pans over to an insurance agent in a suit and tie. He says, "Now that I've got your attention, let's talk about your car insurance..."

Obviously, an ad like this is not going to work. While you may initially catch your prospect's attention and get a high view rate, you won't be able to turn this initial attention into sales.

That's because the Skip Stopper was not RELEVANT to the ad.

The transition to the Big Promise and the rest of the ad is jolting. Just because you got the prospect to pay attention to your bikini models does not mean he's interested in your insurance pitch. Once your gimmick that caught his attention is gone, he'll hit the skip button and you're dead.

Even worse, the viewer will feel TRICKED. His first impression of you will be that you're shifty, dishonest and manipulative. He'll feel like you wasted his time and will be far less receptive to any other ads he sees from you in the future.

And while this example was with a teenage boy, customers in every market feel the same way when they're tricked by irrelevant Skip Stoppers.

That's why it's not enough to just catch your prospect's attention. You have to catch their attention, AND you have to smoothly relate your Skip Stopper to the rest of the ad so that your ideal prospects continue to watch.

How To Create A Great Skip Stopper

First of all, you should study everything you can about creating Skip Stoppers. Obviously, you're off to a good start by reading this chapter. And you can take your knowledge to a deeper level by investing in my video course, where I cover this topic in greater detail.

But other than what I've created myself, there is shockingly little information out there about how to create great Skip Stoppers. That's why in addition to studying my material on how to create great Skip Stoppers, **you need to start studying Skip Stoppers created by other top YouTube advertisers.**

There are absolutely GENIUS Skip Stoppers in many different markets created by some of the most brilliant YouTube advertisers in the world. And you can watch them all for free right on YouTube. You just need to know how to recognize a great Skip Stopper, and how to break down the principles behind it to apply to your own business.

When you're looking for great Skip Stoppers, don't just look at ads that are running a lot right now. You should also look at older ads which got millions of views years ago, but which are no longer used.

That's because these ads are the ones that are the most thoroughly proven to be winners. And because the principles behind great Skip Stoppers are universal, you can usually apply these principles to your concept to create a successful new ad.

At the end of this chapter, I'm going to analyze one of the greatest ads in YouTube history and show you how you can use the principles behind them in your own advertising. I'll also show you how you can start building your own "swipe file" of great YouTube ads, and how to break down the principles behind them to apply to your own campaigns.

The Believable Promise

After you've caught their attention and stopped their skip reflex, you then need to hook your viewer's attention in on a deeper level. And you accomplish this through your **Believable Promise.**

Your Believable Promise will NOT be a promise about what your product will do for them — it will be a promise about what they'll get from spending their time watching your ad.

Remember, they'll be hearing this 10-20 seconds into the ad, right after their first impression of you was some type of attention-getting skip stopper. Even if your product is a screaming bargain and it can solve all of their problems, telling them this will not be BELIEVABLE to someone who has just met you a few seconds ago.

Developing a relationship with a customer is similar to romantic relationships in this way.

You wouldn't ask a woman to sleep with you twenty seconds after meeting her. You wouldn't ask a man to marry you before you've gone on a date. Immediately asking for what you want right away never works in human relationships, because the other person doesn't know or trust you enough to take that big of a step.

The same thing applies to relationships with customers. The goal of each part of your commercial is just to get them to take the next step.

Your Skip Stopper gets them to watch your Believable Promise. Your Believable Promise gets them to watch the rest of your ad. The rest of your ad convinces them to watch your sales video. **And your sales video is what ultimately convinces them to buy your product.**

It's also important to note that what your customers learns from the ad needs to ultimately lead to buying the product.

You'll be sharing genuinely valuable information with your prospect that he can use whether she buys or not. But what he learns will also educate him about why your product is the best solution, so he'll be primed to buy later.

Here are a few examples of what I mean by this…

Example #1: Testosterone Boosting Supplements

BAD: I'm going to show you why Testo-Boost 5000 is going to boost your T and make you more manly!

GOOD: In today's video, I'm going to show you five herbs that can naturally boost your testosterone — and I'll show you the scientific studies proving they're effective.

Example #2: Specialty Car Parts

BAD: Here's how you can make your car way faster by installing our custom-built turbocharger!

GOOD: Here are the three best "bang for your buck" modifications that you can make to your car, so you can get the most performance boost for the least money.

Example #3: Tax Strategist

BAD: Today I'm going to show you how hiring me can save you boatloads of money on taxes!

GOOD: Today I'm going to show you four money-saving tax deductions that most people aren't taking advantage of.

You get the idea. You promise them that they'll get a small, simple, helpful piece of knowledge from watching your ad. It doesn't have to be a huge promise — it just has to be something a customer believes is worth spending a few minutes of their time to learn. You don't need to over-sell or over-promise.

It's also important to note that all of the Believable Promises above promise that the viewer will learn something that will later lead to him believing your product is the best solution to his problems.

In the testosterone booster example, you show him five herbs that boost testosterone, and the proof they work. This could later lead to you showing the prospect how your supplement is the only product to include these herbs or that it's the most convenient and practical way to get them.

The First Call To Action

Your Call To Action, or CTA, is where you ask people to take the next step by going to your website. Your call to action can be to watch the next video (your sales video), or to take a quiz. **When using this formula, it should not be a direct appeal to buy your product — that's what your sales video is for.**

Here's the most important thing you need to know about creating your Call To Action...

Your potential customers are all different types of people, who react to ads in wildly different ways. **So, there is no one single best time to make your call to action.**

Some will be willing to go to your website and watch your sales video after a very short amount of video. Others are more skeptical, and will need more convincing before they're willing to leave YouTube.

If you make short ads, many people in the latter group will never go to your site. And if you wait too long to bring out your call to action, many people in the first group will get bored and will never make it to your call to action.

So how can you appeal to both groups?

It's simple: **You deliver a quick, early call to action where you ask the viewer to go to your website within the first 1-2 minutes.**

You leave a graphical call to action on screen for the remainder of the commercial, so your viewer can go to your website whenever she's ready.

And you deliver a final, longer call to action at the end. In the final Call To Action, you go more in-depth. And you give your viewer more details about why they should spend their time going to your website.

This multiple CTA structure has been proven to work in many different commercials for my own companies and for my clients.

It's effective because it allows customers who are ready to go to your site after a minute or two to do so. This prevents having this type of person skip before your Call To Action comes.

It also gives more detail for harder to convince people, so you don't lose this type of person either. And since the Call To Action is on screen for most of the commercial, people who are in the middle can leave the ad at any point when they're ready.

A common mistake in creating YouTube ads is imagining they're like a novel or a film, where you have to watch them from beginning to end. They're not.

Remember: an ad is not a work of art. It's a tool intended to get qualified prospects to your website. If someone watches a minute of your ad then goes to your website, and never sees the rest of your ad, that's great!

The ad did its job, and you should welcome your potential customers doing this.

Examples Of Good And Bad First Calls To Action

Example #1: Facebook Advertising

BAD: Click "Buy Now" below to get my course so you can make bucket loads of money with Facebook ads!

GOOD: If you liked these tips, I've put together a video that teaches you my full Facebook advertising system. To learn my full system for advertising on Facebook, click "Watch Now" below.

A text graphic that says, "Click Watch Now To Learn My Full Facebook Advertising System!" appears on screen, and stays on the bottom of the screen for the rest of the video.

Example #2: Natural Skin Care

BAD: Now that you've learned how dangerous chemicals in conventional sunscreen can be for your skin, click "Shop Now" to buy my all natural facial sunscreen. It's only $19.95, and I offer six varieties for all different skin types!

GOOD: So now you know how dangerous the chemicals in conventional sunscreen are for your skin. But what should you look for in a sunscreen to know it's safe and effective? It depends on your skin type. And that's why I put together my free Skin Type Quiz. Click "Take Quiz" below to get started.

A text graphic that says "Click "Take Quiz" To Find Out Your Skin Type" appears on screen, and stay on the bottom of the screen for the rest of the video. After the prospect takes your quiz, your website recommends one of your six varieties of natural sunscreen based on her skin type for her to buy.

The Conditioning Content

The Conditioning Content will make up the bulk of your ad. It's "content" because it's genuinely useful information that entices people to spend their valuable time watching your ad. And it's "conditioning" because it subtly conditions your prospect with beliefs that will later lead them to see your product is the best solution.

A small minority of people are "hyper-responders" and are willing to click through to your site right away. But most people aren't like that.

Conditioning Content is meant for these average people who aren't hyper-responders. These people who need more convincing, and they need a compelling reason to keep spending their valuable time on your ad.

It's critical to note that it's not enough to JUST teach prospects something valuable in your Conditioning Content. It needs to be something valuable that later leads to the sale.

A few examples to illustrate…

Example #1: Exercise Equipment

BAD CONDITIONING CONTENT: Giving five nutrition tips to help them build muscle, then saying "go to my website to learn more about my exercise equipment which can also help with building muscle."

This doesn't work because the content didn't condition them to buy. Even if you give them brilliant, helpful nutrition tips, it doesn't instill them with the belief that your exercise equipment is the best solution.

GOOD CONDITIONING CONTENT: Showing a short workout that uses your exercise equipment, and pointing out the advantages of the equipment throughout the workout.

This works because it's engaging content the prospect will learn from, and it also conditions them to buy. They are learning the advantages of your product throughout the content, but it's not a "pitch" — they're also learning a good workout at the same time.

Example #2: Real Estate Investment Advice

BAD CONTENT: Walking the prospect through in detail exactly how you put together your last deal to buy a 200 unit apartment building

This content won't work even if you're showing them brilliant, mind-blowing real estate investing techniques. Your prospects will probably believe you got this deal because you're more skilled than them, or more experienced, or because you have more money. They won't believe that your system can teach them to do what you're doing. They'll come away from the ad thinking you're great, but will not be conditioned to buy your product.

GOOD CONTENT: Teaching the prospect the top five advantages of investing in real estate

This content will work because it can lead naturally into a call to action where you tell them that your system is the only one designed to fully maximize all five major advantages of real estate investing. For example, you could point out how the tax advantages of real estate investing are critically important, and then show them how your system is the only one to fully maximize real estate investing tax breaks.

The Final Call To Action

In your final Call To Action, you'll be telling your prospect in more detail about why he should spend more of his time to go to your website.

For most websites, you will just want to talk about the free content they'll be getting and not mention your product at all.

For other types of websites, it makes sense to mention your product explicitly in the final call to action.

If you're sending your prospect to a quiz or to get something for free in exchange for giving their email, you SHOULD NOT mention the product you'll ultimately be selling. You just want to get them to the next step, and you can talk about the product later.

The same thing applies if you're sending your prospect to a sales funnel. You should just talk about what they'll learn from the next video, and let your sales video sell your product.

The only exception to this rule is if you're using an eCommerce (Shopify) store.

If you're sending your prospect to an eCommerce store, or to download a mobile app, you SHOULD talk about how they'll learn more about the product for sale in the final CTA. These types of landing pages are obviously commercial when the prospect lands of them.

So, by putting this in your final Call To Action, you'll seem more congruent and honest about what they'll see when they click.

If you don't know what these types of sales websites are yet, don't worry! You'll learn all about them later in this book.

For now, just write the final CTA of your ads to sell THE NEXT VIDEO, not the product, unless you are advertising an app or Shopify store.

How To Create Great YouTube Ads

To review, the elements of the Master Formula are:

- **The Skip Stopper**
- **The Believable Promise**
- **The First Call To Action**
- **The Conditioning Content**
- **The Final Call To Action**

You can use this formula to create an infinite variety of profitable YouTube ads.

Now that you've got the Formula, let's talk about the PROCESS of creating great YouTube ads. How can you come up with great ideas for ads that use the Master Formula — and how exactly do you turn those ideas into great scripts?

Like every other complex process, it can be broken down into a series of simple steps.

The First Step: Brainstorm Ideas For YouTube Ads With Skeleton Outlines

I've come up with many different ads which have made millions for my companies and for my clients. From this fact, you might assume I'm some kind of genius at coming up with YouTube ad ideas.

In fact, I am not. **I have just come up with FAR MORE ideas than most entrepreneurs do — and I have a better system to identify the best ideas, and to refine them into polished ads.**

The single biggest mistake I see YouTube Marketers make in the script-writing process is that they don't brainstorm NEARLY enough ideas for ads. Many marketers will brainstorm five ideas, then make three ads out of them. Or even worse, they'll make every idea they have into an ad.

This is a huge mistake. Even if you're a great YouTube marketer, it's not realistic for every idea for an ad that you have to be great. At most, only 20-30% of the ideas that you come up with will have the potential to be winners.

It's like baseball in this way. Even the best hitter can't hit a home run every time. And even the best YouTube marketers cannot come up with "home run" ideas every time.

That's why you want to brainstorm a TON of ideas — and then take the cream of the crop, making only your best ideas into scripts and ads.

There are two ways to do this — by yourself, or with a group of other skilled copywriters.

How To Brainstorm Ideas For Ads By Yourself

The key to a successful brainstorm is writing down ideas FAST and as soon as they flow into your mind.

When most people brainstorm, they have their one foot on their "mental brakes." This means that they only want to write down good ideas, so they think about each idea too much before writing it down.

Like trying to accelerate a car while hitting the brakes, this doesn't get you anywhere.

That's because censoring the ideas that pop into your head blocks the flow of your creativity, and prevents your great ideas from coming out. And if you're brainstorming with one foot on the mental brakes, it'll take you forever to brainstorm even a small number of ads.

You shouldn't worry about practical considerations at all when you're brainstorming.

Maybe your ideas are too expensive or too difficult to shoot. Maybe they'll cause some compliance problems with Google Ads. Maybe your spokesperson will object to saying this or that thing.

Don't worry about these types of mundane practical considerations while brainstorming. It's time to be creative!

When you cull your ideas later, they'll be plenty of time to think about solutions to these problems. And once your ideas come out, you might be surprised that you find a way to solve any practical challenges that come up later.

So, when you're brainstorming, you want to take your foot off the "mental brakes" of finding objections and not writing down your bad ideas. And hammer your creative "mental gas pedal" to the metal!

Write down EVERYTHING that comes into your head — whether it's a stupid idea or not.

In fact, if you're new to marketing brainstorming, you should start off by purposely writing down a few outlandishly stupid ideas just to practice getting your foot off the mental brakes.

You'll find that as you come up with ideas, the flow of your creativity will be unleashed. You might need to come up with 4-5 mediocre ideas before the good stuff starts coming out — and that's perfectly fine. The more you hammer down on the mental gas pedal — and the more you resist your urge to hit the mental brakes — the better your ideas will get.

To avoid getting excessively committed to ideas during the brainstorming phase, you only want to write down the bare bones details of the idea. You don't need an extensive outline — just what I call a "skeleton outline" of the most important parts of the ad.

This way, you can rapidly write down many ideas, and you won't feel bad about discarding the majority of them later.

When you're just starting off, you use the Master Formula as a template. Think of it as a skeleton to hang the "flesh" of your commercial on. You start with the template, write a sentence or two about each of the important sections, and you've got your outline!

Here are a few examples of what your skeleton outlines should look like, from one of my own commercial brainstorms for Social Response Marketing:

Skeleton Outline Example #1: The Most Horrifying Enemy Of YouTube Marketers

- **Skip Stopper**
    - This is the most HORRIFYING enemy you face as a YouTube marketer

- [DAN REACHES DOWN TO SKIP BUTTON. USING EDITING, HE APPEARS TO GRAB IT AND HOLD IT UP IN THE AIR. CAMERA ZOOMS IN ON THE SKIP BUTTON IN DAN'S HAND WITH A DRAMATIC HORROR MOVIE STYLE FEMALE SCREAM]

  - The Skip button. Over 90% of YouTube ads are skipped. And if people are skipping YOUR ad, that means your campaigns are going to lose bucket loads of money.

- **Believable Promise**
  - That's why in this video, I'm going to show you how to create a great "Skip Stopper" — something that draws your viewer's attention in, and gets them to watch your ad.

- **First CTA**
  - I made a free video on my site that teaches my full YouTube advertising system, click "Watch Now" to check it out.

- **Conditioning Content**
  - Show an example of a great Skip Stopper from a past winning ad I've created

  - Break down what makes a great skip stopper work

    - Catches attention
    - Is relevant to the content of your ad
    - Flows in a Believable Promise

- **Final CTA**
  - Watch the free video on my site to learn my full YouTube advertising system

- Show more examples of winning ads I've created and other items that establish credibility — media appearances, book, etc.

- Give more details about what they'll learn in the next video

---

Skeleton Outline Example #2: Surfing The Technology Wave

- **Skip Stopper**
  - o [CRAZY LOOKING FOOTAGE OF DAN SURFING. START WITH GOPRO FOOTAGE AND THEN CUT TO CAMERA SHOT OF DAN SURFING AN INCREDIBLE WAVE]

  - o [DAN GOES UP TO CAMERA, STILL IN THE WATER]

  - o That was incredible! And I'm showing you this because there's an important lesson we need to learn from surfing about making money on the internet.

- **Believable Promise**
  - o Because I've found the key to making money online is surfing the "technology wave."

  - o If you know how, you can surf the wave of technology to wealth and a great lifestyle. And I'm going to show you exactly how to do that in today's video

- **First CTA**
  - o To learn my full system for making money online, watch the next video

- **Conditioning Content**
  - Show them proof of how rapid improvements in internet technology are

  - Show them how not all forms of making money online benefit equally from technological progress

    - Text ads and banner ads benefit the least
    - Video benefits the most

      - Faster streaming every year
      - Higher resolution every year
      - Better devices, screens, etc. every year

    - And long form video benefits the very most. This means that YouTube is the site best positioned to surf the technology wave

  - Show them why advertising is the best way to make money from YouTube

- **Final CTA**
  - Show them why they should trust me — track record with SixPackAbs.com, client results, book, media appearances, etc.

  - Tell them to watch the next video to learn the full system

  - Give them more details about what they'll learn in the next video

Notice how these outlines are short, rough, and written FAST. But they still have enough detail in all the major parts to get the idea of the ad.

I don't let myself get bogged down by practical considerations when I'm being creative.

For example, I have no idea how to surf. I tried once in Hawaii without taking lessons, and a lifeguard had to come rescue me from almost getting dragged out the sea by the current.

But thinking about it afterwards, there could be a few good solutions to this problem. I could just hire a professional surfer cheaply to film this part. Or I could learn how to surf, which is something I've wanted to do anyways. Maybe I can solve this problem or maybe I can't, but I always think about that later. I don't let any potential problems with ideas inhibit my creativity.

When brainstorming by yourself, I recommend writing out at least 50% more skeleton outlines than ads you want to create.

This way you can cull the bottom third of your skeleton outlines, and focus only on the "cream" of your brainstorm.

Let's say you want to create four ads. You should write out a minimum of six skeleton outlines and cut your worst two. If you can write eight or ten, and narrow it down to your top four, that's even better!

It seems like a lot of work, I know. But when you get good at brainstorming, you can crank these skeleton outlines out FAST.

And it will SAVE you a ton of work producing ads which you ultimately can't use because they're unprofitable. Not to mention all the time you'll save having to make changes to your Google Ads campaigns because your ad creative isn't working.

Once you've got plenty of ideas, take a short break. This resets your mind and lets you see your ideas with a fresh perspective.

Then come back and choose the best ones to make into ads.

Try and visualize what the ads will look like once they're made, and pick the ones with the best Skip Stoppers, the most Believable Promises, the best Conditioning Content, etc.

The Key To Group Brainstorms: Only Include Skilled YouTube Marketers

It's possible to brainstorm great ideas solo — I did it myself many times in the early days of Six Pack Shortcuts. But it's a big advantage if you can brainstorm your ideas with a group of other skilled YouTube marketers.

Why?

First of all, you'll get a greater variety of ideas if you have multiple people contributing.

Skilled YouTube marketers can also play off each other's creativity. Someone coming up with an idea can spur multiple other people in the group to come up with related ideas.

It's also a big advantage to have multiple people contributing to the process of choosing the best ideas. We all get attached to ideas we came up with, and it's easy to think all our own ideas are good. But if another skilled YouTube marketer agrees, it means the idea has a significantly better chance of being successful.

But here's the most important thing to know about group brainstorms…

You have to make sure your group consists of ONLY skilled YouTube marketers!

I really can't stress this point enough. Too often, I see business owners including amateurs in their brainstorming sessions out of politeness or a misguided sense of democracy.

I did this myself in the early days of my fitness business. We'd invite everyone to join in brainstorming ideas — customer service reps, accountants, developers, the office manager, etc. But I found out quickly that including YouTube marketing amateurs in the brainstorm has a TERRIBLE effect on the quality of ideas.

YouTube marketing is a skill that needs to be developed — just like computer programming, accounting, or any other skill.

And asking your accountant or your amateur friend to contribute marketing ideas will be just as disastrous as asking a copywriter to work up complex financial statements.

You'll feel pressure to choose at least SOME of their ideas since they spent their time brainstorming with you. They'll seem like they could work at the time, because you don't want to believe your friend's ideas are awful and that they know nothing about YouTube marketing. But this bias towards your friend will lead to you creating poor ideas and money-losing ads.

Having amateurs in your brainstorm will also degrade the quality of your own thinking. Iron sharpens iron, and to come up with your best ideas you need professional YouTube marketers around you. If that's not possible, you're better off doing the brainstorm yourself — otherwise your thinking will descend down to the level of the group.

There are three ways to get skilled YouTube copywriters to brainstorm with you...

The first way is simple — hire them. But to hire a skilled YouTube copywriter full time, you should expect to pay AT LEAST $100,000 per year in salary, plus another $20,000-$50,000 per year in benefits and performance incentives. I know because I've hired many of them.

Why so much? If someone has the ability to create money-making YouTube campaigns — and has a track record of doing this in the past — they'll have a ton of employment options. And if someone is working for less than this, chances are it's because they don't have a strong track record of creating successful YouTube ads.

You COULD definitely hire a low-skilled copywriter for less.

But when your ad campaigns bomb and lose you thousands, you'll realize you didn't save any money in the end.

Because of this, I only recommend hiring a copywriter as an employee if you can afford a premium salary.

You can also hire freelance YouTube copywriters on a contract basis to brainstorm with you.

This is a much more affordable option for most entrepreneurs, and can be a great investment if you don't know any skilled YouTube marketers on your full-time team.

If you have a small business, and you don't yet have an established network of YouTube marketers, this will be your best option.

A final option is to meet other skilled YouTube marketers through networking, and to brainstorm ideas together for each other's businesses.

If you have successful YouTube marketers in your network, this is the best option. It's also a great choice if your budget is limited.

If you're totally broke AND you don't have any YouTube marketers in your network, don't worry! You can start by brainstorming ideas yourself, just like I did. Just keep your eyes open for people who are also interested in YouTube marketing that you can add to your network.

If you actively search for other skilled YouTube marketers at events and online, you should be able to find good people to brainstorm with within a few months.

How To Brainstorm Ideas In A Group

First, make it clear to everyone that **there will be absolutely no negative feedback allowed on any idea until the brainstorm is over.**

That's because if people start shooting down each other's ideas during the brainstorm, it'll make people more hesitant to contribute ideas out of fear of being embarrassed. There will also be a "tit for tat" effect, where the person whose ideas were shot down is negatively biased towards ideas coming from the person who criticized them.

You will lead the brainstorm, and be the one who writes all the ideas down.

If you're new to YouTube marketing, start off your Skeleton outlines with the elements of the Master Formula:

- **The Skip Stopper**
- **The Believable Promise**
- **The First Call To Action**
- **The Conditioning Content**
- **The Final Call To Action**

Copy and paste this in your document a bunch of times, and fill in each section as you come up with ideas.

If you're an experienced YouTube marketing, you can write your ideas free-form or by using one of the advanced copywriting formulas you'll learn later.

Then open up the discussion for everyone to contribute ideas.

Write down your ideas in each section of the formula as you go. Flesh out the elements of each idea. If someone has a great idea for a Skip Stopper, ask them what they think the Believable Promise should be...what the Conditioning Content should be...etc. The outlines don't need to be fully complete, just complete enough to get an idea of the ad.

Write down EVERYTHING that's contributed, even if it's completely absurd or horrifically stupid.

Remember, you can always discard these ideas later. Having their ideas written down will give the person a small emotional reward of recognition for contributing, which will encourage them to contribute more.

Once you've got plenty of ideas, tell everyone it's time to choose.

Everyone who contributed should get to choose at least one idea. And the rules are that nobody can choose their own ideas.

If you're doing this with your employees, it'll be important to make it clear that you want the best ideas regardless of who came up with them. Otherwise, the pressure will be too great for everyone to choose your ideas to flatter you.

The number of ideas each person chooses should be relative to their YouTube marketing skills and experience.

Each person should NOT choose the same number of ideas.

For example, in an eight commercial brainstorm, I'll typically choose four ideas, have my CMO choose two, and have each of our two copywriters choose one.

The end result of this process is that you'll choose the cream of the crop — only the very best ideas. These are not just ideas you think are good, but ideas which other successful YouTube marketers agree have potential.

Write Out Your Full Scripts

Once you've got your skeleton outlines, write out all your ideas into full scripts. And if you've following all of the steps above, this part should actually be very easy!

All you need to do is to hit the points in your outline, and to make your marketing message flow smoothly. So, you should be able to write these scripts very quickly.

Since you already know the major points you want to hit, so you don't need to worry about this. Instead, focus on phrasing your points so they read well when they're put into the teleprompter.

Don't correct mistakes as you go. This will just slow down your writing. It's much better to leave all mistakes you make in the script, and then to correct them all in the editing process.

If you're an advanced copywriter, writing these scripts from your skeleton outlines should be easy. If you're having trouble writing, add more detail to your outlines first and then write out your scripts to make the process easier.

This process should totally prevent what people call "writer's block." If you ever find yourself just staring at the blinking cursor and not knowing what to write, STOP DOING THAT!

You don't need to waste a single second on writer's block since it's a problem that's easily solved.

If you do get writer's block, just write a more detailed outline or a rough draft of your script before writing the full final draft.

You'll feel less pressure to make everything perfect, and you'll build momentum. By adding this additional step, even novice writers can quickly crank out quality scripts. Even if you need this additional step, the process will still be fast if you just keep typing and never let yourself lose momentum.

For your first commercial, you may have to write 3-4 outlines and rough drafts before your final draft. This is perfectly fine!

This is part of the learning process, and you'll soon be able to easily write scripts from short skeleton outlines like my examples above.

Just remember: NEVER spend a single minute staring at a white screen with a blinking cursor. Just start typing even if it's not perfect. You can always refine your script later or just write an entirely new draft.

Once your scripts are fully written, it's time for copy editing.

Again, it's a huge advantage if you can get another skilled YouTube marketer to do this for you. They'll spot holes in your script in a way you might be blind to, and they'll help you tremendously to improve your scripts before they're filmed.

If that's not possible, you can copy edit yourself. Try and think like one of your potential customers as you do this. Tighten up any parts that seem boring, or which don't flow well, or which don't support your ultimate sales message. Make the language as conversational and natural as you can.

The Editing Trick I Use To Make Massively Improve My Ad Scripts

One thing I recommend doing EVERY time you copy edit commercial scripts is to READ YOUR SCRIPT OUT LOUD.

It's weird, I know. But if you care about making your ads profitable, you'll do it anyway.

By reading it out loud, you'll immediately spot parts that will sound unnatural on video. Your script will flow much better than if you just read it over in your head. You'll hear immediately how your script will sound, and you'll make important adjustments based on this.

During the copy editing process you mainly want to focus on ways to make your MARKETING MESSAGE flow better. Of course, you want to fix typos and grammatical errors — they'll create a hassle if they get put into the teleprompter.

But customers aren't going to flood your business with cash because you have perfect grammar. Customers buy because your marketing message is great, and achieving a seductively smooth marketing message is the main goal of copy editing.

Once your scripts are copy edited, you're ready to film! And now the REALLY fun part begins.

And I'll show you in detail how to film and edit a great commercial in the next chapter.

Why This Process Will SAVE You Time

I know, it seems like a lot of work to go through this process.

Why not just come up with an idea, write it out, and produce an ad without doing so much work brainstorming and refining ideas?

While it seems like a lot of work, I've found that this process will actually SAVE you a ton of time and work in the end – while also making you more money.

That's because a thorough brainstorming and idea refining process will produce far better quality ideas than just writing out the first thing that pops into your head. This means your ads will convert better.

With high converting video creative, it'll be easy to make your Google Ads campaigns profitable. But if your ad creative is mediocre, you'll need to use advanced ninja level ad management skills to even squeak out a small profit.

With this process, your chances of getting a large-scale hit ad are drastically improved. This means that you'll spend much less time creating more ads to replace ones that failed.

So do the up-front work required to get brilliant ad creative.

Once you've got this asset, the money will roll in for years with much less work required.

How It All Ties Together: An Analysis Of The Squatty Potty Unicorn Ad

At SixPackAbs.com, we scripted many ads that stuck closely to the Master Formula. If you were following the ads back at that time, you've probably seen many ads that followed this structure.

But to wrap this chapter up, I'm going to analyze an ad from a different marketer rather than one of my own. You can use this same process to analyze other ads from elite YouTube advertisers. With this process, you turn any successful ad into a free seminar from a marketing genius.

We'll be breaking down one of the most successful ads in the history of YouTube — The Unicorn ad created by Harmon Brothers to advertise the Squatty Potty.

If you haven't seen it yet, watch the ad here now so you understand the analysis:

15StepsBonuses.com/UnicornAd

Chances are, you've probably seen it before. But now that you understand the Master Formula, you'll have a deeper understanding of what's making the ad work.

The Unicorn ad does not stick to the Master Formula exactly, but it's pretty close. They use some advanced techniques that I don't recommend when you're first starting off, like heavily relying on humor and directly pitching their product. But nevertheless, it's one of the greatest ads in the history of YouTube and we can learn a lot from studying it.

I'm analyzing this ad rather than one of my own for a reason.

Now that you know the Master Formula, I want to show you how you can use it to break down the principles behind any successful YouTube ad you see. Once you know what these principles are, you can figure out how to adapt them to your own product and your own market.

This analysis will not make any sense unless you've watched the ad, so watch it now if you haven't already.

15StepsBonuses.com/UnicornAd

The Skip Stopper: A Unicorn Pooping Ice Cream

The ad begins with one of the most brilliant Skip Stoppers of all time: a unicorn pooping soft serve ice cream. It's such a weird, disgusting, and cute all at the same time. You can't help but watch.

To make their Skip Stopper even more attention arresting, they started the commercial with a close-up shot of the unicorn pooping. Seeing rainbow poop close up in your YouTube player is shocking, but also funny and intriguing at the same time.

To draw your attention in and engage you even further, the Squatty Potty spokesman than takes a huge lick of the pooped ice cream. He does a great job acting, and it's absolutely hilarious.

The Skip Stopper for this ad relies heavily on humor. It's effective because the Harmon Brothers are masters of using humor to sell products, and because of the nature of the product. A serious ad about bowel movements would be unwatchable, so adding humor makes sense for this type of product.

I don't recommend beginner YouTube marketers use humor in their Skip Stoppers, because it's an advanced technique that often backfires on newbie marketers. But this is an example of how humor can be an incredibly powerful tool to use for skilled marketers in certain product categories.

The Believable Promise: You'll Learn How To Poop Better

Once the viewer's attention is deeply hooked, the spokesman makes the Believable Promise. He tells the viewer "you know who sucks at pooping...you do!"

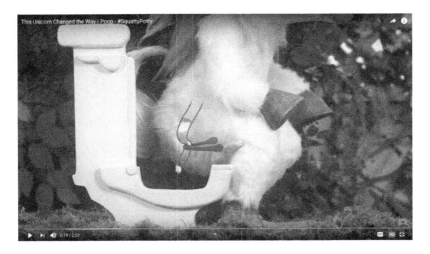

The shot then goes back to the unicorn, who's now on a toilet. And now the viewer is looking at an internal diagram of the unicorn's colon.

The spokesman then shows you how the way we sit on toilets is the wrong angle for our colons to release properly. And then he reads off a list of problems this can cause — hemorrhoids, constipation, etc.

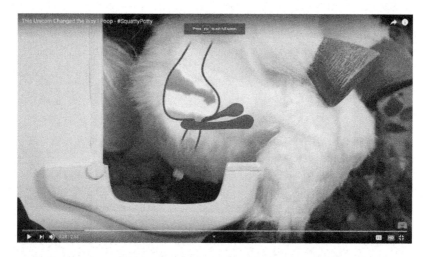

The implication is clear — the spokesman is going to show you how to poop better. And he's going to do it in an entertaining, funny way. It seems unlikely the ad is being run just to spread a message of doom about how our toilets suck, so the viewer anticipates a solution coming.

This hooks the viewer's attention in even more deeply. They're not just watching a weird video of a unicorn pooping for entertainment anymore. Now they're curious about how they can start pooping better.

This can be a great way to make your Believable Promise. Bring a problem your viewers have to the top of their mind, and imply that you have a way to solve it.

The First Call To Action

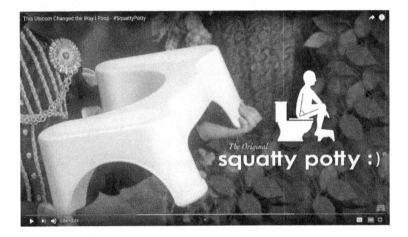

At just 55 seconds into the commercial, the first call to action comes out. Some people get the idea right away, and this call to action is for people like this who are immediately ready to buy.

The Harmon Brothers use another advanced technique here — pitching the product directly in the ad. It works in this case because of the simple nature of their product, and the overtly commercial nature of their website.

I don't recommend doing this in the first Call To Action unless you're an advanced marketer selling a simple to understand product like the Squatty Potty. But for advanced marketers selling products like this, it can clearly be effective.

What you should learn from this part of the ad is how quickly the first call to action comes out. People are given the chance to buy immediately, and the ad continues for people who need more convincing.

The Conditioning Content: Teaching The Viewer The Importance Of Squatting For Colon Release

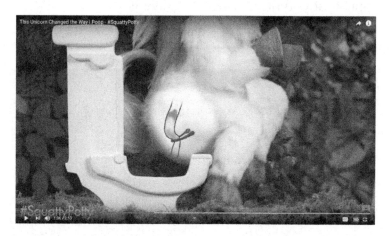

The bulk of the commercial consists of the spokesman educating us about how our colons work. He shows how a seated position causes our colon muscles to be kinked...

And how squatting unkinks our colon muscle, leading to better elimination.

130 sec
average sitting time

50 sec
average squatting time

SOURCE: Digestive Diseases and Sciences, July 2003, Volume 48, Issue 7, pp 1201-1205

He also teaches the viewer how a scientific study has shown that squatting can also lead to faster bowel movements, and less time spent on the toilet. And he does it in a funny way, which is critical to making Conditioning Content about bowel movement studies watchable.

Once the viewer is educated about the importance of squatting it's easy to present the Squatty Potty as the best solution.

Of course, you could just build your own toilet stool, and get the benefits of squatting without buying their product. But who really wants to waste time doing this?

The Squatty Potty is a cheap and convenient solution to the problem viewers now know they have. Once the belief that squatting produces better bowel movements is installed in the prospect's mind, it's easy to convince them that Squatty Potty is the best solution to get the health benefits of squatting.

The Final Call To Action

The spokesman gives more detail about why they should go to the website and learn more about the Squatty Potty. He tells them how the Squatty Potty was featured on a bunch of different major media sources to give it more credibility, and to deepen the viewer's interest.

He also shows them how it's gotten a five star Amazon review from over 2,000 users.

The commercial wraps up with the spokesman again giving a direct appeal to buy the product. And for a simple to understand product like the Squatty Potty, this clearly makes sense in the final call to action.

For people selling information products like video courses or more complex physical products like supplements or cosmetics, this type of Call to Action is not ideal. But this is a great example of how to do it for a simple physical product.

What you should take away from this final Call To Action is how they quickly build credibility for their product before asking people to go there. And you can use the same technique in your final Calls to Action, even if you're not directly pitching your product and you're just telling people to watch the next video.

Start Analyzing YouTube Ads Yourself!

There are two ways you can watch a YouTube ad.

You can be a mindless consumer, and just watch the ads to see which cool products you can blow money on.

Or you can buy cool products when you see them, AND ALSO analyze YouTube ads like this so you learn from them and improve your own marketing skills.

That's what I did when I first saw this ad. I watched the whole thing immediately, and then I went to the website and bought five Squatty Potties — one for each bathroom in my house, and one for my parents.

The next time I saw the ad, I recorded it to make sure I'd have it in my archives to study later. You can record ads you seen show up Instream with the QuickTime Player on the Mac, or with the Xbox Game DVR on a PC. Both of these programs are free and come installed with your computer. They record your screen, allowing you to save skippable Instream ads which normally you can't get back to.

I then went through and analyzed each part of the ad — The Skip Stopper, the Believable Promise, etc. I also noted where they deviated from the proven formula, and why it worked for them (great use of humor, a simple product, etc.)

And you should start doing this yourself when you see a great YouTube ad. You'll be getting a world-class marketing education whenever you watch YouTube, while everyone else is just mindlessly wasting time.

Your Action Steps From This Chapter:

1. Go to **15StepsBonuses.com/Top5Ads** to see what I believe are the five greatest ads ever created in YouTube history. Watch all of these ads, and take notes breaking them down similar to how I did above.

2. Brainstorm at least eight ideas for your first batch of ads using the process I described in this chapter. Use the Master Formula for all the scripts in your first batch. If you can brainstorm 10, 15, or 20 ideas, that's even better!

3. Choose the five ideas you'll make into your first batch of ads

4. Write your scripts from your outlines.

5. Copy edit your scripts. Now you're ready to film!

Step 5: Film And Edit Your First Batch Of Ads

From your action steps in the last chapter, you now have your first batch of killer YouTube ad scripts. Now it's time for lights, camera, action!

While a great marketing message in your scripts is the most important factor in creating great YouTube ads, having good video production helps significantly. This chapter will show you how to turn your scripts into great commercials, even if your budget is limited and you have no video skills whatsoever right now.

Why Video Production Matters

You don't need to have movie-level video skills to be successful with YouTube ads.

But you DO need to know the basics of video production, and how to translate the vision in your script into a finished commercial. And that's exactly what I'm going to show you in this chapter.

If you're a marketing wizard, it IS possible to make your ads profitable while being totally ignorant of video production. While it's possible to skate by like this without learning how to make a decent video, it's not a smart strategy.

That's because well-produced ads can significantly out-sell basic ads that use the same script. You could make 10, 20, or even 30% more sales by improving your video production from the same amount of ad spend.

This may not sound like much. But getting even a little more revenue for every dollar of ad spend will have a tremendously positive impact on your profits.

Let's say your ad campaigns have a 10% profit margin. If you can improve your sales conversion by just another 10% with better production, you've DOUBLED your campaign's profits.

But more profits are only one benefit of learning how to produce great videos...

Well-produced videos are a much better experience for YouTube users to watch. Because retaining users is everything to YouTube, having great video production will help to keep you in their good graces.

If people love watching your ads, you'll have fewer problems with Ad Policy violations, and you'll be given leeway in situations where advertisers with crappy looking ads would get their account suspended.

But here's the biggest benefit of learning how to make polished videos...

If your videos are engaging and edited well, they'll be more interesting to watch. This will significantly increase the engagement from your ads — subscriptions, earned views, likes, comments, etc. And YouTube engagement is tremendously important for building a valuable, long-lasting brand.

Your brand will be the key to making sustainable long-term profits with your company, or to one day selling your business if that's your goal.

So you need to learn the basics of videography. You can't just rely on great ad scripts.

But here's the good news...

You can learn the basic skills you need to produce great YouTube videos in less than a day. And you can buy a great filming setup even with a limited budget — if you know how to spend your money correctly.

And that's exactly what I'm going to show you how to do.

Technology Changes — And My Recommendations Will Change With It

Most aspects of YouTube marketing are long-lasting because they're based on human nature and features of YouTube that are unlikely to change in the future. For example, things like Skip Stoppers and the Six Factor Profitability Analysis will likely be important for decades to come, which is why they're covered in depth in this book.

Filming technology is different though. It rapidly improves and changes, and my recommendations for you need to change along with it.

Because of this, I won't be providing fixed recommendations in this book. Instead, I'll be giving you recommended budgets for your business and your goals — and I'll link you to bonus videos where I discuss my current recommendations for this budget level.

I'll update these videos every year so that you can confidently follow them even if you're reading this book decades after it was written.

If you want to save time, you can just go to the link below and buy all the items on Amazon that I recommend. And if you want to learn more about what you're buying, the video will explain why I believe it's the best option.

The Bootstrapper's Setup — $300 Budget — Smartphone Camera

Go to **15StepsBonuses.com/Bootstrapper** to get my recommendations for a $300 budget.

If you're strapped for cash and on an extremely low budget, the Boostrapper's Setup will allow you to get started making decent videos for a minimal cost.

If you cannot afford the $2,000 Beginner's Setup, I recommend you get started immediately with the Bootstrapper's Setup and upgrade later once you start making money from your campaigns.

The way we do this is by filming with the cell phone you already have — and by adding low-cost lighting, backgrounds, and a microphone to get your videos close to what you'd get from a real camera. And I'll show you great free or almost-free software that you can use to edit your videos.

I've personally made a lot of money with a similar setup to this in the early days of Six Pack Shortcuts, and many other entrepreneurs have as well.

But I still recommend upgrading to at least the $2,000 Beginner's Setup as soon as you possibly can.

This ultra-low budget setup gets you started if there's no other way. But having a real camera, lighting setup, mics, and teleprompter will make a significant difference in your video quality.

The Beginner's Setup — $2,000 budget — One Camera

Go to **15StepsBonuses.com/Beginner** to get my recommendations for a $2,000 budget.

The beginner's setup is ideal for solo entrepreneurs or people making very simple videos that focus on one person. It will allow you to make basic but professional looking videos at a minimal cost.

I recommend the Beginner's Setup for any business which has the cash to afford the $2,000 budget, but which is making less than $20,000 in revenue per month.

The biggest difference from the Bootstrapper's Setup is that you'll be using a dedicated camera to film your videos rather than the camera on your cell phone. While this adds some complexity and cost, it significantly improves your video quality.

The Beginner's Setup will also get you basic three point lighting kit. Again, this makes a big difference in the quality of your videos vs. just having weak lights on your camera rig shining directly at you.

You'll also get an improved mic, significantly increasing your sound quality.

Most importantly, you'll get a tablet-based teleprompter. This will be critical for filming professional quality YouTube ads.

With the Beginners' Setup, you'll be using professional editing software to edit your videos. Again, a big step up.

The Simple Professional Setup — $5,000 Budget — Two Cameras

Go to **15StepsBonuses.com/SimplePro** to get my recommendations for a $5,000 budget.

The Simple Professional Setup is what I recommend for the vast majority of small businesses. If your business is making between $20,000 and $1 million in revenue per month, the Simple Professional Setup is designed for you.

In the Simple Professional Setup, you'll be using two cameras instead of one. Having multiple camera angles significantly improves the look of your videos, especially if you are a video with more than one person.

If you are filming scenes with 3 or more people in them, such as a group workout, having multiple camera angles is essential. And having two cameras lets you keep making videos if there is an accident and one of your cameras breaks.

Spending the extra $3,000 will also allow you to significantly upgrade your camera quality, lighting, and sound.

And you'll even get an aerial drone which you can use to create amazing looking B roll shots (B roll shots are "extra" shots you get to cut into your main video to keep it visually interesting.)

This setup produces significantly better videos but is more complex to operate than a single camera shoot. Because of this, I recommend having a dedicated director/soundman to work your equipment if you have this setup rather than trying to do it solo. I also recommend hiring a professional editor at this stage to maximize the value of your two camera shoot.

The Ultimate Setup — $20,000 Budget — Three Cameras

Go to **15StepsBonuses.com/Ultimate** to get my recommendations for a $20,000 budget.

The Ultimate Setup is the best possible equipment money can buy for YouTube marketing. I recommend it for:

- Any business making between $1 - $2 million dollars in revenue per month that needs complex shots, such as group shots, outdoor shots, or movie-like Skip Stoppers.

- Any business making more than $2 million dollars in revenue per month. If your company is this large, having pro-quality video will be easily worth the relatively small cost.

Most businesses will be fine with the Simple Professional setup. The Ultimate Setup is only for large, established businesses who will clearly get a return on their investment.

At this level of budget, you can shoot with three pro-quality cameras with multiple lenses. You'll have the best lighting and sound setup that money can buy. And you'll be able to get a pro-quality teleprompter.

In my opinion, $20,000 is the maximum any business should spend on their video setup — even the world's largest corporations. This will get you everything you need for the day-to-day needs of your business. On the rare occasions this equipment can't get the job done (like filming a movie-like Skip Stopper) it's more cost-efficient to rent the extra equipment you need rather than to buy it.

With this type of setup, you should have a dedicated director AND a separate dedicated sound man. Having two people will help you pick up on problems, prevent expensive wasted shoots, and will tremendously improve the quality of your footage.

And you should also have a seasoned pro editing your videos at this point. With big three camera shoots, it will make a huge difference.

Reminder: Don't Psych Yourself Out If You Have A Small Budget

If you have a small budget, it might be discouraging to see how much more businesses with large budgets can afford. But don't let this discourage you!

Having a better filming setup is an advantage, and it's worth the investment if your business is large enough. But remember that many YouTube entrepreneurs — myself included — have gotten their start with a cheap, ghetto-rigged setup.

This will be more than enough to get started. And when you get your ad campaigns working, you'll have the money for a better setup in a matter of months.

How To Make Ads Yourself Without A Teleprompter

I've made many of these types of videos myself. This is how we filmed our ads in the early days of Six Pack Shortcuts before we could afford a teleprompter. And to this day, I still make all of my organic content videos this way.

The advantages of filming without a teleprompter is that you'll sound more natural and less scripted. If you do it right, you can also hit all your key points and avoid a rambling, pointless video.

And of course, if you don't have the $200 for a basic teleprompter, this is the only way to get started. If you wait until you can afford something better, chances are you'll lose psychological momentum and never get started at all.

Filming without a teleprompter DOES take more skill and more work. But it definitely can be done!

So, let's talk about the process for making this type of unscripted ad.

You've got your rough outlines you wrote in the last chapter's action steps.

How can you turn these outline into a great videos with a polished on-camera performance?

The key is doing a "practice run" where you can practice fleshing out your points and where you can get everything polished before making your video.

The most important part to rehearse before filming will be the Skip Stopper and Believable Promise. Because these parts of the video are so disproportionately important, I will spend most of my time practicing these parts. In fact, I'll basically memorize these parts and deliver them almost verbatim from my outline when making videos like this.

Putting a lot of effort into the first thirty seconds of your video will ensure you hook the viewer in strongly. It will also help you build psychological momentum, and build your confidence for the rest of the video.

For the remainder, I'll usually run through it once or twice to roughly get my points down. Your Conditioning Content doesn't need to be memorized. You just have to have a rough idea of what points you need to hit.

I'll do one take for each major point I want to make in the Conditioning Content, and then cut before making my next point. This means that I will film myself making one point, then stop the recording and review my outline again before the next point in the outline.

The key thing to keep in mind when filming videos this way is that **practice makes perfect.** If making videos like this seems hard the first time you do it, that's because making videos is a skill that has to be learned. The more time you spend rehearsing and making videos, the better you'll get.

You'll be shocked at how rapid your progress is if you stick to it!

How To Make Videos Yourself With A Teleprompter

Making natural-sounding videos with a teleprompter also requires skill, but it's more easily and quickly learned than the ability to improvise from an outline. And it's a lot easier to make videos with a teleprompter than most people think.

You can get a great tablet-based teleprompter for under $200. You can use the iPad or tablet you already have. If you don't have a tablet, you can buy a cheap one that will work fine for under $100.

To get your script in the teleprompter, you just need to load your script document into your teleprompter app. Then you put your tablet in the prompter, and you'll see the words reflected on the one-directional glass in front of the camera. To the viewer it seems like you're looking directly into the camera, and nobody will be able to see the script on the glass that you're reading.

Most people think that to use a teleprompter you need someone to operate it for you. But new apps have actually made this idea obsolete.

There are great teleprompter apps which can accurately detect what you're saying, and move your teleprompter as it hears you read the words.

The teleprompter app I currently use when filming solo is **PromptSmart Pro**. It does a great job detecting what you're saying and moving your script for you as you talk. You also have the option to move the script at a set speed, or have a person work the teleprompter for you.

PromptSmart Pro is my current recommendation for a teleprompter app, but again keep in mind that technology can change rapidly and the best app may be different if you're reading the book years after it was written.

To get my current recommendation for the best teleprompter app to use, make sure to check out this chapter's bonus material:

15StepsBonuses.com/VideoProduction

Having a teleprompter reduces the need to rehearse before filming your videos. However, I still recommend reading through your entire script at least once to get the flow down — especially if you are new to being on camera.

If you're inexperienced, you may want to run through your Skip Stopper and Believable Promise 2-3 times to make sure your delivery is tight before filming.

Ideally, when you're filming, you'll have your content down pat. And you'll be able to focus completely on your delivery. You'll be like a professional singer focused on hitting the right notes in a practiced song, rather than an amateur karaoke singer struggling to remember his next line.

The Key To Improving Your On-Camera Performance

The best way to improve your delivery is to watch previous videos you've made, and to analyze them for opportunities to improve.

For example, from watching many videos of myself I know that one of my natural tendencies is to talk too fast on video when I get excited about something.

Because of this, I've made this a conscious focus to improve on my videos. When I make videos, I consciously slow down my talking to a pace that seems unnaturally slow when I'm filming. But when I watch the video later, I'm actually still talking at a faster than normal pace — but significantly slower and more understandable than when I didn't think about this.

The key to doing this is to be able to objectively analyze your weaknesses as on-camera talent — while also appreciating the unique value your provide to your viewers.

I personally have many opportunities to improve as on camera talent. I talk too fast, I say "um" and brainfart too much, and I take too much time to get "warmed up" and into my best delivery.

But I appreciate that these are all minor issues in the big picture. I know that you bought this book and you watch my videos because I've helped you to improve your YouTube marketing. And I know that building a successful business with YouTube marketing has life-changing effects. That's what's most important to me, and I know it's what's most important to you as well.

Of course, I want to improve my on-camera skills as much as I can. But I don't let minor flaws in my delivery get in the way of my mission and my message. You shouldn't either.

Video Casting: An Important Skill Everyone Needs To Learn

Knowing how to cast great talent for videos is a critical skill.

Many of you reading this will be doing the marketing behind the scenes, and you'll need to hire someone to be your spokesperson on camera. If you're an expert at doing this, you can get incredible talent very inexpensively.

Even if you or another partner in your business is the main person on camera right now, it's still important to learn how to cast for videos. You'll still need people to play other roles, such as someone to interview your spokesperson, or extras to create certain types of Skip Stoppers. And eventually your business will grow to the point where the owners cannot possibly make all the videos a business needs.

Some business owners who were originally the face of their brands have actually found that they can out-perform their own videos by hiring talent to deliver their scripts for a few hundred bucks on Craigslist.

The fact is that acting is a skill, and there are many people out there who have dedicated their lives to this skill and are probably much better than it than you.

In addition to this, if your business is completely dependent on a single spokesperson, it can put you in a terrible position if your sole on-camera talent leaves.

Unfortunately, I learned this lesson the hard way.

The first trainer I hired for Six Pack Shortcuts decided he wanted to leave the business for spiritual pursuits, and in one sense I was glad that he'd found his personal path to happiness.

But it left our business in an absolutely terrible position for the next few months. It was only because we'd established a relationship with talent that we'd cast in a minor role in previous commercials that we were able to establish a new "face" of the company and survive.

Where To Post Your Casting Ad

The first step of the casting process is to write up an ad for your gig and to post it on casting sites. Here's an example of an ad I posted for a client recently:

My name's Dan, and I'm the Casting Director for Social Response Marketing. We're a YouTube Marketing Agency located in [MY CITY.] We are seeking 50+ male and female talent on behalf of our client [CLIENT NAME REDACTED] to perform in YouTube commercials and other YouTube videos.

This is a paid gig, and may lead to the opportunity to be cast in more filming in the next few months. Our client's YouTube commercials have received over three hundred million views and receive over seven million views per month, so this is also a great way to get more exposure and build your portfolio if you're an actor/actress or a model.

The ideal person for this job will appear at least 50 years old, and preferably will appear to be over 60 years old (the target market for this product is 50+). The initial videos we'll shoot will be a series of short YouTube commercials where you'll be on green screen and reading from a teleprompter script.

Experience creating commercials or reading from teleprompter scripts in the past is a major plus but is not required.

The initial shoot will pay $250 for approximately two hours of filming ($125/hour). If the client is happy with the initial videos, we'll be looking to shoot more content for their YouTube channel, and more commercials in the next few months.

Future shoots will pay $400 for a half day shoot (four hours), and $700 for a full day shoot (eight hours).

If you're interested in this position, send us your headshots along with links to any relevant videos you've made in the past (commercials and teleprompter-based videos are ideal.) Please also include your email and phone number.

The three most qualified male and female candidates will be invited to audition, and you will be notified if you've been cast within 4-5 days of your audition.

The audition will take approximately 10 minutes, and will consist of you reading one of the company's existing commercial scripts against a green screen. If you are not cast for this role, our company regularly produces commercials with 50+ talent and you may be invited to participate in future paid shoots without being required to audition again.

Here are the important things you want to make sure to have in your job ad to attract the best talent:

- **Make it extremely clear who you're looking for — the more specific, the better.** You'll usually want someone who is a fairly close demographic match to your target customer.

- **Make it clear EARLY IN THE AD that it's a paid gig if you are paying.** Many gigs that are posted on casting sites are unpaid. Even if you are offering a tiny amount, it will really mean a lot to the majority of actors who are struggling to land any paid gigs.

- **Think from the talent's point of view, and emphasize how your gig can benefit their career.** The most important things an actor will be looking for are exposure to a large audience, and a great-looking video they can add to their demo reel to get other gigs.

  If you can provide them with that, make sure to emphasize those benefits early in the ad.

- **If there is a possibility of long-term work, make sure to mention that as well.** You should also lay out the specifics of how much this long-term work will pay.

  Many actors will really value the possibility of steady long-term work, and will audition for a small initial gig if they know your goal is to hire someone to work with regularly after this.

You can use my example ad as a template if you want, and just switch it out for the details of your own commercials, what you're paying, your company name, etc.

Once you've got your ads, it's time to post it on casting sites. Here are the sites I've had the most success with in the past:

- **Backstage.com** — I've had tremendous success casting for commercials with Backstage.com, and it's my top recommendation to cast for roles that require speaking and acting. Posting a well-crafted ad here can get you hundreds of responses, many from people with impressive acting and commercial work backgrounds.

  Not only this, but experienced actors are often willing to drive for HOURS to audition for a low-paying gig on Backstage.com. This can be especially important if you live in a smaller town without much talent in your local area.

  Backstage.com is designed for acting casting, so it's easy to see the person's headshots, video portfolio, resume, and other important items right on the site. You can also easily sort your applicants to quickly decide which one of the many people you want to audition.

- **Craigslist.com** — Craigslist is usually thought of as a site for hooker ads and selling junk, but it's actually shocking effective for casting YouTube commercial gigs. You won't get as many applicants as Backstage, and they usually won't have as impressive of an acting resume. But you'll still be getting many quality applicants from significantly different pool of talent than Backstage.

  Because Craigslist is not designed for acting casting, you'll get a lot of applications with no video reel, no headshots, no resume, etc. But since you'll be getting hundreds of applications between all the sites you're posting on, you can safely ignore these and focus only on the best candidates who send you everything you asked for in your ad.

- **ModelMayhem.com** — Model Mayhem is a model casting site, and is not good for casting people in speaking or acting roles. If you need models for a photo shoot for your video thumbnails, Model Mayhem is a great place to look. It's also great if you are looking to cast extras to look good in the background while someone else talks. For most roles though, I recommend sticking to Craigslist and Backstage.

While casting sites are not changing as frequently as video technology does, it will still be subject to change over time. If you are reading this book in 2021 or later, go to 15StepsBonuses.com/VideoProduction to get my current recommendations for the best casting sites to use.

If your ad gets a good response, at this point you'll have hundreds of quality applicants wanting to audition for a gig. If you don't have enough, make some adjustments to your ad and post it again. Consider broadening the demographic of talent you're searching for and offering more money.

How To Do Auditions

It's critical when you're casting for any role that you audition talent before putting them in your video. There's simply no other way to know how well someone will perform on camera.

There have been many times I've auditioned people with incredible demo reels and resumes who were terrible when they auditioned with me — and people with much thinner resumes have often done a great job.

Auditioning takes time, but it's well worth it to find great talent.

And the good news is that actors and models will almost always audition for free, even if they're in demand and making good money right now.

I recommend auditioning your ten best candidates for each role you want to cast. For the audition, have them read one of your actual commercials scripts to get the best possible test for how they'll do on camera.

You can make this process MUCH more efficient by hiring a virtual assistant who can filter through the resumes and choose the best candidates for you. You can hire an excellent VA in the Philippines or in Colombia for $5-$10 an hour, and this can save you hours of work filtering through demo reels and scheduling auditions.

To schedule your auditions, I recommend using Calendly or similar scheduling software. This will allow the actor to see all the times you have free to audition, so they can choose the time that's most convenient for them for themselves. It'll also create a Google Calendar reminder for both of you when they choose their time.

Choosing their own times makes it much easier for people to audition with you, and saves you a ton of time coordinating appointments and sending Google Calendar invitations.

The auditions must be efficient — each one should take no more than 5-10 minutes. When they come to your house or office, be friendly, offer them coffee or bottled water, and go out of your way to make the audition a good experience for them.

If they enjoyed auditioning with you, they'll be more likely to accept your gig if you offer it to them later, even if you're offering less money than they usually make.

How To Edit Videos Yourself

If you're new to video editing, I recommend using low-cost consumer grade video software like iMovie or Windows Movie Maker.

This type of software is very easy to learn how to use. You can pick up the basics just by watching YouTube videos about your software and by playing around with the features to create a video or two.

While it's now possible to do basic video editing on your phone or tablet, I strongly recommend you don't do this unless you have no computer and you're totally broke. You'll edit videos faster and better on a computer — mobile device editing is only appropriate for amateurs.

When you're making videos like this, the most important advice I can give you is to keep your editing simple and minimalist. Let your message be the star, and keep the graphics, effects, and fancy transitions down to a minimum.

To make a minimalist video, you'll just need to go through your footage and choose which clips you want to use. Then you clip out any "junk footage" at the beginning and end of each clip, and join them together on your video timeline.

Here are a few simple guidelines to get you started if you're a video editing beginner:

- Avoid "jump cuts" or cuts between clips with no transition or graphic between them which makes it seem like the person has "jumped" from one place to another in the camera shot. Use basic digital zooms or full screen images between clips to avoid this.

- Add in text graphics to emphasize key points, but keep them light and minimal.

- Break up long monotonous shots of a single person speaking with B roll clips and images. These are basically "extra" clips you can cut in to add visual variety to your video. You can purchase these on stock image and footage sites, or you can use videos and images you already have.

While these basic guidelines for editing commercials will help, you should watch at least a few YouTube videos teaching you more about your software before editing your own commercials. I include some recommendations for basic video editing tutorials I recommend in this chapter's bonus page:

(15StepsBonuses.com/VideoProduction)

If you're already experienced with video editing and you can use software like Final Cut Pro or Adobe Premiere, of course you should use your pro software. But I still encourage you to keep your videos simple and to avoid spending too much time on editing to ensure your main focus is on creating a great marketing message and managing great ad campaigns.

Now, I recommend that you hire a professional video editor to edit all of your commercials for you as soon as you can afford it. Even if you have video editing skills yourself, video editing is incredibly time consuming and will distract your focus from creating your marketing message.

And you can get killer editing done cheaply if you know how to hire and manage editors.

There are two ways to hire an editor. You can either hire someone locally, or hire someone remotely from an outsourcing website.

How To Hire A Remote Editor Cheaply & Easily

If your budget is limited and you need to get someone to edit your videos quickly, an outsourcing site like Upwork.com is your best option. You post your project on the site, and freelance video editors will bid to complete the work for you.

Once your freelancers have bid, you can choose which one you want to work with based on the price, their portfolio of work, and their ratings. Then you upload your footage, and they download it and edit it based on your directions.

When you're outsourcing video editing, it's critical to describe in detail what you're looking for. If you can provide examples of similar videos you want it to look like, this helps a lot as well.

I find the best way to get good work from inexpensive remote editors is to have a VERY thoroughly written description with examples they can refer to, and to also talk to them on the phone or Skype as well to make sure they understand what you need.

Once the editor completes the project, they'll send you the video. But you're not done yet! **You should regard this first video as a draft video, and make revisions to improve it further.**

Watch through the video, and make detailed notes for which revisions you'd like the editor to make. Include the timestamp of the video where you want them to make a change and screenshots when needed.

If you're detailed in your description and revisions, and if you've chosen your contractor well, you can get quality editing using this method. It'll be cheap, you'll have the flexibility to ramp up or down contract editors as needed. And it's a great option if you live in a rural area without much access to editing talent.

Remote editors do have some drawbacks though. A remote editor cannot film for you, and in the early stages of your business it can be a big advantage to have the same person filming and editing. They can get the footage exactly as they want it and own the project from beginning to end — something many editors appreciate.

It can also take a lot of time to upload and download footage, especially if you're editing long videos filmed in high resolution. And the communication is not as good as someone who you have an in-person relationship with.

Because of this, I recommend hiring a local editor if you can afford the extra cost, and if you live in at least a medium sized city.

How To Hire A Local Editor

To find a local editor, you can post your editing gig on Craigslist, Indeed, and other job sites. Pick the top three candidates for your gig based on the quality of their portfolio.

Generally, editors who have created many similar commercials before will do the best job with yours. **While film experience can help, you should value experience making marketing videos much more highly than experience making artistic videos.**

Once you've got your top three, do brief phone interviews with each of them to see who you communicate best with among your top options. Ensure they're close enough so that they can also film for you, and see if they have additional equipment that they can use on your shoots which could make them better.

Once you've chosen your editor, set a filming date if they're shooting for you. If you've already shot the footage, upload it for them to download or have them pick up a hard drive with the footage from you if it's an extremely large video file.

Give detailed instructions and revise the video similar to how I described above. And don't be afraid to ask for additional rounds of revisions until the video has all the important changes that you want.

When doing these one-off video editing gigs, you should view them as a tryout for a permanent video editor position. This is the best way to get your videos done in the long term — to consistently work with an editor who knows your business and who will require few revisions on their videos.

If the project goes well, consider offering the editor regular monthly work if your business can afford it.

By doing this, you can usually get the editor to reduce their hourly or project rate. Since many editors work a per-gig basis, their income fluctuates severely from month to month. If you can provide them with a base guaranteed income and if they like working on your projects, they'll edit your videos at a significant discount.

The ideal person to have in your long-term editing role will:

- Be available to shoot in person for you

- Have excellent equipment that can enhance your shoots

- Have a powerful computer designed for video editing, and be an expert in Final Cut Pro or Adobe Premiere

- Have a library of stock footage and clips they own which they'll include in your videos for no additional cost

- Be reliable in meeting deadlines and responsive to your communication

- **Most importantly, the best editors for YouTube commercials have a basic understanding of marketing and appreciation of its value.** I've found that some incredibly skilled film and TV editors produce terrible commercials, because they hate creating marketing videos and they view it as prostituting their artistic skills.

  So, focus on finding someone with a marketing orientation, even if this means hiring an editor with more basic technical skills and equipment.

Having a great editor to work with regularly will be incredibly valuable, so keep an eye out for your long term match when you're hiring for editing gigs. If you get a chance to work with someone great, do everything you can to lock them down long term.

How To Upload Your Video To YouTube

Once you've got your final edited video, it's time to upload! Now the really fun part begins :)

When you're uploading your videos, it's important that you upload the highest resolution that you possibly can.

YouTube has great technology which can detect how fast your device can load video without buffering, and it will create different sized video files and serve the person the highest quality version their device can handle. So, uploading a huge, high resolution video file will not cause your video to load slower for users on a slow connection.

Most people are watching YouTube on their phones in a low resolution right now. But technology is improving rapidly, and soon many more people will be streaming in 1080, 4k, and even higher resolutions.

Uploading a large, high quality file will make your video "future-proof" and keep it from looking outdated for longer.

Give your video a simple, memorable title that lets users see what they'll learn from watching your ads.

Titles that directly describe what the user will learn, like "3 Simple Ways To Make More Money With YouTube Marketing," are great.

Titles that seem like your ad will be a blatant pitch like "Why Social Response Marketing™ Is The World's Leading YouTube Ad Agency" will turn viewers off.

Your video's description will not be visible in InStream advertising, and most users won't view your description even if they click a Video Discovery ad where they have the option to.

You shouldn't spend much time on it, but there are a few things you should include.

In the first two lines of your description, include a call to action and a link to your website.

Something like this:

Get The #1 Best-Selling Book On YouTube Marketing:
https://SocialResponseMarketing.com

Make sure to include the "http://" or "https://" in your link, otherwise YouTube will not make it a clickable hyperlink.

Below this, include a brief paragraph summarizing what the viewer will learn from your video. This should be targeted towards people who view your ad in the Video Discovery format, who want to quickly learn what a video's about before committing their time to watching it.

Very, very few people will read further than this. However, the Google Ads Policy team, YouTube Policy team, and some business owners who are evaluating your credibility will read your entire video description.

Because of this, the rest of your description should be targeted to this type of person – not to customers. Rather than trying to sell your product or why they should watch your video, put in content and links which show that your business is credible and trustworthy.

Examples of this include:

- Any awards your business has gotten, such as being in the Inc. 5000 or having a good rating from the BBB

- Links to media appearances

- Links to positive reviews on Amazon or other third-party platforms where reviews cannot be faked

- Any degrees or certifications you have

- For any videos containing testimonials, you should also include a legal disclaimer in your description explaining that the testimonials you're getting are a showcase of the best results people are gotten, and are not the average or typical results you're promising the viewer.

Sounds tedious, I know. **But the good news is that you don't have to re-type this description every time you upload a video.**

You can set a "default" description that shows on EVERY video you upload, and just customize the top call to action and paragraph. The rest you just have to type out once, and you can set it to automatically be added to the description of every video you upload. It's a tiny bit of effort, and it might prevent you from getting a YouTube strike or having your Google Ads account suspended later.

And you're done! You've now scripted, filmed and edited a batch of killer YouTube ads using the Master Formula. And you've uploaded them to YouTube, and set them up so they're ready to use. You're just a few steps away from making money!

And you're just a few steps away from explosively growing your YouTube subscribers and the value of your brand.

Your Action Steps From This Chapter:

1. Pick your filming setup budget based on the guidelines I gave earlier in this chapter.

2. Buy your equipment, or any critical pieces of the setup you don't already own. Here is the link to this chapter's bonus content, where you can get each of my recommended setups and all of the other current recommendations I discussed previously: **15StepsBonuses.com/VideoProduction**

3. Film your first batch of five ads

4. Edit your first batch of five ads, or hire someone to edit them for you.

5. Upload your videos to YouTube, and set them up with titles and descriptions.

Step 6: Create A Website Designed To Convert Your YouTube Traffic Into Cash

Having great YouTube ads is important, but it's only half the battle. The other half is having a website that reliably converts your YouTube traffic into buyers.

The type of website that converts YouTube traffic into sales is very different from the type of website that works well for Facebook, Google Search, email marketing, or other traffic sources. You must learn how to create a website specifically optimized for YouTube marketing for your ads to succeed.

Why You Need A Separate YouTube Sales Process — And How I Learned This The Hard Way

You're about to learn the importance of having a separate YouTube sales process on your website the easy way — by reading about my experiences in this book.

Let me tell you how I learned the hard way...

When we first started Six Pack Shortcuts, YouTube was our only way of getting website traffic and sales. So, our website was naturally designed for YouTube only.

But then something amazing and unexpected happened!

We got image ads (sometimes called banner ads or display ads) working on a small scale. Then we started scaling them up like crazy — while still keeping large profit margins!

Every week it seemed like we got more and more sales from banner ads. We were ecstatic, not only to get more sales but also to get advertising outside of YouTube working.

We performed many "split-tests" on our website, where we tested one version of the site against another to see which produced more sales. And as I explained previously, continually improving your website conversion through split-testing is the key to developing a great sales website.

We got some huge split-test wins, increasing the sales conversion of our website significantly every week or two. Or so we thought.

Then something weird started to happen...

As our image ad campaigns explosively grew, our YouTube campaigns started getting less and less profitable. Eventually I had to cut our spending on YouTube ads because of this. The net effect was that most of our gains from image ads were cancelled out by the decline in our YouTube marketing.

While our image ad campaigns were blowing up, we still making about the same amount of sales overall.

I didn't understand why this was at first, but after talking with some business owners who were experienced at buying media it became clear.

What was happening was that as more of our traffic shifted to image ads, our website was gradually becoming more and more optimized for image ad traffic. This led to us buying more image ad traffic and less YouTube traffic...which further reinforced this trend...and so on and so forth.

In one split test, we achieved a monster improvement in conversion by testing a much longer and more detailed sales video. But our YouTube sales tanked right after this supposed "win!"

It's obvious why this happened in hindsight. The video was super detailed, and great for people seeing a random banner who'd never heard of us before. It wasn't appropriate for people coming from YouTube, since most of these people had watched 30+ minutes of video and multiple different commercials before even coming to our website.

It was only once we split our YouTube traffic into a separate part of our website, which was split-tested independently, that our YouTube campaigns started to grow again.

You should learn an important lesson from this mistake I made which cost me hundreds of thousands of dollars.

Always make sure that you are sending the people who have seen your YouTube ads to a separate part of your website that's specifically optimized for YouTube traffic only.

Why YouTube Traffic Is Different From Every Other Traffic Source

I've performed hundreds of different split tests YouTube traffic. I've also done hundreds of these split tests on other traffic sources.

And I've seen very different sales processes work on YouTube vs. other traffic sources. When you think about the YouTube user base and how they're getting to your site, it makes sense why this is.

First of all, YouTube is a website exclusively dedicated to long form video. Because of this, visitors coming to your site from YouTube will like watching video more than the average internet user. They will also be more likely to have high bandwidth internet connections and quality devices to make watching online video enjoyable.

This means that no matter what type of sales process you build, the critical element that converts your YouTube traffic into sales will ALWAYS be another video on your website.

Secondly, to get people to your website from YouTube, you'll usually have to promise some type of content. This could be a video they'll learn from, a quiz that will show them something, a free ebook...something that's in it for them.

You need to deliver the content in your YouTube ads clearly and up front, otherwise people will get disgruntled and click back to YouTube.

For other traffic sources like Google Search, this isn't the user's expectation. They're explicitly searching for a product, and promising them free content in the ad will seem irrelevant to what they want.

Another important difference: by the time YouTube users get to your site, they're much more qualified and they trust you more than traffic coming from other sources.

This is because if someone's watched a YouTube ad, you know they've seen at least a few minutes of video with you before they clicked through. And the vast majority of people will not just watch one ad. They'll watch many different ads before clicking, and probably watch some of the content videos on your channel as well.

This puts them in a drastically different mentality towards you compared to someone who just clicked on an image ad, and who has not seen a single second of video from your business.

A final difference is that although YouTube users have typically watched a lot of your video before going to your site, YouTube does not provide "social proof" for your brand and product as strongly as some other traffic sources do.

"Social proof" is basically evidence that other people like you and your business. It's a natural human tendency to look for "social proof" of others who've had a positive experience with a business before buying. It's embedded in human nature to imitate the behavior of others we see around us — which is why social proof can be so powerful.

With Facebook and Instagram advertising, social proof is embedded in the nature of the platform. They can see how many people liked their ads, if any of their friends did, view the comments, and easily see how popular your page is.

On YouTube the social proof elements of the platform are far less emphasized. They can still go to your channel and see how many subscribers you have, but they can't see if anyone they personally know likes your business. On InStream ads, likes and comments on your video won't even be visible.

If you get a lot of your traffic from affiliate marketing right now, this is also going to be a critical distinction to learn about.

When someone endorses your product for a commission, they are coming to your website after hearing positive things about you from an authority they trust. This means that it's not as important to demonstrate social proof, since you've got a lot of it coming in.

By contrast, demonstrating social proof is critical in your YouTube sales process because the viewer hasn't already seen it. Unlike Facebook or affiliate marketing, you aren't "socially proofed" from the beginning — so your sales video needs to accomplish this for you.

I hope I don't have to belabor this point any more. **What works to convert YouTube traffic is much different than what works to convert other traffic sources. And by creating a separate YouTube sales website, you'll be giving yourself a HUGE advantage over most marketers.**

The Three Types Of Websites That Convert YouTube Traffic

There are three different types of websites that can convert your YouTube traffic into cash:

- Sales funnels
- Quiz funnels
- Ecommerce stores

If you're an advanced marketer who said "DUH!!!" when you read this, you can skip this section and just focus on the advice to improve your specific type of website.

But if you don't know the differences between these types of sales processes, I'll show you in the next few pages. I'll also show you how to choose the best sales process for your unique product and business.

Sales Funnels: The Best Solution For Most YouTube Marketers

Dean Graziosi's "Expert Secrets" website is an example of a video-based sales funnel could work well for YouTube traffic.

Sales funnels are simple websites intended to sell one "flagship" product initially.

The biggest advantage of sales funnels is that it's easier to perform split tests on sales funnels vs. other types of websites. And this is a huge advantage in the hands of a skilled marketer!

Let's revisit split testing, and talk about why it's so important.

Split testing is the scientific process for improving your sales process that all the world's top marketers use. Rather than guessing at whether a change to your website might improve it, you test it and measure the results objectively.

Improving your website through continuously split testing is KEY to success with YouTube marketing — and any other type of marketing as well. And sales funnels make the process of split testing simple and easy.

Sales funnels are also the simplest and fastest type of website to build. Again, if you are building this site yourself and are not hiring developers to do it for you this makes a huge difference.

Sales funnels also generate more upsell revenue than eCommerce stores. This is because on a sales funnel, you can charge the user for the initial product and then offer them one click upsells after the sale. This means they can add additional products to their order without having to fill in their credit card information again.

This can make a HUGE difference in your upsells and the average revenue per customer you get.

So, sales funnels have a lot going for them. Unfortunately, they also have a few downsides.

The biggest downside of sales funnels is that they are not a good experience for repeat customers.

When someone buys for the first time, a long, detailed video is necessary to make the sale and to help them understand what they're buying. But when they're buying something they've bought for years, sales funnels can be annoying. This leads to fewer repeat sales for businesses that use sales funnels.

Poorly designed sales funnels can also lead to more Policy problems with Google Ads.

Because many scammy products have been sold using sales funnels in the past, Google trains their Policy team to give extra scrutiny to businesses using this model. However, later in this chapter I'll show you how to make a few small changes to your site to minimize the chances of these types of problems without hurting your sales conversion.

Sales funnels are great for most businesses, but they're not appropriate for some business categories. For example, it would be difficult to sell shoes using a sales funnel. Because tastes in shoes are so divergent, it would be difficult to build a business around a single "flagship" style that everyone has to buy first before they're offered other products from you.

You also need to provide many different sizes, which is more difficult to do in a sales funnel shopping cart.

Generally, these types of businesses should use sales funnels:

- If your website exists to generate leads, you should use a sales funnel. Examples include a car dealership generating sales leads, a doctor generating leads for patient appointments, or an ad agency generating leads for clients.

- If you are in the business of selling information or services, you should always use a sales funnel. Personal trainers, landscapers, nutritionists, accountants, lawyers, dating coaches, and business training all fall into this category.

- If your business has fewer than five products, you should be using a sales funnel.

Later in this chapter, I'll show you how to build sales funnels — and the software I personally use.

Keep in mind your YouTube sales funnel does not have to be your only website! You can still have a traditional corporate style company website with multiple pages, navigation, and all the usual bells and whistles most websites have.

You just won't send your YouTube traffic to this company site. You'll be sending it to a funnel specifically optimized for YouTube ads.

An expertly designed quiz funnel created by my client company Mind Movies. Check out their affiliate program if you're in the personal development market!

I've seen huge success advertising quiz funnels in the past few years, both for myself and for my clients. **It is likely that quiz funnels could be the future of YouTube marketing — so it's important to learn about them.**

In a quiz funnel, the user answers a short series of questions when they first land on your site. After they fill out their responses, they're usually asked to give their email to receive the results. And after they do this, they get a sales video **customized to their unique situation** that incorporates the information they gave in their quiz responses.

Everything after this is the same as a regular sales funnel. They're offered a single product based on their responses, and upsells they can buy with one click after they checkout.

Quiz funnels have a few HUGE advantages over regular sales funnels…

First, they give you a GREAT call to action for your YouTube ads.

My testing has shown that asking viewers to take a quiz leads to a much higher rate of people clicking through to your website than asking them to watch another video. If your sales process works, more people to your website will usually mean more sales.

Second, a well-designed quiz funnel can convert visitors to sales at a higher rate than a conventional sales funnel.

This is because customers are different, and it's impossible for a single sales video to talk to all of their needs. A sophisticated quiz funnel delivers a sales message crafted specifically for each individual customer – another huge advantage.

Finally, quiz funnels are less likely to have problems with Google Ads Policy compliance.

Because they're a better experience for users, Google's Policy team will give your website less scrutiny if you're using a quiz funnel.

These are some HUGE advantages...but of course, there are also some downsides to quiz funnels.

The biggest downside of quiz funnels is that they are significantly more complex to create.

To build a sophisticated quiz funnel, you will need to hire a developer to code the quiz. There are some software options to create basic quiz funnels yourself though, and I'll walk you through them later in this chapter.

It's also more complex to perform split tests on quiz funnels.

Because your users are served different sales videos depending on their responses, it adds to the complexity and time needed to perform split tests. But I'll show you how you can overcome this if you're working with a good developer in the next section.

You can get started with quiz funnels with a fairly small level of customization. For example, one of my clients who sells relationship advice segments her customers into three "buckets" based on her quiz — single people, people in a relationship, and married people. She serves a different sales video to each group which talks specifically to their needs. It's a very simple quiz funnel, but far more effective than serving a single sales video to everyone.

On the other hand, I've also worked with a large corporate client who had eighty-seven (!) different sales videos they served based on the user's responses to their quiz. The logic behind this quiz was stupefyingly complex, and required a large team of developers to set up. And creating eighty-seven different variations of their sales video required a small army of copywriters and video editors.

However, the work this client does is clearly worth it for them because they make tens of millions of dollars in revenue every month from this funnel. And for large businesses, it's worth it to invest in a sophisticated quiz funnel like this.

If sales funnels are appropriate for your business AND you have a good developer, you should consider building a quiz funnel. While they require more technical work, they usually out-convert regular sales funnels while also providing a better customer experience.

ECommerce Stores — The Best Solution For Businesses That Sell Many Products

An example of a well-designed eCommerce store created by my friends at Organifi.

While sales funnels are the best solution for most businesses, they aren't right for every business. Certain types of businesses will do better with an eCommerce store — or a website designed to sell many different products.

Unlike a sales funnel, in an eCommerce store there is no one "flagship" product that everyone has to buy before they get offered other product. An eCommerce store is more like Amazon.com, where they customer is offered an array of different products, and where many different products are advertised.

The biggest advantage of eCommerce stores is that there is excellent, cheap software available for building them.

I'll walk you through this software (Shopify) and how to use it to build your site later in this chapter.

eCommerce websites are also a better experience for repeat customers, which leads to more repeat business. This can significantly add to your customer value and your ability to buy advertising.

eCommerce is also most appropriate for businesses with many products. It's much easier to create a new product listing on an eCommerce store than it is to create a whole new sales funnel. If you have more than ten products, and more than one that you're already advertising, this means you should probably be using an eCommerce store.

eCommerce websites are FAR less likely to have problems with Google Ads Policy compliance than sales funnels. Since most people using the eCommerce business model are trustworthy companies, Google will be more lenient to your website when doing Policy reviews. You'll also be able to push the envelope more with your marketing claims compared to if you were using a sales funnel.

Most importantly, eCommerce websites are the only type of website that can access TrueView For Shopping campaigns.

These are campaigns where the user is offered different products on your site based on Google's algorithms predicting what they'll be most interested in. We've seen these campaigns usually out-perform non-shopping campaigns, so getting access to them is a big advantage.

So, eCommerce stores have a lot of advantages for some businesses...but there are drawbacks as well:

First, eCommerce stores are significantly more difficult to build and maintain than sales funnels or even quiz funnels. Because there are many more products on your store and because the software behind it is more complex, it's significantly more difficult to build this type of site yourself if you're not a developer.

It's also far more difficult to perform split-tests on an eCommerce store. It can be done, and I'll show you how later. But the difficulties in split-testing an eCommerce store are a major disadvantage, and will reduce the rate at which you can improve your site.

Finally, eCommerce websites are not ideal for selling monthly subscriptions. Again, it can be done...it's just much harder to get it to work. When the user has the option to buy many products, it's harder for them to understand what subscription goes with which product and why.

If you are using a "forced continuity" model where every user has to purchase a subscription to buy from you, you'll probably be better off using a sales funnel.

eCommerce stores are best for any business which sells more than ten products, where it is impossible to create a single "flagship" product all customers must buy. This includes most larger companies that are selling physical products in categories like fashion, cosmetics, kitchenware, car parts, or tools.

The Best Of Both Worlds: Use Sales Funnels AND An ECommerce Store

If your business is making less than $100,000 in revenue per month, you should just pick one type of sales website and focus on that. You don't want to make things too complex when your team is small and your resources are limited.

But for many larger businesses, I've found that it's ideal to have BOTH sales funnels and an eCommerce store.

That's why we used quiz funnels, regular sales funnels, AND an eCommerce store at SixPackAbs.com. If you have the technical and marketing bandwidth to do it, this approach gives you the best of all worlds. Many top YouTube marketers are using this approach, and in certain product categories in particular it makes a lot of sense.

When you're using this approach, you send most of your advertising to your quiz or regular sales funnels. They're usually the highest converting sales process for new customers, and you can usually acquire new customers more cheaply this way.

But once someone has bought, you shift to mainly promoting your eCommerce store to them. This way the product they want is simple to find and easy to buy, and the repeat buying experience is good.

You can also use your eCommerce store to access TrueView for Shopping campaigns. This gives you the huge advantage for these campaigns, while also allowing you to use a funnel strategy in other campaigns.

The Best Software For Building Sales Funnels

NOTE: Software is technology and subject to rapid change. If you are reading this book in 2022 or later, go to **15StepsBonuses.com/SalesWebsite** *to get my most current recommendations.*

My #1 Choice: ClickFunnels — ClickFunnels is by far the best software out there to build regular sales funnels, and it's what I use myself. Its simple, drag and drop interface makes building sales funnels easy.

There are also many pre-built site templates that you can buy in the ClickFunnels Marketplace. And the customer support is excellent if you're having problems figuring something out.

ClickFunnels also has a great team making ongoing improvements to the product. I've also gotten a chance to talk with Russell Brunson, the founder of ClickFunnels, at a few different events. He's a great guy who cares about his customers, and I can wholeheartedly recommend doing business with him.

In this chapter's bonus material, I include a video review of ClickFunnels and all of the other software I recommend in this chapter.

You can sign up for Clickfunnels at:

15StepsBonuses.com/ClickFunnels

My #2 Choice: Leadpages — Leadpages is similar to ClickFunnels, but it's cheaper and its functionality is more limited. It can work well for businesses who generate leads online and close them on the phone or in person. But if you want to actually take sales online ClickFunnels is much better. And it's well worth the additional cost.

If you want to sign up for Leadpages, you can sign up here:

15StepsBonuses.com/LeadPages

The Best Software For Building Quiz Funnels

My #1 Choice: Bucket.io — If you can't afford to hire a developer to code a quiz funnel for you, I recommend using bucket.io. It's got a simple drag and drop quiz creation interface, and it also provides some great templates for building your quizzes. It also gives you tools to segment your users based on their quiz results, which can be very useful for YouTube marketing.

I have not found any other good quiz creation software on the market right now, so bucket.io is my first and only recommendation.

You can learn more about Bucket.io here:

15StepsBonuses.com/Bucket

The Best Software For Building eCommerce Stores

My #1 Choice: Shopify — Shopify is the industry leader in eCommerce software, because it's simply the best. It's easy to use, has powerful functionality, and it has a vibrant marketplace of developers and designers experienced with the software.

It also works great for drop-shipping (marketing a product online while having another company handle the inventory and fulfillment.) And it has excellent integrations with Google Ads, Facebook Ads, Google Analytics, and other important software.

You can learn more about Shopify here:

15StepsBonuses.com/Shopify

My #2 Choice: BigCommerce — BigCommerce isn't bad. In a world where Shopify didn't exist, it would work fine. But as someone who's used both, Shopify is clearly better than BigCommerce in just about every way. Use Shopify for your eCommerce software unless you're already committed to BigCommerce or another platform.

Learn more about BigCommerce here:

15StepsBonuses.com/BigCommerce

Should You Develop Your Own Site From Scratch?

All of the software above can be great options for smaller businesses. But if you have a business doing more than $10,000 a month in revenue, you should seriously consider coding your own site manually from scratch.

There are many technical advantages to doing this, and it also gives you ultimate freedom to customize your site to fit your needs. This is why I've mostly used custom coded pages in my own businesses, and why all of my large clients do as well.

You can also hire someone cheaply to code a site for you even if you have no technical skills. I certainly have none, yet I've created dozens of custom coded sites by knowing how to hire the people.

Your Sales Video: The Ultimate Key To Making Any Sales Process Work

Once you've chosen your software, it's time to build your site!

There are many details about building each type of site that are different. But ultimately, **the key to success with any type of YouTube sales website is going to be creating a great sales video.**

With a great sales video, you can make even a basic sales website work. But if your video sucks, then even the world's most amazing website with the most eloquently written text won't save you.

The text and images on your sales page are necessary to comply with Google Ads policies. But my testing experience has shown me that they don't make nearly as much of an impact on your conversions as your sales video does.

Most marketers waste way too much time on the "window-dressing" around their video while not spending nearly enough time on the video itself.

Doing this is like spending all your time on your YouTube's video's description, rather than spending your time on your actual video. It makes much more sense to focus on what people will actually watch — the video — rather than text that most people will never read.

In the next few pages, I'm going to show you my Simple Sales Video Formula. This is sales video formula designed specifically for YouTube traffic, which is simple and easy for any copywriting beginner to learn.

You can easily learn this formula and make a sales video with it in just a few weeks. And if you're new to creating sales video, this will be the best place for you to start.

The Simple Sales Video Formula

Here is a simple formula that I've used to create many winning sales videos:

- Hook their attention
- Demonstrate empathy & understanding of their problems
- Show them how all of their problems have a single root cause
- Show them that the root cause of all their problems has a solution. Not a product, but a system.
- Give them Conditioning Content that teaches them more about your solution
- Present your product, and show them why it's the best option to get the solution you've taught them
- Give the first call to action
- Give your money-back guarantee
- Give the final call to action

I'll walk you through each step, and how you can apply it to your product.

Hook Their Attention

This is the same idea as a Skip Stopper, but with one key difference — **the customer is not given an explicit option to skip your sales video after five seconds.** Because of this, the best sales video hooks are usually slower developing and more integrated into the main video than the best Skip Stoppers.

There are infinite ways to hook customers' attention. I could write an entire book about this alone, and going deep into this topic is beyond the scope of this book.

But I'll link you to a few excellent courses that have helped me tremendously to create sales videos at the end of this chapter. And to get you started, I'll give you a few ideas that have consistently been winners for me in the past:

- **Media appearances** — A TV News clip not only hooks the viewer's attention; it also establishes credibility right off the bat. Before your sales message even starts you'll be perceived as a quasi-celebrity, and they'll be much less resistance to your sales message.

In Step 12, I'll walk you through in greater detail how anyone can buy sponsored media appearances for a minimal cost. And I'll also teach you how you can get double mileage out of these appearances by also using your media clips as a YouTube commercial.

To get a media appearance to work as your hook, the key is the editing. Make sure you have the rights to edit the clip, and edit it down to 30-45 seconds maximum. You want to establish credibility and hook attention, but if your clip is too long, it'll get boring and reduce conversion.

Don't be afraid to aggressively edit your media clip intro down and to make it a little choppy. My testing has shown aggressively edited intros usually convert the best.

- **A promise of content they're very interested in** — In some markets that are highly engaged, a simple promise of content can be the most powerful type of hook. For example, many great sales videos in the golf market start off by simply promising to teach the viewer a new way to improve his golf game.

- **An attractive member of the opposite sex** — If your product is targeted to a single gender, this is a simple and shockingly effective way to hook in attention. All you need to do is have an attractive man or woman introduce you. It'll cause your audience to immediately pay attention, and it will build your credibility in their eyes before you even start talking.

  For example, let's say that you're a woman selling dating advice exclusively to other women. A great way to hook attention in would be to hire an actor with male model looks and a British accent to introduce you.

  Your prospects will listen in rapt attention as he explains how you've helped thousands of women around the world meet the man of their dreams. And when he explains you're the world's leading expert in attracting men, they'll take it as a statement of fact.

Demonstrate Empathy & Understanding Of Their Problems

Before someone is open to hearing your marketing message, you first need to show them you understand their problems. And not just an intellectual understanding — you must show that you empathize with your prospect, and that you literally "feel their pain."

If you've gone through the problem yourself, the easiest way to do this is to show them how you had many of the same frustrations and fears that they had before you found the solution. If you have not gone through this problem, talking about the experiences of a client you've worked with is usually the best way to demonstrate empathy.

For example, when I'm making sales videos targeting entrepreneurs, I don't just acknowledge they're unsatisfied with the money they're making and they want to make more money with less work.

I tell them about how I was dead broke myself just a few years back, and how it ruined my self-esteem and my life. I tell them what it was like to not be able to afford basics for my daughter because my ad campaigns weren't profitable enough. I tell them about the gut-wrenching feeling of despair I felt when Google Ads suspended my ad account in the past.

And I also show them how I share their hopes and dreams. How they're like me because we both share the same vision of building a business, we love that makes us wealthy.

If you haven't gone through the problem yourself, the best way to empathize with the prospect will be to tell the story of someone who had the problem that you helped.

This can be a client or a friend who you helped informally before you started the business.

When you tell the story of someone you helped, it will be even more important to include details that will show your prospect you understand what they're going through. Even if you have a great story of successfully helping a client, it will fall flat if you don't use the right emotional language.

Don't just share the bare facts of what happened, like "my client Mary improved her advertising ROI by 48% with my software." Tell them how Mary FELT before and after getting your solution.

Something like this...

"I know what a struggle it can be to keep track of many different ad buys. My client Mary was going through exactly what you were just a few months ago. Mary's a friend of mine, and she's a single mother of three kids. She also runs a thriving business — but when she saw her ROI on some of her ad buys begin to tank a few months ago, she began to panic.

It seemed like nothing she was doing would work to get her business profitable again. She told me she was having trouble sleeping because of her financial problems, and she felt constant anxiety that she wouldn't be able to provide for her kids.

I helped her get set up with my software, and within a few months we'd improved her ROI by 48%. She called me in tears to thank me, and she told me she was so relieved she didn't have to worry about sending her kids to college anymore. She's now financially free, and her days of stressing about how to provide for her family are over."

Of course, if you use a client story, it has to be a real story. But you should make sure to include these types of emotional details that mediocre marketers leave out. Most business owners have helped at least one customer like this, and it's just a matter of telling that story the right way.

To make a great sales video, you MUST demonstrate deep empathy for your prospect — not just a surface-level understanding. You must literally "feel their pain." And you should literally feel the thrill when your customers achieve success as well!

Later in this book, we'll dive into advanced strategies for developing this money-generating sense of empathy.

Show Them How All Their Problems Have A Single Root Cause

Let's say you're selling a course on how to make your marriage better. A prospect coming to your website may have many marriage related problems.

Maybe he's fighting with his wife too much, maybe they're not having sex enough, maybe they disagree about how to raise the kids, maybe it's money...or any number of other things.

Your job in this section is to show the prospect how all of these problems have a single cause.

Later in the video, you'll give him the solution and show him why your product is the best way to get that solution.

For example, let's say I was hired to sell the book "The Five Love Languages" in a sales video. The way I'd do it is by showing the prospect how all of their marriage problems just come from not knowing their prospect's love language, or their unique way of receiving love. Once they learn their love language, the fighting, lack of sex, parenting disagreements, etc. will all be solved.

Once the prospect has accepted this premise, selling the book later will be easy.

Show Them That Their Problems Have A Solution.

Once you've identified the problem, the next step is to show them their problem has a simple solution. Not your product — that comes later in the video. You want to show them the solution to their problem in general terms, and imply that they'll learn more about it in your video. Later, you'll show them why your product is the best way to get the solution they've learned about.

For example, let's say you're selling a virtual dating assistant service. These are services that will cheaply hire a virtual assistant in the Philippines for you, and get them to do all the tedious work of online dating. They'll make your profile, message men or women who fit your criteria, and set up dates.

If I were selling a product like this, I would first show the prospect why the main reason why haven't seen success in online dating is that it's incredibly time consuming, and they're too busy to spend multiple hours every day on it.

Then I would show them how the solution to this problem is a virtual dating assistant — someone who will spend multiple hours every day doing the repetitive, tedious work of online dating for you.

With your product, do something similar. Show them the solution in general terms, and later show them why your product is the best way to get that solution.

Give The Conditioning Content That Teaches More About Your Solution

This part of your sales video will be similar to the Conditioning Content you created for your YouTube commercial. But because this is a sales video without tight time constraints, you'll want to make it longer and more in depth than a commercial.

Let's say you're selling a financial advisor looking to generate leads for clients who want to save money on their taxes.

You've taught them that the root cause of their financial problems is that they pay too much in taxes. And that the solution to this problem is to learn the tax avoidance strategies used by billionaires, who generally pay a far lower effective tax rate than the rest of us.

In your Conditioning Content, you can teach them about some legal and ethical solutions they could use to immediately start paying less tax. Examples of this would include a captive insurance company, an SEP-IRA, renting your house out to your own business, and starting an overseas corporation.

(Google these if you're curious, they are all completely legal ways to save on taxes commonly used by the rich.)

Ideally, when your prospect hears your Conditioning Content his mind will be blown. And he'll become deeply committed to your solution. In our tax example, the prospect might have accepted that the amount of tax she's paying is a problem, and that she could save a huge amount by doing what billionaires do.

But once she's learned the specific tactics in your Conditioning Content, it becomes much more real for her.

She becomes more committed to this solution — which sets you up for an easier sale later.

Present Your Product, And Show Them Why It's The Best Option To Get The Solution They Learned

If you've done your job with the previous sections, this part should be easy. All you have to do is show your prospect why your product delivers the solution you taught them better than anything else out there.

Let's go back to our financial advisor / tax savings example. Once the prospect has learned your tactics, they have a few options open to them.

They could try and do it themselves — but this is nearly impossible, since the tax avoidance strategies above are all incredibly complex and nearly always done by professionals.

They could get their local CPA to do it — but this sucks as well because 99% of CPAs have no idea how to use strategies this complex, and most will not even be willing to use aggressive tax avoidance strategies.

Or they could fill in their information in your form, where they'll get a free call from someone on your team who will give them customized tax savings recommendations. If they like the recommendations, they can work with you to implement them.

It'll be easy to show your prospect why this makes the most sense. Once they've accepted your tactics are the solution, doing it themselves and having their accountant do it are clearly not viable options. It makes the most sense to work with someone like you, who's an expert in these strategies and who's done it hundreds of times before with other clients.

With your product, you want to accomplish the same thing. Show the prospect why the other options in her head are not viable now that she's accepted what you've taught her in the Conditioning Content.

Give The First Call To Action, The Money Back Guarantee, And The Final Call To Action

After you've done this, it's time for action! Explicitly tell them what to do next to buy. Tell them to click the button below the video, to fill out the forms on the next page, and when to expect their product in the mail.

When you do this, some prospects will click over to your order form and not watch the rest of the video. That's good! The video has done its job, and they don't need to watch the rest.

However, many prospects will have some last minute reservations and will not order immediately when you give the first call to action. For the benefit of these prospects, you should then go through your money back guarantee to ease their fears.

I recommend giving as aggressive of a money back guarantee as you possibly can.

If you are selling a quality product, very few customers will take you up on it and your guarantee won't cost you very much. However, it'll go a long way towards easing customer anxiety about buying if they know they have a way to get their money back in the worst case if things don't work out.

The minimum guarantee I recommend offering is a 60 day unconditional money-back guarantee.

That means that you'll give anyone a refund who asks for one for any reason, as long as they ship their product back within 60 days.

If you can offer a bolder guarantee, it will probably work even better!

For example, I recently attended a copywriting seminar that cost $25,000. It was taught by Justin Goff, an internet marketer I've known for a long time who'd recently sold his company. I wasn't going to sign up for his seminar when he first pitched me on it. But then, he sent a physically mailed letter to my house that convinced me to go.

What could he have possibly written in this letter to get me — and many other business owners — to pay him twenty five grand?

It's simple: he offered a DOUBLE your money back guarantee. He was so confident I'd love the seminar that he would give me FIFTY THOUSAND DOLLARS if I told him I wasn't satisfied and I wanted a refund later.

This showed serious confidence, since I knew nobody would make this guarantee unless they were very confident in their content. So, I went to the seminar, along with about thirty other people. We all got more than our money's worth, and not a single person asked for a refund.

If you can offer a seemingly insane guarantee like this, it's the ultimate way to alleviate customer fears and get more sales.

Double their money back, triple their money back, mailing them a $100 bill on top of refunding their purchase...all of these are great guarantee tactics that have worked out very profitably for business owners with quality products.

It's likely that when you do this, you'll have to refund 5-10% of your sales even if you have a top quality product. But that's OK! You'll be making far more in additional sales than what you're losing if your refunds are at this level.

If your refunds are higher than 10% of your sales, this indicates there's a problem with your product or customer service. You should work on improving these until your refunds are lower, and you can afford to offer a more confident guarantee.

After you've given your guarantee, give your final call to action. Tell your prospect again to buy, and again give explicit directions as to what he should do next.

We're Only Scratching The Surface

You can create a profitable sales video using the basic sales video formula I gave you above. If you're just looking to build a small lifestyle business, you can do it just with the Simple Sales Video Formula alone, and you won't even need to advanced formulas.

However, if you're looking to make large scale profits and build a valuable brand with YouTube marketing, you'll need to get a deeper understanding and go beyond the basics.

Make sure to later study the advanced sales video formulas I give you later in this book. Since your sales video is so important, it's worth devoting some time to really mastering this skill.

In Step 13, I'll go more in-depth into advanced sales video formulas and website optimization strategies. But to wrap this chapter up, I'll just give a few of my best tips to get you started with each major type of sales website.

Later, we'll kick your conversions into high gear with the advanced tactics in Step 13. But get some experience under your belt with the basic formula now, and you'll get much better results with the advanced formulas later.

Tips For Building A Great Video Based, Standard Sales Funnel

- Use the YouTube player to serve your sales video. Our testing has shown the YouTube player usually beats other video players in split tests. This is probably because YouTube users trust the YouTube player more, and because it serves faster and better videos for some users. It also has the advantage of being free!

- Avoid making aggressive marketing claims in the text content of your page, and keep any marketing claims within the video itself. The text of your page will be heavily scrutinized by the Google Ads Policy team, but will be skipped by the vast majority of your prospects.

  Focus this content on images of your product and information about it rather than selling its benefits.

- Make sure you have the compliance content on your site the Google Ads Policy team requires. The most important pages are a Legal Disclaimer Page, a Contact Information page, and a Privacy Policy.

  In Step 13 I'll teach you more about these compliance pages and how to create pages that minimize your chance of ad account problems

- Include a video or audio clip on your SHOPPING CART page. Most marketers neglect to do this, but adding this can massively increase your conversion and sales.

- Include at least three one click upsells after the customer buys your product. If you don't have three more products to sell, partner with another business owner to sell one of theirs in your upsells. This is a great opportunity to get more sales for no additional advertising cost, and it's just as important as the first parts of your sales funnel.

Tips For Building A Great Quiz Funnel

- The key to building a great quiz funnel is to divide your customers into "buckets" in the best possible way. This should strike a balance between talking to all the different types of customers you have, and creating a manageable amount of different sales videos and complexity to your quiz.

  If you're a solo entrepreneur, generally you should limit yourself to 4-5 buckets of customers who each get a unique sales video. If you have a large organization, it will be worthwhile to create many more buckets, more complex logic in your quiz, and possibly even multiple different products the customer is sold based on their bucket.

To minimize the amount of work needed to create sales videos for each individual bucket of customers, you can create one single "base" video that all customers see.

To customize your funnel, you then create a unique first 5-10 minutes of each video that talks specifically to your customers' needs, and edit this in front of your base video. When you're presenting the details of your product, the call to action, the money back guarantee, etc. there won't be much difference in what prospects need to hear. So, you can keep this content the same, and only make the beginning of the video specific to their responses.

Tips For Building A Great eCommerce Store

- Use Shopify. It's the best, and I've tried multiple alternatives.

- VERY IMPORTANT: You MUST customize your Shopify theme to add a VIDEO to each product listing page if you are serious about making money from YouTube marketing. I cannot stress the importance of this enough.

  Remember, people coming from YouTube love video and hate text. You can massively increase your sales conversion by adding video, yet many eCommerce store owners are not doing this.

  Generally for an eCommerce store, you'll want longer and more in depth sales videos for a few of your best-selling, most advertised products. You'll also want short, simple videos for all your other products — these can be just a minute or two long

- On a related note, I highly recommend creating a unique Shopify store that is ONLY for your YouTube traffic. Remember, all traffic sources are different. If you are building a website that's mainly optimized for Facebook or email traffic, it's going to be harder to achieve success with YouTube marketing.

- Focus your advertising on a small number of products, so you can focus on creating truly great videos and listing pages for these.

Your Action Steps From This Chapter:

1. Choose which type of sales website you'll be making for your YouTube traffic if you don't have a website already. Your alternatives are a regular sales funnel, a quiz funnel, or an eCommerce store.

   Choose the software based on my recommendations above. Go with my #1 recommendation unless you have a strong reason not to. If you run a large business, consider having your developers code a custom site made without any software.

2. Outline your sales video using the Simple Sales Video Formula

3. Write and copy edit your sales video script

4. Film and edit your sales video

5. Write the text for your sales page, shopping cart, and upsell pages.

6. Create your basic sales website using the software and guidelines I gave you above.

7. Find a solution for processing credit cards, and integrate this into your website. I recommend using Stripe or PayPal.

8. Test your site out and put through a transaction to make sure everything works

Step 7: Set Up Your Google Ads Account, And Create Your Remarketing Campaigns

You've got your channel, your website, and you've made your first ad. Now it's time to start advertising!

*The first ad campaigns we'll be making are your **remarketing** campaigns.*

If you already have traffic coming to your websites from other sources, these campaigns will be the easiest to make a small-scale profit with. This will not only build your bankroll — it will also build your confidence. Once you see your first few sales coming in from remarketing, you'll be able to re-invest that money in more scalable YouTube campaigns.

Remarketing: The Holy Grail Of Advertising?

Congratulations! If you've made it this far — and if you've been doing the action steps in each chapter — you've now got your channel, website, and ads set up. You've laid a great foundation for success, and now it's time to start advertising!

But now you're probably wondering...what type of YouTube campaign should I set up in Google Ads first?

What I recommend is setting up your **remarketing** campaigns first. Remarketing is an incredibly powerful advertising tool. Many business owners even call it the "holy grail" of digital marketing.

If you're not familiar with remarketing, the way that it works is that when someone visits your website or watches one of your YouTube videos, Google places a "cookie" on their computer.

This is a small data file that tells Google this person has been to your site or watched your videos.

You can then target your ads to this person no matter what kind of video they're watching. And since you know the people seeing your ads are already interested in your product, remarketing campaigns are usually extremely profitable.

You can also remarket to people in email list or customer database through a feature called **Customer Match** remarketing. Once you hit the Google Ads requirements to be approved for this, all you have to do is upload a list of your customers' emails to Google Ads. Google will place cookies on their computers, and you can serve ads to them the same way.

Have you ever seen ads that seem to follow you around the internet no matter what type of video you were watching?

Chances are you were seeing a remarketing campaign in action. Most likely, the reason why you kept seeing those ads is that they were making a big profits for the advertiser.

If you already have traffic going to your websites, you are going to LOVE remarketing.

You will probably make a fat profit immediately, and with very little effort, just by showing YouTube ads to your existing audience.

If you don't yet have any traffic going to your website, that's OK! The next chapter will show you how to start getting some from YouTube. And once you do, your remarketing campaigns will start running.

You should still set up your remarketing campaigns first even if you have no traffic to your website right now. This way when you start buying cold, non-remarketing traffic using what you'll learn in the next chapter, you'll be positioned from the start to fully maximize it.

First Step: Create Your Google Ads Account

If you don't already have a Google Ads account, this is the first thing you'll need to do. Go to ads.google.com to set one up — it's super simple and easy.

There's just one important thing you need to know...

When you're setting your account up, make sure you choose the "Advanced" account setup option. Avoid "Smart Campaigns" (previously called "Adwords Express") or any other options meant for beginners.

It's really only "smart" to use Smart Campaigns if you suck at advertising and you're too lazy to learn how it's done. For skilled advertisers like us, they should really be called Dumb Campaigns.

Advanced campaigns will give you much more powerful functionality than so-called "Smart" campaigns. And even if you're totally new to Google Ads, you'll pick up these advanced features fast now that you have this book.

A Crash Course In The Mechanics Of Google Ads

There are many great tutorials on YouTube which will teach you the mechanics of Google Ads. **By "mechanics," I mean what to click on or type to access certain functions (as opposed to the concepts & ideas behind what you should do.)**

However, there are very few people who can teach you how to create a marketing message that can actually make you a profit, and the concepts behind running profitable ad campaigns.

There's a big difference between knowing how to create a Google Ads campaign and knowing how to create one that makes you money.

Because of this, I'm going to focus mainly on the marketing aspects of Google Ads and YouTube in the remainder of this book. But I'll give you a quick "crash course" in how everything works now, so you know enough to get started.

You can skip this section if you're already familiar with Google Ads. And if you're totally new to Google Ads, there are many other videos and articles you can watch later to learn more about mechanics.

The first thing to know is that there are three levels of organization inside your Google Ads account:

- Campaigns
- Ad groups
- Ads

Your ad groups are groups of ads that run on the same targeting (for example, they're targeted to the same keywords or remarketing audience)

Your campaigns are groups of ad groups that share similarities. Campaigns share important settings like budgets, bidding strategies, geographic targeting, and other settings that are crucial to how your ads run.

To get started, you'll first need to make a new campaign. Then you'll need to make an ad group within this campaign...and then finally at least one ad within your ad group.

And later in this chapter, you'll learn exactly how to set up your campaigns, ad groups, and ads to position you for success.

CRITICALLY IMPORTANT: Set Up The Right Data Columns

If you're an advanced marketer who skipped the last section, STOP SKIPPING NOW! This part is critical, and I've seen many advanced marketers mess this up.

When you run Google Ads campaigns, you are provided with a plethora of data that you can view. There are nearly infinite options for information about your ads to view — how many people watched it, the view rate, the average watch time how many people clicked to your site, the conversion rate, how many sales you made, your return on investment, and many, many other options.

It's like you're being drowned in an overwhelming ocean of data. **What data should you be looking at — and which data can you safely ignore?**

This decision is critical to the success of your account. If you view too much data, it'll be impossible to use and managing your account will take forever.

If you're missing important data though, it can be even worse.

Not having the right columns in your Google Ads account is similar to being blind — you won't have the information you need to make good decisions.

But having the BEST possible columns set up is like giving yourself X-Ray vision. You'll be able to see things in your ads other marketers can't, and all your decisions will be better because of this.

So, it's absolutely critical you set up your columns the right way.

I've spent many years experimenting with different Google Ads columns. After thousands of hours and millions of dollars spent, this is the most important realization I've made:

You should always arrange your data columns from the most important metrics on the left, to the least important metrics on the right.

Why this way? It's because in English, we read from left to right. You'll intuitively look at your leftmost metrics first, and then move to the right.

Because of this, your most important data should be on the left. If you don't have enough data to make a decision based on your most important metrics, then you move to the right. If you still don't have enough information, you move to the right again.

This system of organizing your columns will save you a TON of time. It will also tremendously improve the quality of the decisions you're making in your Google Ads account.

And I'll show you the exact columns I recommend in just a minute.

How To Split Test When Using The Universal Data Columns

One of the most important things you'll be using your columns for is **split-testing** your ads.

Split-testing is an extremely complex subject, and I could write an entire book about this alone. **Most business owners are not split-testing their ads correctly, and it is costing them a ton of money.**

Over the years, I've experimented with many different ways of split testing. And I've found this is the most effective way to split test your ads:

- When you have enough data, you always split test based on **ROI**

- When there is not enough ROI data, you split test based on **cost per lead**

- When there is not enough cost per lead data, you split test based on **cost per click to your website.**

Here's why you need to split-test this way:

If you have enough data, then ROI is the ultimate source of truth. If one ad is making a better ROI than the other ad, preliminary metrics like cost per lead and cost per click become unimportant. Who cares if one ad is getting you cheaper leads if another is more profitable in the long run?

ROI is the ultimate measurable goal of your campaigns, and the best data to split test on when you have it.

Of course, ROI isn't the ONLY goal of your campaigns. You also want to build your brand, and build your social engagement as well. But since it's difficult to measure whether one ad is building your brand better than another, we won't use engagement or branding metrics to test ads in most campaigns.

I will show you how to run an advanced type of "Modern Branding" campaign that is split tested based on engagement generated later.

This is an exception to the rule though — in most campaigns, we'll be using ROI metrics to compare ads to one another.

When using this approach, it's important that you're only making ads that build your social engagement and brand, and that you are not using marketing tactics that devalue your brand. Of course, it's no good to make a short term profit from an ad if it ruins your brand in the long run.

But if all your ads are designed to be brand-enhancing, ROI is the best way to compare them to each other. And I'll show you more details about how to make sure your brand and engagement are good in Step 14.

So, ROI is the best way to split test ads when you have enough data. But there is a problem with only using ROI to split test...

I recommend spending at least 2x the price of the product you're advertising, and a minimum of $50 before making split testing decisions on ROI.

For example, if you're selling a $50 product, you should spend at least $100 per ad before doing ROI-based split testing. If you're selling a $300 product, you'll need to spend a minimum of $600 per ad.

Any less data than this, and you may be seeing a single fluke sale that isn't indicative of long term performance. And if you sell a very expensive product - like a high-end seminar - you'll need to spend a HUGE amount per ad to get sufficient ROI testing data.

If you're a smaller advertiser – or if you sell a very expensive product – this could mean you'll NEVER have enough data in many ad groups to split test based on ROI. And even if you're a large advertiser selling a cheap product, you'll still have many ad groups where your ads aren't spending enough to test based on ROI.

And this is where cost per lead split testing comes in…

Your "cost per lead" is how much it costs you to get one person to give you their email address or phone number for follow-up.

If you've designed your funnel well, your cost per lead from your ads will correlate highly with ROI. That means if your cost per lead is good, your ROI is likely to be good as well. It's not quite as good as ROI data, but it's real close and it's available faster.

So, when you do not have enough data to test based on ROI, you should split test based on cost per lead.

By doing this, you can make meaningful improvements to your campaigns even when your spend is small. And doing this is often the key to making better ROI.

For advertisers selling high priced products, testing based on cost per lead is critical. For example, let's say you're selling a high end business course that costs $5,000.

You will need at least double your initial sale price spent on each ad to test based on ROI at the minimum. This means you need to spend **more than $10,000 per ad** to make ROI based decisions.

But when you split test based on cost per lead, you can make improvements much sooner.

To test based on cost per lead, each ad you are testing should have gotten at least five leads.

Since you can usually get leads for between $1-$10 depending on the industry, this usually allows you to make testing decisions much sooner.

But what do you do if you don't even have enough spent on each ad to get five leads?

If you are using InStream ads, **you should split test based on cost per click to your website.** This data is shown in the "cost per click" column.

While the correlation with ROI is not as strong as cost per lead, it is still significant enough to make early improvements to your campaigns. You can use this method of split testing once you've gotten at least thirty clicks to your website from each ad tested.

With Video Discovery ads, the cost per click to your website data is not available. So, in this case, you should split test based on the **view rate.** For Video Discovery ads, this is the rate at which people click on your ads and watch the beginning of your video.

Because the view rate on Video Discovery ads does not correlate strongly with ROI, I only recommend small, low-budget advertisers use this method of split testing.

For large advertisers, you should wait until you have cost per lead data, and forgo split testing on Video Discovery ads until you do.

The Universal Data Columns

Here is how I recommend setting up your columns from left to right.

- Cost
- All Conversion Value
- All Conversion Value / cost
- Conversions
- Cost / Conversion
- Value / Conversion
- Clicks
- CTR
- Average CPC
- Views
- Impressions
- View Rate
- Average CPV
- Earned Subscribers

If you haven't seen these metrics before, I know that looking at all these weirdly named columns might seem complex. But don't get discouraged!

Once you've read the next few pages, you'll see how they these columns actually make managing your ads shockingly simple.

You should use these columns for EVERY view in Google Ads. When you look at campaigns, ad groups, ads, devices, geographic locations, or anything else, they should ALL have these same columns.

Having one universal set of columns for everything in Google Ads tremendously simplifies your life. It'll reduce confusion, and you'll be less likely to make errors when managing your account. You're already dealing with an array of complex metrics, and it's important that your view of the data be as simple and manageable as possible.

They should look like this when they're set up:

□	Campaign	Budget	Status	Cost	All conv. value	All conv. value / cost	Conversion	Cost / conv.	Value / conv.	Clicks	CTR	Avg. CPC	Views	Impr.	View rate	Avg. CPV	Earned subscribers

I'll explain what each metric is, and why they're set up in each way.

ROI Metrics: The Ultimate Source Of Truth

Cost	All conv. value	All conv. value / cost

Your three leftmost columns are ROI metrics. They are:

- Cost (how much you've spent)
- All conversion value (how much you've made)

- All conversion value / cost (your ROI, which is equal to your All conversion value divided by your cost)

You will use ROI metrics to split test your ads when you've spent at least twice the cost of the product you're advertising, and at least $50.

That means if your product you're selling costs $100, you spend at least $200 on each ad before you use ROI split testing. If you have the budget to spend more than this, this is even better and will make your testing more reliable.

If you are selling a very inexpensive product, like a $1 app, you should spend at least $50 before doing ROI split testing.

This will make it less likely that a fluke sales day will throw off your testing.

And if your product is very expensive (say, a $2,000 sales training course) this means that you'll NEVER use ROI split testing unless your budget is extremely large. And that's OK, because you can still use cost per lead split testing.

You'll be using your ROI metrics for many important decisions outside of split testing as well. They'll be the basis for how you bid in different geographic locations, how you bid on different devices, whether to increase or decrease campaign budgets, setting your CPA bids, etc.

Lead Metrics: The Next Best Thing To ROI

Conversions	Cost / conv.	Value / conv.

Your lead metrics are:

- All Conversions
- Cost / Conversion
- Value / Conversion

If you've set up your leads as a conversion, the vast majority of your conversions will be from leads. I recommend changing your campaign settings so you are ONLY counting leads in your "Conversions" column.

If you're not familiar with how to do this in Google Ads, see this chapter's bonus video.

This will make your "conversions" columns purely data related to your leads, which is what we are going for.

You will use your lead metrics to split test when you don't have enough ROI data, but when you do have at least five leads for each ads you're testing.

This way you can make meaningful improvements to your campaigns before spending a large amount on each ad.

Click Metrics: The Fastest, Cheapest Way To Test

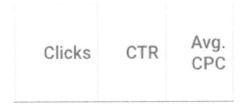

Your click metrics are:

- Clicks
- CTR
- Average CPC

It's important to note that "clicks" means people clicking through to your website from an InStream ad. **This is not the rate that people view your ads on YouTube — that is the view rate.**

It does not mean the rate at which people click on your Video Discovery ads. This shows up as your View Rate, and click metrics do not appear in Video Discovery campaigns.

You'll use click metrics to split test when you have at least thirty clicks on each ad, but when you don't yet have enough data to split test based on cost per lead.

How To Use Your Columns To Perform Split Testing

Now that you've set up these columns, split testing will be simple.

You look at your ROI metrics, and test based on that when there's enough data.

If you don't have enough ROI data, you move to the right and test based on cost per lead metrics.

If you don't have enough cost per lead data, you test based on cost per click (or view rate for Video Discovery ads if you're running a small campaign.)

This is the big picture idea behind how the Three Level Split Testing System works. This split testing system has given me a massive advantage in my YouTube advertising career, and it's one of the biggest reasons why I'm financially free today. I know the system will help you tremendously as well.

And you should congratulate yourself for learning this system! Most advertisers are not intelligent enough to educate themselves like you did, and to learn a proven split testing system. Many advertisers just "eyeball" what they think is the best ad based on their feelings and gut instincts.

Now that you're using the Three Level Split Testing system, you are going to SMOKE these lazy advertisers in the Google Ads auction.

Later in this chapter, I'll walk you through some specific examples to help you understand more details of the system.

The Technical Setup Required To Make Your Metrics Work

In order to get conversion data in your Google Ads account and to create remarketing lists, you'll need to install a piece of code on your website called **the Google Ads global site tag.**

Currently, the global site tag looks like this:

—

<!– Global site tag (gtag.js) - Google Ads: 123456789 –>
<script async
src="https://www.googletagmanager.com/gtag/js?id=AW-123456789"></script>
<script>
  window.dataLayer = window.dataLayer || [];
  function gtag(){dataLayer.push(arguments);}
  gtag('js', new Date());
  gtag('config', 'AW-123456789');
</script>

—

You need to install the Google Ads global site tag on EVERY page on ALL of your websites.

You'll also need a small piece of code called an **Event Snippet** on each page where you want to track a conversion.

This is a smaller piece of code that looks like this:

—

```
<!– Event snippet for [NAME OF YOUR CONVERSION] –>
<script>
  gtag('event', 'conversion', {'send_to': 'AW-
123456789/_BuqClbGt6sBEPCN09cC'});
</script>
```

—

To make installing your global site tag and event snippet code easy, I recommend using a tool called **Google Tag Manager.**

It simplifies the process of placing your tag on every page, and is a godsend if your site has hundreds of pages. All you have to do is drop the code in your tag manager, and it'll handle placing it on every page on your site for you.

To make sure your tags are working, I recommend using **Google Tag Assistant.** It will check all of the tags on each page, so you can make sure your global site tag is on all your pages.

To keep the focus of this book on marketing, I won't go too deep into the technical details of tag installation and the advanced ways you can set it up. There are many excellent tutorials on how to do this on YouTube, though, and there are developers who can do it for you very inexpensively as well.

I've collected a few of the best YouTube videos on tag installation and put them together for you on this bonus page:

<u>15StepsBonuses.com/TagTutorial</u>

You can also get the links to download Google Tag Manager and Google Tag Assistant on that page.

How To Set Up Your Remarketing Lists

The way you set up your remarketing lists will be crucial to your success with remarketing ad campaigns. If you don't set them up the right way, your remarketing campaigns will lose money and you won't know why.

There are MANY advanced ways that you can set up your remarketing lists, and many ways you can combine them with other forms of targeting. And you'll learn all about these advanced tactics later in the book.

But if this is your first time setting up remarketing with Google Ads, the key to making remarketing work for you will be to **keep it simple.**

The Simple Remarketing List Setup

When you're first starting off, I recommend you create remarketing lists for these three groups of people:

- People who visited your sales page (or eCommerce store landing page)
- People who visited your shopping cart
- People who have purchased your product
- People who have watched any one of your YouTube videos

To make your lists, you'll be using **rules** that you set up inside Google Ads. These rules will tell people which people to add to your list by telling them which pages should trigger a user to be added.

For example, let's pretend I had a sales funnel like this:

Sales page: https://socialresponsemarketing.com/sales
Cart page: https://socialresponsemarketing.com/cart
Page customer sees immediately after they buy:
https://socialresponsemarketing.com/upsell1

The simplest way I could set up these lists is by telling Google to add a user to that list once they visit a that exact URL.

For example, I could make a list that would target page by making a list with these rules:

When using this method, **be careful if you are split testing on your site or if the URL of any part of your funnel may change.** If this happens, it will break your remarketing list and the users going to the new URL will not be added.

Another method which can sometimes prevent these issues is to tell Google to add anyone who visits a page with a certain term in the URL to your list. For example:

A visited page must match **every** rule in this group

URL   ▾   contains   ▾   /sales   AND

This makes sense if you're testing many different sales pages, like:

socialresponsemarketing.com/sales/variation1
socialresponsemarketing.com/sales/variation2
socialresponsemarketing.com/sales/variation3

Users who visit ANY of these pages will be added to the list.

When you're using this method, just be careful that you are not unintentionally adding people to your list from other pages.

For example, if there is a page on your site with the URL:

socialresponsemarketing.com/salesblog

Users who visit this page will be added to your list as well. If it's not the page you intend to target, this usually results in you losing money.

If your remarketing campaigns are bombing, check your list rules and make sure that this is not happening to you.

I recommend starting by creating lists for people who have watched any videos on your channel, and people who have watched any of your videos as an ad.

What Duration Should You Make Your List In?

Membership duration	Enter the number of days people should remain in the audience
	30 days
	The maximum membership duration is 540 days

The **duration** of your remarketing list is how long someone will keep a person in your remarketing list after they've gone to your page or watched your video. If your duration is too long, your remarketing campaigns won't be profitable. And if it's too short you'll miss out on a lot of potential profit.

Because of this, it's important to **test** different remarketing list durations and to not just make them all the same duration. To make this easy, I recommend creating ALL of the durations you'll need for each list to start with.

If this is your first time using Google Ads remarketing, I recommend setting up your lists in these durations:

- 7 days
- 30 days
- 365 days

These will give you a few different options to test without being overwhelming.

This means that for each list, you'll actually be creating **three** remarketing lists with the same rules and different durations.

To make sure you keep your remarketing lists straight, I recommend naming them with an easy to understand naming convention.

So, for your sales page lists, you'll have three lists that are named the following:

- Visited Sales Page | 7 Day
- Visited Sales Page | 30 Day
- Visited Sales Page | 365 Day

The first part of the list tells you what the list is, and the second part specifies the duration.

Google Merchant Feed: Critical Extra Feature For eCommerce Stores

If you are using an eCommerce store, I also recommend setting up a **Google Merchant Feed** before you start your ads. This is basically a data feed you upload to Google Ads which gives them information about the products in your store.

The reason why this is so important is that **uploading your merchant feed is necessary to use TrueView For Shopping campaigns.**

I've found these campaigns are exceptionally effective for my eCommerce clients, especially in remarketing campaigns.

If you're using Shopify, uploading your merchant feed will be easy. There are many great videos on YouTube that teach you the mechanics of how to do this, and I've put together a few of the best ones on this page:

15StepsBonuses.com/MerchantFeed

InStream Remarketing: The First Campaign To Set Up

Finally, it's time to make your campaign!

If you're not familiar with the mechanics of how to set up a Google Ads campaign, make sure to check out this chapter's bonus content. It has an up-to-date guide on the mechanics of how to set everything up in Google Ads, and it will show you exactly what you need to click on to accomplish what I'm talking about in this chapter.

You can get your bonus videos at:

15StepsBonuses.com/CampaignSetup

In that video, I will also show you exactly which campaign settings I currently recommend for the first campaign you set up. These settings are very important, so make sure to watch that video if you're new to Google Ads.

Here are the campaign settings I recommend using once you've learned the mechanics of what to click on to set up your campaign:

Bidding strategy: Target CPA
Network: YouTube videos and video partners on the Display network
Language: English
Inventory Type: Expanded inventory
Excluded Types And Labels: Embedded videos, live streaming videos
Digital Content Labels To Exclude: None
Devices: All eligible devices
Frequency capping: 2 impressions per user per day
Ad schedule: All day

If you don't know what all of these settings mean yet, don't worry. The bonus video will explain everything in detail.

Your **Location Targeting** should be set to the location where you get most of your customers from right now. If you're a local business this will be around your local area. For most businesses shipping out products or selling a digital product, it makes sense to start off targeting the United States and Canada.

Your **budget** should be set to a daily amount you feel comfortable with. Start very small if you're new to Google Ads — just $10/day is fine. You can see your ads run a little bit, get comfortable with how everything works, and gradually increase your budget higher over time.

In the video, I'll discuss your geographic targeting, device bid modifiers, content exclusions, and the other good stuff that makes your campaign work.

I'll also show you what budget you should set, and how you should increase your budget over time.

I'm not covering these settings in depth in the book, because they change frequently with updates to Google Ads. But they're critically important, so be sure to check out that video if you're unsure about anything.

15StepsBonuses.com/CampaignSetup

How To Create Your Remarketing Ad Groups

Once you've created your campaigns, it's time to create your ad groups.

I recommend creating one ad group for each remarketing list you've created. So, if you are using a regular sales funnel, your campaign will look like this:

- Ad group 1: People who visited your sales page or eCommerce store
- Ad group 2: People who visited your shopping cart

- Ad group 3: People who have purchased your product
- Ad group 4: People who have watched any one of your YouTube videos

Target your ad group to these list durations to start with:

- People who visited your sales page or eCommerce store — 30 day duration

- People who visited your shopping cart — 60 day duration

- People who have purchased your product — 365 day duration

- People who have watched any one of your YouTube videos — 7 day duration

The bonus videos will walk you through exactly how to do this.

This will divide your customers into groups based on how much interest they've shown in your business. Setting your campaign up this way will be much more effective than targeting everyone who's interacted with your business in the past together.

Each ad group will have a different starting duration for the remarketing audience it's targeted to. That's because each group of customers has engaged with your business on a different level. Someone who has bought a product from you is very engaged, and will usually be worth showing ads to for a year or more.

On the other hand, someone who's just watched a few YouTube videos but hasn't yet been to your website is far less engaged and may not even remember you after a week.

You'll be testing different remarketing list durations over time, but these durations are a good place to start.

If you need step by step directions showing you how to set this up watch your bonus video at:

15StepsBonuses.com/CampaignSetup

Create Your Ads, And Paste Them Into Each Ad Group

In the bad old days, you had to manually re-create each ad for every ad group you added it to. Fortunately, Google has used the magic of technology to make this process much easier.

You can now copy and paste your ads into ad groups, just like you'd copy and paste text on your clipboard.

The easiest way to do this is to create an "Ad Bank" campaign where all your ads are stored. This campaign will not actually run, but it will just be a paused out campaign you'll use to hold all your ads in an organized way.

Copying and pasting your ads out of an organized Ad Bank campaign will be much easier than digging through your live campaigns for the ad you're trying to find.

Create your ad bank campaign first. You should have at least five ads if you've been following the action steps at the end of each chapter.

Once you've created all of your ads, paste them into each ad group.

The bonus videos **(15StepsBonuses.com/CampaignSetup)** gives you a full walkthrough on the mechanics of doing this.

Set Your Bids

The final step before your campaign runs will be to set your bids. **If you've set your conversions up the way I recommend, this will be the amount you're willing to pay Google for each lead (NOT EACH SALE!)**

Start your bids by taking an educated guess at how much a lead is worth to you. If you know that your business typically needs ten leads to make $100 worth of sales, and your goal is to acquire customers at break-even, then you should bid $10 per lead to start off with.

This will just be a starting point, and you'll refine your bids over time as more advertising data comes in.

Create Your Video Discovery Remarketing Campaign

And you're done! Congratulations, you've just made your first campaign with Google Ads!

While most wannabe entrepreneurs just talked about it, you actually took action and put yourself on the road to success. So, pat yourself on the back for making it this far!

Now it's time to make your second remarketing campaign: your **Video Discovery** remarketing campaign.

Remember, Video Discovery ads are not the skippable ads that show up in the YouTube player. They're the ads that show up in the "Up Next" recommended videos on the side or below the video player that look like this:

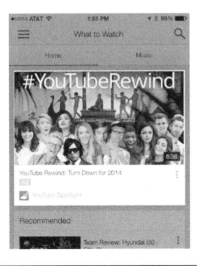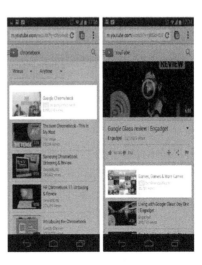

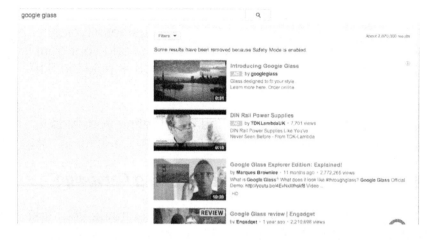

A few examples of how Video Discovery ads will look to your viewers. You will be creating ads which can appear in all of these formats, and a few other more minor formats as well.

This means that when you're creating a Video Discovery campaign, you'll need to create a **custom thumbnail image, a headline, and ad text.**

How To Create A Custom Thumbnail

The best thumbnail images for Video Discovery Ads are attention-getting, but are also clearly related to the video.

You want to strike a good balance between getting someone to click and not tricking them into clicking when they ultimately won't be interested.

Here are some guidelines for creating your custom thumbnails:

- Many times, a simple centered image of your face (or your spokesperson's face) will be the best choice for a thumbnail – especially for remarketing campaigns.

- Most advertisers should **avoid** putting text in your thumbnail image. If you do put in text, make it only a few words, and make those words as large as possible.

  The reason for this is that most YouTube viewing takes place on phones, and small text you can easily read on your computer will be too hard to read on a phone.

- If you don't have photos to use, the best way to make a custom thumbnail is simply to screenshot an exciting moment from your video. For example, if you're making a video for entrepreneurs with a Lamborghini in it, that should be in your thumbnail image.

You can also get someone to create these thumbnail images very inexpensively on outsourcing sites like Upwork. If you're hiring a designer to make your thumbnails for you, ask them to brighten and color correct the image. This will make your thumbnail image stand out more when people see your ad.

The tutorial at **15StepsBonuses.com/CampaignSetup** walks you through how to create and upload a thumbnail image step by step if you need more details.

How To Create Your Video Discovery Ad Headline

Make your headline something that catches attention and promises content to the viewer.

For example, if you're selling a dessert cookbook, and your commercial shows them a kiwi cheesecake recipe, a headline like "Kiwi Cheesecake Recipe." paired with a delicious looking image of the cheesecake is a good starting point.

You should avoid explicitly selling in your headline. "Buy My Cookbook $27" is an example of what to avoid.

In most Video Discovery ads, you should avoid using your brand name or product name in the headline. But for remarketing campaigns specifically, this can sometimes work well because it helps your customers remember when they saw you before.

In remarketing campaigns, I've also seen a lot of success with putting the spokesperson's name in the headline of a Video Discovery ad, like "Mary's Cheesecake Recipe."

You get up to 100 characters for your Video Discovery ad headline. However, on most devices, only 25 characters will be visible.

Make sure that your headline is good if the person can see only the first 25 characters, and you can also add in extra content beyond that for the few people who can see more.

A headline like "Mary's Cheesecake Recipe — Learn How To Make Delicious Kiwi Cheesecake" will work well if just the 25 characters are visible (Mary's Cheesecake Recipe), and it's even better in the formats where all 100 characters are visible.

You'll learn much more about how to write headlines for Video Discovery Ads later in this book. But for now, keep it simple and don't spend too much time on your headline.

Your thumbnail image is much more important than your headline for driving clicks to your video, so focus most of your attention on the image.

How To Create Your Ad Copy

Your ad copy is the small text that appears underneath your video's headline in some Video Discovery ad formats. And many marketers spend a ton of time crafting killer ad copy for their Video Discovery ads.

Unfortunately, they're completely wasting their time.

That's because in most Video Discovery ad formats, only your headline is visible and your ad copy does not even show up 95% of the time.

And on the rare occasions a user can see your ad copy, it's much less important than your headline in influencing them to click — and FAR less important than your thumbnail image.

That's why I recommend using the same ad copy on EVERY Video Discovery ad you create to save time.

Write something that could be a good description for any ad your business runs, and then you won't have to spend any time writing ad copy that hardly anyone sees when you're managing your campaign.

Going back to our cookbook example again, something like this would be good:

Headline: Mary's Cheesecake Recipe

Ad copy line 1: Learn delicious dessert recipes
Ad copy line 2: from award-winning chef Mary.

Your body copy should tell people what they'll get out of watching your channel generally, so it makes sense when it shows up with any ad.

Spend some time crafting some good universal body copy to use on every Video Discovery ad you run, and then you'll never have to think about this again.

Set Up Your Video Discovery Remarketing Campaign

Because you can't have Video Discovery and Instream ads in the same campaign, you'll need to create a new campaign for your Video Discovery remarketing ads.

Set up your campaign with the same process as before. Use the same settings, and create all of the same ad groups. If you're using a regular sales funnel these should be:

- Ad group 1: People who visited your sales page or eCommerce store
- Ad group 2: People who visited your shopping cart
- Ad group 3: People who have purchased your product
- Ad group 4: People who have watched any one of your YouTube videos

For Google Ads beginners, I walk you through the mechanics of doing this in this chapter's bonus videos:

15StepsBonuses.com/CampaignSetup

And You're Done!

Your remarketing setup is complete — congratulations! Now it's time to start running your campaigns.

Before turning your campaigns on, do one last double check to make sure your targeting, campaign settings, and ads are all set up correctly. It can be easy to make mistakes when you're setting up many ad groups, but a quick double check will catch these errors.

Keep in mind that if you do not have anyone going to your website or watching your YouTube videos right now, your remarketing campaigns will not start running yet.

And that's perfectly fine! The next step will get you started advertising to "cold" prospects, so you start getting some people to your site and channel.

Once you've done that, your remarketing campaigns will start running. And by setting these up from the beginning, you'll be maximizing the value of the cold traffic that you're about to buy.

If you already have viewers on your YouTube channel or people going to your website, your remarketing campaigns will receive traffic right away. For most advertisers, it'll be easy to make a profit on these "warm" prospects who are already familiar with you and your business.

If you make a profit on a small scale with these campaigns right off the bat, get excited! Because in the next few chapters you're going to start campaigns to "cold" prospects who aren't on your remarketing lists yet.

Once you do, your remarketing lists will grow. And your remarketing profits could scale up by 10x...50x...or even 100x!

Your Action Steps From This Chapter:

1. Watch the bonus material at 15StepsBonuses.com/CampaignSetup. It's especially critical for this chapter, and it will show you the mechanics you need to know to set these campaigns up.

2. Create your Google Ads account

3. Set up your columns using the Universal Column Formula

4. Place the Google Ads global site tag on ALL pages on EVERY website you own, and set **Event Snippets** to track each of your conversions. I recommend using **Google Tag Manager** to make this process easier, and using **Google Tag Assistant** to verify your tag is on every page.

5. Put through a test transaction on your website to make sure everything is working.

6. Set up your Instream remarketing campaign

7. Create the thumbnail images, headlines, and ad copy for your Video Discovery Ads

8. Set up your Video Discovery remarketing campaign.

Step 8: Learn The Targeting Ladder, And Start Your First InStream Cold Traffic Campaign

Since most YouTube ad inventory consists of skippable InStream ads, it makes sense to focus on Instream ads for your first cold traffic campaign. InStream ads are also better than Video Discovery ads for driving direct response ROI — which you can use to later fund your brand and engagement oriented ad campaigns.

In this chapter I'll show you how you can create your first InStream campaign. I'll also teach you the Targeting Ladder — a breakthrough YouTube advertising concept that will make choosing the targeting for your ads simple.

The Targeting Ladder — My Proven Ad Targeting Strategy

Your targeting determines who will see your ads. And there are so many targeting options in Google Ads, it could make your head spin.

There's keyword targeting, topic targeting, age targeting, gender targeting, income targeting, and a dizzying array of different types of audience targeting. So how do you know which option you should use?

The best way to decide is to use the **Targeting Ladder**, a targeting strategy that I've developed through years of experience and millions of dollars in ad spend.

The Philosophy Behind The Targeting Ladder

The philosophy behind the targeting ladder is that you should start with the tightest (most specific, least scalable) forms of targeting. You should then expand your campaigns into broader (less specific, more scalable) forms of targeting.

Here's how this works...

Some targeting options on Google Ads, like keyword targeting, are very specific and targeted to your customer.

Let's say you're selling a kettlebell workout course to men.

The keyword "kettlebell workouts for men" will target your videos to prospects who are very likely to be interested in your product. They'll be more likely to buy from you — but this targeting will not be very scalable.

That means that the people you can reach with a very specific keyword like this are limited, and you'll have trouble increasing your ad spend and profits with ultra-specific keywords like this.

Your ads will also tend to "saturate," or wear out faster, when you're targeting a smaller audience. This means you're limited in how much you can spend.

On the other hand, other targeting options are very broad. For example, if you used demographic targeting and advertised your course to all men on YouTube, you'd be far less likely to show your ads to someone who is interested in your product.

The upside of broad targeting is that it's easier to scale your campaigns. If you get a campaign profitable targeted to all men on YouTube, you could spend tens of millions of dollars every month on it – and make a massive profit. And you could spend many millions on each ad before it starts to wear out.

But creating a profitable campaign on broad targeting is very difficult to do. If it were easy, then every business owner would be driving around in a Bentley full of YouTube cash.

All forms of targeting have their upsides and downsides. So which form of targeting should you use when you start your first campaigns?

The Targeting Ladder

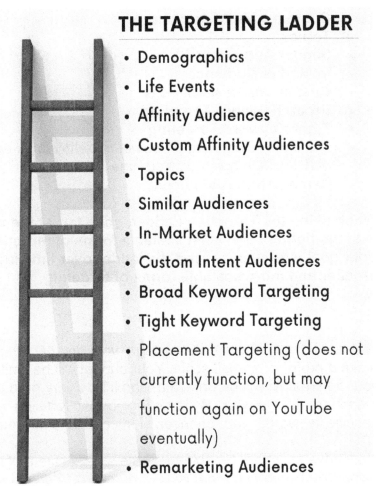

THE TARGETING LADDER

- Demographics
- Life Events
- Affinity Audiences
- Custom Affinity Audiences
- Topics
- Similar Audiences
- In-Market Audiences
- Custom Intent Audiences
- Broad Keyword Targeting
- Tight Keyword Targeting
- Placement Targeting (does not currently function, but may function again on YouTube eventually)
- Remarketing Audiences

This is the Targeting Ladder. I'll explain what each targeting option the ladder is and how it works in the next few pages.

You can use the image above as a "cheat sheet" that you have next to your computer when you set up your campaigns.

In case you're reading this on your phone and you're having trouble reading everything in the image above, here's the Ladder again in text format:

- **Demographics**
- **Life Events**
- **Affinity Audiences**
- **Custom Affinity Audiences**
- **Topics**
- **Similar Audiences**
- **In-Market Audiences**
- **Custom Intent Audiences**
- **Broad Keyword Targeting**
- **Tight Keyword Targeting**
- *Placement Targeting (does not currently function, but may function again on YouTube eventually)*
- **Remarketing Audiences**

When using the Targeting Ladder, you start at the bottom with the tightest and least scalable forms of targeting. Your goal is to then ascend the ladder over time into broader and more scalable forms of targeting.

Why is this?

When you first start a new campaign, your first priority is to make a profit on a small scale. Your budget will be limited, your ad creative will be untested, and it'll be very hard to get broad targeting to work. By targeting your advertising to very specific keywords, your chances of success are far better.

Most advertisers will be able to create small scale profits by doing this. But the problem is that you can only spend so much advertising on very specific keywords.

To scale your campaigns, you can then expand into broader keywords. Rather than ultra-specific keywords like "kettlebell workouts for men," you use broader keywords like "workout" or "fitness."

This will massively expand the amount of people you can reach. It also makes it harder to make your ads profitable. But by this point you've got some profits to reinvest. You've also tested and improved your ad creative and YouTube sales website. So, your chances of success are much better now than when the campaign first started.

Once you're making a profit on broad keywords, you can then expand into Custom Intent Audiences — the next rung on the ladder. You repeat this process and "ascend" the ladder until you reach the top.

I've used this strategy many times to create a small profitable campaign, and then to parlay that success into bigger and bigger profits over time.

Now that you've got the concept behind the Targeting Ladder, let's review what each targeting option on the ladder is.

The Quick & Dirty Guide To Google Ads Targeting

I'm going to keep these explanations brief so that this chapter doesn't get too long. And if you're already familiar with the Google Ads targeting options, you can skip or skim through this section.

If you want a more in-depth breakdown of the Google Ads targeting options, watch this chapter's bonus video at:

15StepsBonuses.com/TargetingLadder

Remarketing audiences — Like we discussed in the last chapter, these are people who have been to your website or watched one of your YouTube videos. You can also remarket to people on your email list once you're approved for this feature.

Remarketing lists are the "warmest" possible traffic you can advertise to and usually produce better ROI than any other traffic source. However, you're limited in how much you can advertise to remarketing lists by the size of your cold traffic advertising campaigns.

Placement targeting — Placement targeting is when you target an individual website, YouTube channel, or YouTube video to show your ads on. In theory placement targeting is the tightest, most granular type of targeting available and many people think it's the logical place to start when running ads.

However, in practice I do not recommend placement targeting.

That's because it does not function on YouTube at the time of this writing — and it has not functioned properly on YouTube for years.

You can target your ads to certain channels or videos.

However, when you do this, Google will serve only a tiny percentage of your ads on the placement you chose, and 99% of your ads will be served on irrelevant channels outside your chosen placement.

You can tell this is happening by looking at the "Where Your Ads Ran" placement report. If you're not sure how to access this report, watch the bonus video for a walkthrough on the current way to get to it:

15StepsBonuses.com/CampaignSetup

It's kind of a sneaky trick on Google's part. Newbie advertisers think they're advertising on a specific channel when they target their ads to a placement. But in reality, their ads are running on completely random shit. Their ad campaigns will be doomed to lose money because of this, no matter how good their creative is.

This is why I do not recommend anyone use placement targeting to target YouTube ads right now. If placement targeting does begin functioning properly again in the future, it will be the first step on the Targeting Ladder, and the best form of targeting to start new cold traffic ad campaigns with. I'll update you immediately on my YouTube channel if it does begin working again.

Tight keyword targeting — Keyword targeting is when you give Google words or phrases related to your product. Google then serves your ad on pages related to those keywords, or to people who may be interested in those keywords. Tight keyword targeting is when you use very specific keywords, like "kettlebell workout for men."

Broad keyword targeting — Broad keyword targeting works the same way, except you'll be using general keywords for your product category. Rather than "kettlebell workouts for men," broad keywords would be "workout," "fitness," or "exercise." Once you've maxed out tight keyword targeting, expanding with broad keyword targeting is the next logical step.

Custom Intent Audiences — Audience targeting is when Google shows your ad to someone based on their interests and web browsing history, rather than targeting the ad to related web pages.

This means that with audience targeting, you are targeting the ad to the person watching the video — not the video they are watching.

Custom intent audiences are audiences you generate yourself by giving Google a list of keywords. Because you can specify keywords tightly related to your product or service, I consider this type of targeting more specific and tight than other types of audience targeting.

In-Market Audiences — In-market audiences are users that Google believes have strong intent to purchase a certain product or service soon. This could be because of their search history, because they've recently bought similar products, or because they've clicked on ads or visited webpages that show purchasing intent.

In-market audiences are one of the tightest audience targeting options. Because most people don't show strong intent to buy a product or service soon, these audiences are much smaller than affinity audiences. However, I've found these audiences usually produce better ROI than any other audience type outside of custom intent audiences.

Similar audiences — Similar audiences are made of users that Google has determined are similar to users in one of your remarketing lists. For example, if you remarket to people who have visited your sales page, Google will also generate a similar audience of people who are similar to these users.

The best way to use similar audiences is to create an audience of people similar to customers who have purchased your product. While this has worked well for me, I have not seen much success with Similar Audiences outside of customer lists.

They simply do not work as well as Facebook's Lookalike audiences, and they will play a much more minor role in your campaigns than Lookalike audiences typically do in Facebook campaigns. But again, I'll update you on my YouTube channel if Google improves this feature in the future.

Topic Targeting — Topics are a contextual targeting option, which means that your ads will be targeted to users viewing a video about your chosen topic. When you target an ad to a topic, you're targeting pages that Google has determined fit into the general "theme" of the topic. Topics are an "in-between" targeting option. They're significantly broader than keyword targeting, but still far more tightly targeted than affinity audiences or demographics.

Custom affinity audiences — Custom affinity audiences are created by giving Google URLs, apps, or keywords that represent the interests of your customer. People in these audiences are only showing affinity, or interest in your product or service — not necessarily buying intention. Because of this, these audiences are much larger than in-market audiences.

However, because you can tailor these custom affinity audiences to your specific product or service, they are still significantly tighter targeting than regular affinity audiences.

Affinity audiences — These are people who have an interest in a certain product or service, but not necessarily buying intention. Unlike custom affinity audiences, affinity audiences are predefined by criteria Google chooses. They are not generated from your keywords or URLs.

Affinity audiences are VERY broad targeting. They're more difficult to make work. But if you can get them to work, they're incredibly scalable.

Life events — Life events target someone when Google detects they're going through a significant life change. Some examples include getting married, buying a house, starting a business, and retiring.

In some situations, life events can be very specific to your product or service. Let's say you're a wedding planner. For your business, targeting people who are about to get married will be one of the best possible targeting options for you.

However, most advertisers will not have a Life Event that corresponds perfectly with their product or service like this.

But they can be used to find a demographic of customers who may be a good fit. For example, a financial advisor could target retirees since they tend to have the most assets.

Demographics — Demographic targeting is broadest form of targeting available on Google Ads. This makes it the most challenging targeting option to make profitable — but there are HUGE rewards for any advertiser who can make it work.

Demographic targeting shows ads to users based on their gender, age, parental status, or household income.

And if you want to build a large-scale business with a brand you can sell, your ultimate goal should be to make demographically targeted ad campaigns profitable.

How To Use The Targeting Ladder To Set Up Your Campaigns

The Targeting Ladder gives you a blueprint for setting up your Google Ads campaigns. You start at the bottom, and progressively ascend the targeting ladder as you are able to make broader and broader targeting work.

Here's how to do this:

Start a remarketing campaign. If you already have significant traffic on your website, focus on this campaign only until you are spending at least $200/day, and this campaign is consistently profitable for you.

At this point, start a keyword targeted campaign with a small budget. Keep expanding your remarketing campaign at the same time. Use tight keyword targeting to start off with.

Once you are spending more than $200/day and making a profit on tight keyword targeting, create ad groups with broad keyword targeting in your campaign.

Once you are spending more than $200/day profitably on these broad keywords, create a new campaign targeted to Custom Intent Audiences. And keep expanding your existing keyword targeted campaign!

When this Custom Intent Audience campaign is profitable on $200/day, start a new campaign targeting In-Market audiences. And again, keep building out your existing campaigns as you do this.

And so on and so forth...until you ascend to the top of the Targeting Ladder and are targeting huge, broad demographic groups.

At this point, you can go buy a gold-plated Lamborghini and start swimming in your YouTube cash Scrooge McDuck style.

When To Go Outside The Targeting Ladder

The Targeting Ladder is a great rule of thumb, and a strategy that makes sense almost all the time. It also helps to simplify the many different Google Ads targeting options to reduce confusion and overwhelm when you're first starting off.

However, there are certain situations where it makes sense to go outside the Targeting Ladder, especially if you're an advanced advertiser who's very familiar with the Google Ads targeting options.

For certain advertisers, there will be a broad targeting option which happens to be perfectly aligned with your product or service. Examples of this would include a wedding planner targeting the "about to get married" life event, or for a parenting coach to target the "parents" demographic.

In exceptional cases like this, you should go outside the targeting ladder and go after this ideal broad targeting option right away. This only makes sense for a few advertisers though. For most people, sticking to the Ladder is the best strategy.

Another situation where you may want to go outside the Targeting Ladder is if you are running a local advertising campaign — for example, targeting your ads to a single city.

In this case, you'll want to go broader on your targeting in the beginning, since your geographic targeting is already very tight and restrictive.

Finally, it can make sense to go outside the Targeting Ladder if data from other campaigns indicates a broad targeting option may be the best place to start.

For example, if you're already profitably advertising to a demographic on Facebook, it may make sense to start your YouTube campaigns with the same demographic targeting.

There are some exceptions to the Targeting Ladder strategy and situations where it makes sense to go outside it. But 95% of the time, the Targeting Ladder is the best strategy to scale up. I've personally used it to build many multi-million dollar advertising campaigns, and I know it will work for you as well.

Keyword Targeting: The First Step Beyond Remarketing On The Targeting Ladder

Enough theory. Now it's time to put the Targeting Ladder into action!

We'll start at the bottom, and work our way up.

We already made our remarketing campaigns in the last chapter. And because placement targeting does not currently function correctly for YouTube ads, we're skipping that broken rung on the ladder.

That means the first cold traffic campaign we create will be a keyword targeted campaign.

We'll start with tightly targeted keywords, and then later expand our campaign to broader keywords.

The Keyword Targeting Sub-Ladder

First, make a new InStream CPA campaign. If you need to review the mechanics of how to do this in Google Ads, revisit the Step 7 bonus video:

15StepsBonuses.com/CampaignSetup

Next, we'll be making our ad groups within this campaign.

To do this, we'll first brainstorm some tightly targeted keywords that we can use to start the campaign. After this, I'll show you exactly how to build these keyword ideas out into ad groups.

Now, there are an infinite number of keywords that you could use to target your ads. How do you know what the best ones to get started with are?

The best way is to look at keyword targeting as a "sub-ladder" within the overall Targeting Ladder. Like the main targeting ladder, you start with the tightest keywords and then build up to the broadest.

The keyword targeting sub-ladder looks like this:

THE KEYWORD TARGETING SUB-LADDER

- Keywords for content on YouTube unrelated to your product or service, but which you know your customers are interested in
- Keywords broadly related to the product or service you are selling
- Keywords targeting your competitors' brand names, product names, or personal names
- Keywords very closely related to the product or service you are offering
- Keywords for brands, products, people, and channels highly related to your business
- Keywords related to your brand name, product name, and spokesperson's name

Here's the keyword targeting sub-ladder again in text, for those of you reading this on a phone:

- Keywords for content on YouTube unrelated to your product or service, but which you know your customers are interested in

- Keywords broadly related to the product or service you are selling

- Keywords targeting your competitors' brand names, product names, or personal names

- Keywords very closely related to the product or service you are offering

- Keywords for brands, products, people, and channels highly related to your business

- Keywords related to your brand name, product name, and spokesperson's name

Basically, the idea is the same as the Targeting Ladder. You start at the bottom of the ladder, and ascend to the next step when you start seeing profits.

Let's go through each step on the ladder, and some examples of keywords you can use for each step.

Keywords Related To Your Brand Name, Product Name, or Spokesperson's Name

The easiest possible prospects to convert will be people who have already shown some interest in your business. That's why I recommend that advertisers start their keyword campaigns by advertising on terms related to their business.

This includes the name of your company, the name of the product you're selling, the names of any channels or websites associated with you, and your product spokesperson's name.

That's why the first keywords I used for my campaign advertising this book were:

social response marketing
daniel rose
15 steps to profitable video marketing

Unless you already have a large business, you will receive very little traffic from these keywords when you start off. And that's OK! You'll receive a small amount of quality traffic even if your brand isn't well known right now. And once you start buying more advertising, it will create a larger audience that's interested in these keywords.

Similar to setting up your remarketing first, this will allow you to fully maximize the value of the colder traffic you're buying later.

Keywords for brands, products, people, and channels highly related to your business

Once you've brainstormed all of the ideas related to your business, the next best prospect you could advertise to is **someone interested in a person, brand, product or channel that's highly related to your business.**

For example, let's say that you just did a collaboration video with a YouTuber that has a large channel. It would then make sense to target their name and their channel's name, since some people on this channel would already be familiar with you.

Other examples include influencers you've bought sponsorships from, people who have promoted your products as affiliates, vendors that you promote as an affiliate, industry experts you've interviewed, and other people or brands related to your company.

Here are a few examples I used in my own campaigns:

sixpackabs.com (the name of my last company that I was the founder and CEO of)

Flight Club / Glen Ledwell / Alex Cattoni (a $25,000 mastermind event I spoke at, and the owners' names)

Mark's Mastermind / Mark Ling (a different $25,000 mastermind I spoke at)
Capitalism.com / Ryan Moran (a friend of mine in Austin who I did a YouTube interview with)

ClickFunnels / Russell Brunson (the software I use for most of my sales funnels, and a business I promote as an affiliate)

Most people don't advertise on keywords like this because they rarely work for Search or Image ad campaigns. But for YouTube campaigns, these keywords can be some of the highest ROI targeting available to your business.

Keywords very closely related to the product or service you are offering

This is what people who take conventional Google Ads courses are taught to do. This type of keyword can produce interested traffic, and it can work well for your business.

But for YouTube advertising, it's not the lowest hanging fruit.

You should first max out your brand keywords and highly related keywords before building out these ad groups.

Here are some examples of this type of keyword from my campaigns:

youtube advertising book
youtube advertising tips
youtube marketing
youtube marketing tutorial
google ads for youtube

For your business, you would brainstorm similar keywords that are VERY closely related to your product or service. While the traffic you can buy on these keywords will be limited, these types of keywords will usually convert much better than broader terms.

Keywords targeting your competitors' brand names, product names, or personal names

Most people who take conventional Google Ads courses are NOT taught to target these keywords. Because of this, they're often a "sweet spot" where you can get quality, scalable traffic at a low cost.

If someone is interested in a related business, YouTube channel, or product, the chances are fairly good that they'll be interested in yours as well. This type of keyword typically will get you access to a larger audience than anything lower on the Keyword Targeting Sub-Ladder, since you can target the largest players in your niche.

Here are some of this kind of keyword that worked well for me in my own campaigns:

dean graziosi
billy gene
neil patel
graham stephen
think media
youtube secrets

The first four keywords are names of people who run large YouTube channels in the entrepreneurship or marketing niches. Some of these YouTubers also advertise, and have marketing-related courses.

"Think Media" is the name of a YouTube channel run by Sean Cannell, a great guy who I met at a think tank event here in Austin. He teaches filming techniques and how to grow a YouTube channel organically (without advertising.)

"YouTube Secrets" is the name of Sean's book on the same topic.

The important thing to note about this type of keyword is that **they do not have to be selling the exact same type of product or service as you — they just have to be selling to a similar market.**

There are probably VERY few businesses selling exactly the same type of product as you, so it's important to take an expansive definition of who your "competitors" are.

For example, Sean focuses on filming and the organic side of YouTube. Graham Stephen talks a lot about real estate and personal finance. And Billy Gene is mainly known for his Facebook advertising courses.

Their audiences still work to target my ads to because they're selling to similar people, even though their products are different.

It's important to note that although I describe these businesses as "competitors," I don't see myself as "competing" against them in any way.

I am just using the word "competitors" to differentiate these types of businesses from highly related businesses. They're just businesses that sell similar products I haven't collaborated with yet. There's no need for one of us to lose for the other one to win.

If you achieve large profits advertising to the audience of a "competitor," it can benefit you a lot to reach out to them for a collaboration or a cross-promotion of each other's products.

This will move their audience into the "highly related" category, and it will probably make advertising to their audience more profitable.

Keywords Broadly Related To The Product Or Service You're Selling

It's ideal to find someone who's interested in the *exact* product or service you are selling. But chances are that there are few of these people you can advertise to, and you'll tap these keywords out fast.

So that's why once you've tapped out everything lower on the ladder (brand terms, related businesses, highly related terms, and competitors' names), the next step is to go into broadly related keywords. These are keywords that describe the general category your product is in.

Some examples of this type of keywords that I'm using:

online marketing
entrepreneurship
video advertising
advertising
marketing

These terms are much less targeted than keyword types farther down the ladder. But they're MUCH more scalable since you're targeting a bigger audience.

Keywords for YouTube videos unrelated to your product or service, but which you know your customers are interested in

This is the hardest type of keyword to convert, since they're not directly related to your product or service. But these types of keywords are by FAR the most scalable. Your goal should be to make everything lower on the ladder profitable as soon as you can, so you can get into this these types of big money keywords quickly.

I will almost never include this type of keyword when I start a campaign, or in the first month or two of advertising. But in my mature keyword targeted YouTube campaigns (campaigns spending more than $5,000 per day) **more than 80% of the traffic comes from this type of ultra-broad keyword.**

The key to making this type of keyword profitable for you is having a deep knowledge of what unrelated videos your customers will be watching.

Here are a few ways of finding this out that have worked well for me.

- **Seeing where your ads ran, and where they made conversions.** Under the "placements" targeting tab, you'll have an option to see where your ads ran. You can then sort the channels your ads ran on by all conversion value (revenue your ads produced on the channel) to see which channels are getting you sales.

   If you see a certain type of channel getting you a lot of sales, you can use keywords to target that type of content. For example, I once noticed that many sales for one of my clients were coming from channels about sports cars. So, I used keyword targeting to target many sports car related terms, and I was able to massively increase the profits I was bringing in from this type of channel.

- **Surveys.** One of the best questions to ask on a survey is "What YouTube channels do you watch?" You'll probably find some very common answers that aren't related to your product. For example, if a lot of your customers watch comedy channels, "comedy" would be a good keyword to test out in your campaigns.

- **Other targeting types that are working well for you** — Once your campaigns have been running for a few months, you'll have other types of targeting you're using in addition to keyword targeting. Once you do, targeting that works well for you in other campaigns can be a good source of ideas to grow your keyword campaigns.

I once had a client who was doing VERY well advertising on the Left Wing Politics topic with an unrelated product. I was able to scale these results up by targeting left wing political channels and personalities as keywords in a keyword targeted campaign (for example, "the young turks," and "david pakman.")

How To Brainstorm Your Starting Keywords

I recommend starting your keyword targeted campaigns with:

- 2 brand keywords
- 3 keywords for people, channels, or businesses related to your brand
- 5 keywords very closely related to your product or service
- 5 names of competitors' channels, businesses, or YouTube talent

This will give you 15 ad groups, which will let you test a variety of ideas while still staying manageable.

Using this approach, most businesses will "tap out" the first three rungs of the Keyword Targeting Sub-Ladder right from the beginning. There are usually very limited keywords you can use for your brand and things highly related to your brand.

And there are also a very limited number of keywords that exactly describe your product or service. You should seize this low-hanging fruit right away since it's the easiest traffic to convert.

To ascend the Ladder, you'll later focus on expanding the campaign with more competitor-related keywords.

Once you get your first profitable ad group from this type of keyword, you'll still continue expanding your campaign with competitor names. But you'll also start adding in some targeting from the next rung on the ladder — broadly related keywords.

We'll focus on the campaign setup for the remainder of this chapter. But later in this book, you'll learn my process for expanding campaigns and choosing additional targeting in more detail.

How To Build Your Keyword Ideas Out Into Ad Groups

Once you have your keywords, you'll need to build them out into ad groups.

The approach that's worked best for me is to use 5-10 keywords in each ad group. They should all be highly related to the main keyword.

For example, if you're making an ad group targeting "astrology," you should also add related keywords like "astrology signs." Generally, you should avoid keyword variants that do not contain your main keyword — like "gemini" or "horoscope." Keywords like this should be put in separate ad groups.

But what's the best way to find highly related keywords to put into your ad groups?

I've tried many methods of doing this, and what I've found works best is **using the YouTube search auto-complete results.**

For example, one of the terms I used to start my keyword targeted campaign for this business was "youtube advertising." To build out this ad group, I typed "youtube advertising" into the YouTube search bar, and got these autocomplete results:

---

youtube advertising |

_____

youtube advertising **campaign tutorial 2019**

youtube advertising **campaign**

youtube advertising **formats**

youtube advertising **cost**

youtube advertising **music**

youtube advertising **bangla**

youtube advertising **discord server**

youtube advertising **results**

youtube advertising **channel**

youtube advertising **tips**

_____
Report search predictions

I then targeted all of the keywords that appeared in the auto-complete results in my "youtube advertising" ad group, EXCEPT for keywords that I knew would not produce good prospects for my business.

In this case, I targeted all of the keywords except "youtube advertising bangla." That's because this refers to "bangla" refers to the language spoken in the central Asian country of Bangladesh. Most people viewing videos in Bangla (or Bengali, as it's sometimes called) would not have the English fluency or the money to buy my products.

If a term shows up in the YouTube auto-complete results that you know would produce bad prospects for your business, you should also EXCLUDE it from your targeting. For example, in this case, I added "bangla," "bengali," and "bangladesh" as negative keywords, so my ads do not show up on these videos.

Another method that you can use to build your keywords out into full ad groups is **the Google Ads Keyword Planner.** This is a tool that's mainly used for search advertising which can find keywords related to your main keyword for you, and which can also show you the Google search volume.

I prefer using the YouTube auto-complete results over the Keyword Planner. I've gotten much better results from ad groups made this way for many different clients. This is probably because YouTube auto-complete results are based on YouTube search data, while the Keyword Planner is based on Google search data.

Not only this, but it's significantly faster and easier to build out your ad groups with YouTube auto-complete results vs. the Keyword Planner. Because of this, I don't recommend you use the Keyword Planner unless you're a search advertising veteran who's familiar with its advanced features.

Create Your Ad Groups, And Put Your Ads In

Once you create an ad group and target it to a set of keywords, it's time to put in your ads.

The easiest way to do this is to create an Ad Bank campaign like I described in the last chapter, and to copy and paste your ads in from your Ad Bank campaign.

I recommend starting each ad group with three ads. Pick the three ads which you think will perform the best, and paste them into all of your ad groups as your starting point.

The Mechanics Of Setting Up Your First Campaign

Once you've got your list of keywords for each ad group, the mechanics of setting it up will be simple.

If you need to review what to click on to make a campaign, how to make an ad group, or how to put ads into each ad group, review the Step 7 bonus video again at:

15StepsBonuses.com/CampaignSetup

This tutorial will be updated with each major change in the Google Ads interface, so you'll be getting the current instructions for how to set up these campaigns even if you're reading this years after the book was written.

If you're a Google Ads veteran, you won't need this. But if you're new to Google Ads, watch that video again if you're unsure about any of the steps to set up this campaign.

Congratulations! You Made Your First Cold Traffic Campaign

Once you've done this, you're ready to start acquiring new customers through cold traffic advertising! It's a big milestone in your YouTube advertising journey, so pat yourself on the back for making it this far.

Later in this book, you'll learn exactly what to do to manage and grow these campaigns. Not only will you learn how to scale your keyword targeting campaign up, you'll also be expanding into other targeting types soon.

So, keep your progress going by knocking out these action steps. You've come a long way, and you're about to get to the best part of YouTube advertising soon.

The part where you start making massive profits!

Your Action Steps From This Chapter:

1. Familiarize yourself with the Targeting Ladder strategy, and learn what all of the Google Ads targeting options are.

2. Brainstorm ideas for keywords for your keyword targeted InStream advertising campaign. Brainstorm as many ideas as possible on the first four rungs of the Targeting Ladder (brand terms, terms highly related to your brand, terms highly related to your product/service, and competitors' names.)

3. Choose your initial keywords to target. I recommend creating these ad groups to start with:
    a. 2 brand keywords
    b. 3 keywords for people, channels, or businesses related to your brand
    c. 5 keywords very closely related to your product or service
    d. 5 names of competitors' channels, businesses, or YouTube talent

4. Build your keywords out into ad groups by using the YouTube search auto-complete results.

5. Paste your starting ads into each ad group. Use three ads you've made that you think have the best chance of converting well to cold prospects who aren't familiar with your business.

Step 9: Start Your First Video Discovery Cold Traffic Campaign

While most ads on YouTube are skippable InStream ads, Video Discovery ads are also important. That's because Video Discovery ads are better for building engagement on your channel, and for building the long term value of your brand.

When a customer clicks on a Video Discovery ad, it's much easier for them to subscribe to your channel, like the video, or share the video than it is if they see an ad InStream. This means they'll build your subscriber base and views faster than an equivalent amount of InStream advertising.

Video Discovery ads can also produce great direct response ROI for advertisers who have strong content on their channel. And they'll also be key for some of the advanced remarketing strategies we'll discuss later in this book.

Why You Need To Use Video Discovery Ads

Many YouTube marketers don't use Video Discovery ads at all. They think they don't need them because most of the YouTube ad inventory is skippable InStream ads. And for most advertisers, InStream ads tend to produce better direct response ROI.

While this is true, Video Discovery ads still have a few important advantages that make them worth learning how to use.

First of all, **Video Discovery ads will build more engagement on your channel than InStream ads.**

With Instream ads, the user does not have the option to like, share, and comment on your video. It's also harder for them to subscribe to your channel. With Video Discovery ads, they see your ad on the YouTube watch page just like any other video.

Because of this, your Video Discovery campaigns will produce more subscribers, likes, shares, and comments for every dollar you spend compared to InStream campaigns.

Video Discovery campaigns also build more valuable remarketing lists than InStream campaigns.

This is because you're building an audience of people who voluntarily clicked on your video to see your ad. And building these valuable remarketing lists from Video Discovery ads will be important for some of the advanced remarketing strategies we'll discuss later.

Video Discovery ads also allow you to access more inventory than using InStream ads alone.

For your most profitable ad targeting, this is particularly important. For example, if you're making killer ROI with Instream ads on a certain remarketing list, chances are that you'll also be profitable running Video Discovery ads against that same targeting.

The Elements Of A Great Video Discovery Ad

To review what we covered in Step 7, the four elements of a Video Discovery ad are:

- Your video
- Your body copy
- Your ad headline
- Your thumbnail image

In this chapter, I'll take your knowledge to the next level. And I'll show you in detail how to master each element.

Which Videos To Use In Video Discovery Ads

Of course, your video will ultimately be the most important element of a successful Video Discovery Ad. And the principles behind making a great video for Discovery vs. Instream ads are mostly the same.

To keep things simple, use the same five videos for your Video Discovery campaigns as you're using in your InStream campaigns when you're first starting off.

Once you have more creative to choose from, you'll want to focus on a different type of creative in your Video Discovery campaigns vs. your InStream campaigns.

The most effective Video Discovery ads tend to be very content oriented. Because the user is clicking on them — not being interrupted by them — they have a greater expectation that they'll learn something from the video, and that it won't be a straight pitch.

Later in this book you'll learn **The Pure Content Formula** — one of my advanced ad writing formulas. I find ads written with the Pure Content Formula have the highest chance of success as Video Discovery ads, and I recommend you try a few of these in your campaigns once you learn the advanced formulas.

How To Create Great Universal Body Copy For All Ads

Remember, your body copy is usually not visible in Video Discovery ads. I recommend using the same body copy on ALL of your Video Discovery ads because of this.

Your body copy isn't very important since users usually don't see it. But since you'll be using this copy on thousands of different ads, it's worth coming up with something good.

The formula I use to create my body copy is to put my brand name in the first line of body copy, and a description of the content of my videos in the second line. For example, if I was running ads for a client who did dog training, my body copy would look like this:

Amy Jo's Dog Training Tips ®
Learn To Train Your Dog At Home!

You want to keep your body copy very brand-oriented, and you want to avoid making any type of marketing claims in your body copy. Although your potential customers will rarely see this body copy, the Google Ads Policy team WILL be reviewing your body copy carefully. So never "push the envelope" with aggressive marketing claims in your body copy.

In fact, to be safe, in your body copy I would never include ANY claim your product will provide the customer with any benefit whatsoever.

There simply is no upside to making marketing claims that the customer will never see, but which will be heavily scrutinized by Google's Policy team.

How To Write Killer Headlines

Your headline is much more important than your body copy, because people will actually see it every time your Video Discovery ad shows up.

Because of this, you should write a unique headline for every Video Discovery ad you run.

You get a very limited number of characters to convince someone to click on your ad, so it's important that you learn how to make every word count.

The best way to do this is to use **HEADLINE FORMULAS which have been proven to work in many different markets.** And I'm going to give you a few of my best headline formulas in just a minute.

With Video Discovery ads, you can write a headline of up to 100 characters. However, on most devices the headline will be truncated and only 25 characters of your headline will be visible.

Because of this, you should make sure that all your headlines make sense within the 25 character limit.

Many of my best performing headlines are "two part" headlines — the first part targeted to people seeing only 25 characters, and the rest giving more detail about why they should click for anyone on a device that displays the full 100.

I'll give you a few examples of headlines like this as we run through the headline writing formulas.

But one last important thing before I give you the formulas...

When you're writing your headlines, you need to catch your customer's attention and get them to click without deceiving them.

For example, you might be able to get tons of people to click on your ads by promising them "5 Killer Twitter Ad Tips." But if your ad is just a pitch that doesn't actually deliver the content you're promising, it won't be effective. Make sure you deliver on this critical first promise you make to your prospect, and it will go a long way to build trust.

The Content Promise Formula

The Content Promise is the strongest Video Discovery headline formula when you can use it. It's simple, straightforward, and trustworthy. But to make it work, you need to clearly deliver on the content you're promising in your headline. If you can't do that, you should use one of the other formulas.

Let's say you're a dentist, or you're doing the marketing for a dentist client. A good Discovery ad headline could be:

3 Tips For Whiter Teeth

This headline fits within the 25 character limit, and everyone who sees the ad will be able to read the whole thing. But we can make this headline even better by adding a second part targeting to people who can see the full 100.

It would look something like this:

3 Tips For Whiter Teeth — The Three Things Dentists Recommend You Do At Home For Whiter Teeth

By telling people that dentists recommend our tips, and that they can do them at home, we may be able to get more people to click.

To make this headline work well, it's important that our video delivers on the promise of these three tips. If you take too long to get to the tips or if you don't deliver them, prospects will just click on your ad then leave once they realize you tricked them.

These types of headlines often work best if you include a number in them, it seems like they're about to get a more concrete and real piece of knowledge.

Some examples would include "5 Ways To Prevent Cavities" or "4 Alternatives To Braces".

Think about what your market wants to learn. Even if you're selling straightforward physical products — or a boring service like dentistry — there is always something that you can teach your prospect that will be valuable to them.

Find out what it is, make a video about it, and promise that content in your Video Discovery ad headlines.

The Customer Callout Headline Formula

The Customer Callout is a great formula to use for people who sell to a very specific and well defined customer group.

The more specific you are in calling out your ideal prospect, the more effective this type of headline will be.

Let's say you have a dating advice business for women over 40. A good first part of your headline for people who can only see the first 25 characters would be:

Women 40+: Find Love Now

You can enhance this further by adding the second part for people who can see the full 100 characters:

Women 40+: Find Love Now — Mary Shows You How She Found Love At 53 And How Her Clients Have Too.

You should note that when your product is demographically targeted like this, it's important to be targeting a specific group of people.

"Women: Find Love Now" might still work, but it's far weaker than a headline calling out both the customer's gender and age.

"People: Find Love Now" would be a TERRIBLE headline.

Since it's calling EVERYONE out, it's not singling anyone out individually. Few people will click on this ad, and even fewer will buy.

A demographic group is the simplest and most obvious way to use the Customer Callout Formula. But it can be used in limitless other ways as well.

Here are some more examples of headlines calling out a specific group of customers:

Doctors: Get Patients — Learn How From Austin's Leading Medical Marketing Firm

Retirees: How To Invest — If You're Retired And Have A Net Worth Over $500k You Need To See This

You get the idea. If your product is targeted to a very specific type of person, put that in your headline. Your ideal prospect will be interested in the ad if they see it's specifically for people like them.

The From Loser To Awesome Formula

If you're a male who was browsing YouTube 5-6 years ago, chances are you saw one of the best Video Discovery headlines I've written: **From Fat To Six Pack Abs**

I bought millions of views for ads with this headline, and it's one of the best known headlines in the history of Video Discovery ads. Because I used it so much, smart marketers copied what I was doing and adapted this formula to different markets.

For example, Tai Lopez copied my Loser To Awesome formula to create the headline:

Broke To Beverly Hills

You can use this formula for your own business as well. You just need to figure out a way to say the person featured in your video went from being in pain to having the benefits you're promising.

For Tai Lopez, this is going from broke to being rich — and he figured out a great way to adapt my headline formula to his business.

Another great adaptation of my headline formula I saw a fashion advertiser using on YouTube:

From Frumpy To Fabulous

Again, this perfectly captures the idea of the formula. The customer went from being a loser who was in pain, to having their pain relieved and getting the benefits you promise.

If your video contains a story of your spokesperson getting results, or of a customer getting results, consider this type of headline. It can be very powerful when paired with the right video!

The Enemy Hates You Formula

It seems counterintuitive to advertise that people hate you in an ad headline. Aren't ads supposed to convince people to love you?

They are, but marketers have known for years that hate can actually be a very powerful selling tool.

You just have to advertise that the prospect's "enemy" hates you. Because you have a shared enemy, this will intrigue him and make him interested in what you have to say.

The most widely known example of this is the image ads with the headline **"Language Professors Hate Him"** that the Pimsleur approach has been running for years. They've made millions and millions from these ads because they've positioned themselves against their prospect's enemy — boring and ineffective language professors.

They show them right away their approach to learning a language is different. This intrigues the prospect, and prevents them from ruling them out as yet another boring and useless community college language class.

After seeing the Pimsleur ads, I adapted this into **"Trainers Hate Him."** My fitness business used this headline extensively, and many other fitness businesses have used it as well. It works because it shows prospects that you're not just a typical personal trainer, and that your approach is controversial and opposed by personal trainers.

This intrigues the prospect and gets him interested. Most male clients hate personal trainers. That's because most personal training is ineffective, inconvenient, a waste of money, and intended for women. But this video isn't from another lame trainer — it's promising a totally new and different approach.

Think about who your prospect's "enemy" is, and how you can show them that their enemy is against you too.

But here's something VERY important to keep in mind about your prospect's "enemy."

The "enemy" doesn't have to be someone your prospects literally hate, and it usually isn't. **Usually the best "enemy" to oppose in your advertising is a business or person your prospect perceives as a bad solution to her problem.**

A few examples of what I mean:

Divorce Lawyers Hate Her — See How This Relationship Coach Has Saved 27 Different Marriages

Car Salesmen Hate Him — Jim Shows How You Can Buy A Car With Fair, Transparent, No-Haggle Pricing

The Remarketing Recall Headline Formula

For your ads running in cold traffic campaigns, you should assume your prospect has never heard of you or your business. This means you should usually avoid using your spokesperson's name or your brand name in your ad headline. If your prospect doesn't know who you are, these are just meaningless words to them — a waste of your valuable headline characters.

For REMARKETING ads though, the situation is different. The prospect does know you, and adding your name or your brand name to the ad's headline can significantly improve its performance. It helps your prospect remember the ad is from your business which they previously showed interest in. Not only this, it keeps your brand name and your spokesman's name top of mind, even if they do not click on the ad.

A few examples from my own business:

Dan's Five Best Ad Formulas — Here Are The Formulas I've Used To Write Dozens Of Profitable Ads

Social Response Marketing — Dan's Video Shows How To Make A Profit While Growing Your Subscribers

If your business is built around a single spokesperson, or if it's built around you, then using a personal name in the headline will be the most effective approach.

If your business is not built around a single person, using your brand name or product name will usually work better.

You get the idea. If a prospect has shown interest in your videos or business before, remind them you're the business they're interested in before in your headline. They'll come back to watch again, and they'll be more likely to buy.

Your Thumbnail Image — The Most Important Element Of A Video Discovery Ad

Your headline is important for your Video Discovery ad's success — but your thumbnail image matters FAR more.

Other than your video itself, it's the most important thing to focus on.

Many people neglect to create a great thumbnail image, and just accept one of the auto-generated thumbnails that YouTube offers them when they upload their video. **This is a huge mistake.**

Your thumbnail is very important, and by accepting whatever random thumbnails YouTube generates for you you're massively lowering your odds of success.

Sometimes you'll "hit the lottery" and get a brilliant thumbnail that works as a Video Discovery ad from the automatically generated images. But don't count on it!

Hoping to get lucky against the odds with your thumbnail is a losing strategy. It's far better to make your own, so you can consistently make great ones.

Here are a few ways that you can create great thumbnail images.

Screenshotting The Most Exciting Moments In Your Video

If your video contains something visually exciting, this will be the best way for you to get a good thumbnail. And if you don't yet have any photography to use, this is your only option.

What you want to do is identify the most exciting moment in your video, then take a burst of 20-30 screenshots (pictures of your screen playing the video) around it. Similar to a photographer, you want to give yourself many different options to choose from. This will increase your chances of getting a great image.

To do this, open your video full screen on YouTube and set your resolution to the maximum. This is important to make sure you get a high quality thumbnail image.

To take a screenshot on a PC, press *Print Screen* on your keyboard. To do this on a Mac, press *Shift + Command + 3.*

Browse through your screenshots and choose the best one.

Ideally, you'll get one where the prospect is looking at the camera, and where it seems like something unusual or exciting is going on.

After doing this, you'll want to crop your image. Crop out the video player controls at the bottom, the title, and any graphics in the video.

You'll want to crop your image to YouTube's recommended thumbnail size. This is **1280x720 pixels, or a 16:9 width to height ratio.**

Once you've got your cropped base image, it's time to enhance it!

Even if you know nothing about image editing, there are a few simple things you can do to make your images perform better.

For most screenshots, the most important thing you can do is to increase the brightness.

This will make your thumbnail image stand out more among the sea of related videos next to it.

After this, increase the saturation so the image looks vibrant and not washed out.

Increasing the brightness will make your image more noticeable, but it will also make your image look "whiter" and make the colors less vibrant. To counteract this, increase the saturation on your image until it looks good again.

There are other settings you can also play with, like sharpness, warmth, tint, etc.

I recommend leaving these other settings to professional designers. Just quickly enhance the brightness and saturation if you're making thumbnail images yourself, since you've got a lot of other important stuff to do.

Photography For Thumbnail Images

Screenshots are great for videos with something exciting happening in them. But what if your video consists of just a person talking to the camera?

This is where using a photo as your thumbnail image can really help.

If you don't have photography for your business right now, you can start by just using the photos you have on Facebook or Instagram. If you hired a spokesperson for your ad, you can ask them for permission to use their photos that are already online.

When you're using a photo, you want to make sure that you're selecting something attention-getting that people will want to click on.

But it's important that the photo you choose is also somewhat representative of what the viewer will see in the video.

For example, any marketer selling to men could get a very high view rate by just uploading an image of an attractive woman in a bikini. But unless this woman actually appears in your ad, this photo will fail miserably as a Video Discovery thumbnail image.

You'll be charged for tons of horny guys clicking on your ad.

But they'll quickly realize you tricked them, and none of them will buy. If they see another ad from you, their guard will be up since you've deceived them before.

While your photo shouldn't be deceptive, it does not have to be an exact representation of what's in the video. For example, if you're creating an ad about achieving financial freedom, you could use a picture of yourself celebrating on a beach.

Even if you're just talking during the video and the beach does not actually appear, this will still work as a Video Discovery ad because it captures the theme of the video.

I highly recommend doing a photo shoot, and getting a few basic shots of your product spokesperson as soon as you can.

Important shots to get include:

- Your spokesperson looking at the camera and smiling on a variety of backgrounds. **Most importantly, make sure to get plenty of photos on the set you're shooting the video on.** If you have a green screen, make sure to get a few green screen shots as well.

- Once you have straight-up shots, have them do a variety of "expression" shots. **Ask them to avoid model-style posing, and to make the photos look as organic and un-planned as possible.** Shots to get include your spokesperson looking shocked, looking at something like it's really weird, looking angry, looking sad, and celebrating.

- If multiple people appear in your videos, make sure to get some shots of the two of them together. If the video is with a guest who doesn't appear regularly on your channel, simply snap a few photos with your camera after you're done making the video for thumbnails.

- If you have a headline idea in mind for your Video Discovery ads, get some photos that will match that headline. For example, if you were using the headline "From Frumpy To Fabulous" in your ads, you could show a before and after transformation of the customer's previous frumpy look, to the new fabulous look you put together for them.

When you're shooting photos for your thumbnail images, **make sure you are shooting all of your pictures in a horizontal orientation.**

That's because the YouTube thumbnail dimensions are 16:9, and vertically oriented pictures (pictures with more height than width) will often be hard to crop to the right size.

You should also make sure to shoot a little farther away than normal when shooting YouTube thumbnail images. This way, you'll have more room to crop the image to the right dimensions without distorting it.

Once you've got your photos, the process for making the thumbnail image itself will be the same as screenshots.

Go through your photos, and choose one that you think will catch attention without being deceptive. Crop it to the right size, brighten it and increase the saturation, and upload it to your video.

Should You Use Text Graphics In Thumbnails?

As a rule of thumb, it's usually best NOT to include any text in your thumbnail. I've found this usually reduces the performance of Video Discovery ads, because it makes it seem more like an image made by a graphic designer, and it seems less like an actual moment that will appear in the video.

There are some exceptions to the rule though…

For example, check out this thumbnail image for one of Graham Stephen's most viewed videos:

How I Bought This
House For $0

For a video topic like this, there simply is nothing visually exciting Graham could have put in the thumbnail without being deceptive. It's just him standing in front of an average looking house.

The exciting part of the video was that he got the house for $0.

In cases like this where the exciting part of the video can ONLY be communicated through text, you should include a text in your thumbnail image.

If you are including text in your thumbnail, use as few words as you can and make your text as large as possible.

That's because most people who use YouTube watch it on their phones. If your text is too small, it won't be readable to most of your viewers — even if it looks great on your big desktop monitor.

The Masters Of Video Thumbnails To Study

The best thumbnail makers are actually not advertisers — they're YouTubers who rely on organic traffic.

Thumbnail images are critically important to YouTubers like this because they literally have no other way to get traffic. They can't just buy InStream ads like us. Either they make good thumbnail images or their channel dies out.

Here are a few channels I recommend checking out:

Charisma Matrix — Best Thumbnail Post-Production —

Barron Cruz, the guy who runs the channel, is a client of mine and a friend. I originally met him when he was speaking at Mark Ling's Mastermind event, where he gave an excellent talk about how he gets millions of views with advanced thumbnail design.

Many of Barron's thumbnails are just publicly available images. But he edits them to really pop — brightening the image, changing the colors to stand out more, removing empty space to put two people closer together, and more.

Here's one example. This thumbnail was made from this original image:

Trump at The Bush
Funeral – Here's What...

Barron got 2.1 MILLION views on this video, largely because of what he did with the thumbnail. You can see he brightened it, increased the saturation, changed some of the colors to more attention-getting colors, and he did a great job using red lines to highlight the interesting part of the photo. He also moved the people closer together, so people were more recognizable in a small thumbnail.

You can use these techniques on Video Discovery images to take your images to the next level. **However, just note that for advertising, you need to own the copyrights to any images you use, and you cannot use images of public figures like the President in an ad campaign.**

Graham Stephen — Best Thumbnails For Boring Topics — Graham makes videos about personal finance, real estate investing, and other money-related topics. Many of his videos are about inherently boring topics that have no interesting visual component. And by boring, I mean REALLY boring — like how to maximize your credit card rewards, or frugal dating ideas.

Of course, these topics are interesting to the millions of people who watch his channel. But it's definitely more challenging for him to create great thumbnails than it was for me in the fitness market, where I had a variety of incredibly shredded fitness models to choose from for my thumbnails.

Graham not only makes interesting videos on these topics, but he makes interesting thumbnails as well. To do this, he usually combines an image of himself making an attention-getting expression with large, readable text.

If you think there's no way you can create attention-grabbing thumbnails for your business, check out Graham's channel.

And you'll see ANY video topic can have a great thumbnail if you're clever enough about it.

Nicole Arbour — Best Female Thumbnails — Nicole isn't popular just because her videos are funny. She also makes great thumbnail images! Her images are clearly from professional photography, and her team does a great job enhancing the images to make her look better and more attention getting.

Yet, her images are not overly enhanced. They still look natural enough where nobody complains when they see the unenhanced Nicole on camera. She also does a great job making funny, attention getting facial expressions in her thumbnail photos. When the interesting part of the video can only be communicated by text, she does a great job with the text as well.

DEAR FEMINISTS

1.3M views • 3 years ago

Making the women in your thumbnails look as good as possible is extremely important for certain female focused industries, such as fashion, skin care, and makeup. It can also be important to catch attention in male focused industries like men's dating advice, entrepreneurship, or sports cars. If you have women in your videos, study Nicole's thumbnails and emulate her approach.

The Ultimate Key To Great Thumbnails: Hire Someone To Do It For You

As soon as you can afford it, I recommend hiring a designer to make your thumbnail images for you. That's because making these images are incredibly time consuming. But you can find great graphic designers to do this work super cheap, and super-fast.

Even a low level graphic designer will be able to do a much better job enhancing an image than you will (unless you're a professional designer yourself.) You just need to train them in what's important for YouTube thumbnails. And you need to make sure they're doing good work.

Here are some tips for hiring someone to make your thumbnails:

- **The most important thing to communicate to your designer is that your thumbnails need to look ORGANIC.** This means they need to look like a moment that actually appears in the video, not a polished image made by a professional designer.

  Since this is the opposite of what most clients want, it's tough for most designers to grasp this at first.

  You will have to emphasize this point over and over again, since it will be hard for them to believe you really want unprofessional looking images.

But once they get it, professional designers can make far better thumbnails than a non-professional.

- When using photos for your thumbnail, make sure you tell your designer to focus on organic-looking photos that do not appear posed, and to avoid using any modeling-style posed shots. Again, this is the opposite of what most of their clients want to be sure to emphasize this point.

- Tell them that their images must look good as a tiny phone thumbnail image, since this is how most viewers will be seeing it. Make sure they design with the phone first in their mind, and that they always view their image in a tiny phone size before finalizing it.

- If a video has an exciting moment in it and you want them to use screenshots of the videos, make sure you tell them. Your designer can't be expected to watch all your videos to detect these moments — they rely on you for that. You should also make sure to thoroughly train them in how to take a burst of screenshots around the exciting moment to make sure they get an ideal shot.

- Always review the thumbnail images your designer makes and give them feedback on how to improve.

Once they've been doing it for a few months, they'll probably be able to make better thumbnails than you can for your videos with very little required on your side.

However, sometimes you will have an idea for a thumbnail you think is much better. When you do, you should not be shy about asking your designer to re-make it. **Remember, if you are spending thousands of dollars on this ad, even a small improvement in the thumbnail will make a big difference.**

Common Questions From Clients About Thumbnail Images

Should I use stock photography?

No! I strongly recommend you avoid using stock photography in your thumbnail images.

If you're not familiar with stock photography, it's images you can get for free or buy for a small royalty online. Many YouTube advertisers use stock photos for their thumbnail images because they're cheaper and easier to get than original photos.

While it's much easier than taking your own photos, I've found that original photography massively outperforms stock photos in Video Discovery campaigns once you know what photos to take. And using a screenshot as your thumbnail will usually outperform stock photography as well.

The nature of stock photography is that it consists of professional models posing. These posed images are then polished by a professional graphic designer. Because of this, it does not seem like a moment that will occur in the video. And it won't entice people to want to watch.

If you don't have a budget for original photography, then use screenshots or images you already have on Facebook and Instagram. Both of these options will usually outperform stock in advertising campaigns.

What size image should I upload?

You should upload all of your images in the maximum size YouTube allows (2 MB at the time of this writing.)

While most people will view your images on a phone, some of your viewers will be seeing your thumbnail on a large computer monitor or a TV screen. A high quality thumbnail will ensure the image will look good for these people, and YouTube will automatically serve a more compressed image to people on phones.

A high-resolution thumbnail will also "future-proof" your video against coming technology improvements, which will allow more users to load high quality thumbnail images on their phones.

What should I avoid in my thumbnail image?

Because your thumbnail image will be heavily scrutinized by the Google Ads Policy team, it's important that you avoid putting anything in your thumbnail that could cause compliance problems. Here are a few things you should avoid:

- **Suggestive nudity, which can depend on the context.** A woman in a sports bra doing a workout is OK, but a woman in lingerie with identical coverage making a sexy facial expression is not.

- **Text claims in your image.** For example, if you claim a user can "make $10,000 in 30 days," this is a violation of Google's Misrepresentation policy. Google will be reading the text in your image and it could cause your ad to be disapproved.

- **Images you don't own the copyright to.** If you use stock photos you don't own, stock photo sites regularly scan YouTube and can detect this. They will make you take the image down, and could even threaten a lawsuit. Avoid this by simply using your own original photography or screenshots.

Not only will these things cause compliance problems, they also don't work well for marketing purposes. Make sure to avoid them since they're risky and there's no possible upside to using them.

The Easy Part: Setting Up Your Video Discovery Campaign

Once you've created your thumbnail images and written your headlines, the hard part is done! Now you just have to set up your campaign — and this will actually be very easy.

Upload your thumbnails to YouTube, and in your Ad Bank campaign create your Video Discovery ads. You'll just need to add in your headline for each ad and your universal description. The easiest way to do this is to make one ad, then copy and paste it into the same ad group.

This way, you already have the body copy set. You just switch out the video and the headline.

Once you've done this, create a new keyword targeted Video Discovery campaign.

To save time, you can use the same targeting on your first Video Discovery campaign's ad groups that you use on your first Instream campaign. Just re-create the same 15 ad groups with the same exact keywords.

Once that's done, paste your ads into all of the ad groups.

And you're done! Your Video Discovery campaign is now good to go.

This will be super simple for Google Ads veterans. But if you're new to Google Ads, I know this seems like a lot of complex steps. And you might not be sure about the mechanics of how to set everything up.

If that's you, it's important that you review the campaign setup tutorial at:

15StepsBonuses.com/CampaignSetup

It's yours free with this book, and it will walk you through exactly what to click on in Google Ads to create this campaign.

Your Action Steps From This Chapter:

1. Create the thumbnail images for your first batch of videos. Use original photography, screen shots, or photos from your social media profiles.

2. Write your universal body copy you'll use on every Video Discovery ad.

3. Add your videos to your Ad Bank campaign in Google Ads. Write a headline for each ad, using one of the headline writing formulas you learned in this chapter. Paste in your universal body copy.

4. Create your Video Discovery campaign

5. Re-create the same fifteen keyword targeted ad groups you made in your Instream campaign in your Discovery campaign.

6. Pick the three Video Discovery ads you think will perform the best after looking at the thumbnails and headlines.

7. Copy and paste your three top ads into every ad group in your new Video Discovery campaign

Step 10: Learn The Ten Pillars Of Great Ad Management

Now that you've set up your ad campaigns, it's time to learn how to manage them. This is how you get your profits REALLY cranking!

The way you manage your campaign is incredibly important, and it can make the difference between success and failure with YouTube marketing.

There are ten critical things you need to do to grow profitable ad campaigns. This chapter walks you through each pillar of ad management, and shows you exactly how to manage your ad account like a pro. I'll also show you how to make your ad management efficient, so you can bring your campaigns to success quickly and easily.

The Single Biggest Key To Ad Management Success

In this chapter, I'm going to show you high level techniques that I've used to drive hundreds of millions of dollars in revenue from Google Ads. Many of my students have also implemented these techniques, and made millions themselves.

The techniques you're about to learn are powerful. And they're proven to work on a huge scale.

But none of them will do you any good – unless you first have the #1 biggest key to ad management success.

The biggest key to learning how to successfully manage Google Ads campaigns is having a consistent scheduled time to focus only on ad management. Without this, no method of ad management will do you any good.

Many advertising newbies think they just need to make some ads, set up the campaigns, and then passive income will roll in forever with no more effort required!

It'd be nice if things worked like that...but they simply don't.

You — or someone on your team — will need to spend a small amount of time each week to perform important tasks in your ad account if you want to keep it profitable.

You don't need to spend all day managing your campaigns. You can make the process quick, efficient, and simple. But you have to be consistently doing the small things each week that eventually lead to success.

You can make great money with a consistent four hour YouTube marketing workweek. But if you're just haphazardly working on your account here and there "when you have the time," your campaigns are going to lose money.

It's similar to fitness. Even if you have the best exercise advice in the world, it won't do you any good unless you consistently hit the gym a few times a week.

I've coached many clients and given them advice on how to improve their YouTube campaigns. **My coaching clients who achieve the most success are almost always the ones who schedule this focused time.**

Clients who do not schedule a specific time to manage ads rarely do it consistently, and they usually don't achieve large scale profits from their campaigns because of this.

When your campaigns are small, you don't need to spend a huge amount of time managing your ads. But you do need to make sure to consistently check your campaigns and optimize them every few days. It just takes a few minutes each day. Once you get into the routine, it'll be easy.

Like with your YouTube uploads, sticking to a regular schedule is the most important thing.

How To Create Your Ad Management Schedule

Here's the amount of time I recommend blocking off to manage your ads:

- If you are spending less than $500 a day on Google Ads, you should schedule time blocks of 30 minutes 3 times per week.

- If you are spending between $500 - $2,000 a day on Google Ads, you should schedule time blocks of 45 minutes 5 times per week.

- If you are spending $2,000 - $10,000 a day on Google Ads, you should have 90 minutes blocked off 5 times per week for ad management.

- When you're spending more than $10,000 a day on Google ads, you still won't need to spend more than 90 minutes a day on your campaigns. But at this point, you should hire a full time employee to work on your campaigns eight hours a day. If you don't want to hire an employee, you can hire an agency or contractor for an equivalent number of man-hours. And I'll show you exactly how to do this in Step 15.

You'll be using your scheduled time block to make critical improvements to your ad account, like split testing ads, refining your targeting, and expanding your campaigns.

To make sure this time is sacrosanct, schedule it on your calendar for the same time on the same days every week. If you're serious about building profitable YouTube campaigns, you cannot allow this time to be interrupted for any reason. It has to be just as uninterruptible as a meeting with an important client.

If someone asks to meet with you during that time, say "sorry, I have a meeting already scheduled." Because you do have a meeting scheduled. A meeting with yourself to manage YouTube ads.

I recognize that this is a big time commitment, especially for business owners who are already busy with many other things.

If you're managing many other aspects of your business in addition to YouTube marketing, it will not be practical for you to permanently devote the time to ad management that you need to be successful.

That's why I'm going to show you in detail how to hire an agency or employee to manage your ads for you in Step 15. If you're busy with many other things, this will be the best long-term solution for you.

I encourage you to manage your campaigns yourself for at least a few weeks even if you know you don't have the time to manage them long term. By managing your campaigns personally before handing them off, you'll have a much stronger understanding of how to build profitable Google Ads campaigns.

This will make you much better at supporting the person who will be managing your ads long term.

The Ten Pillars Of Great Ad Management

To become a master of managing Google Ads campaigns, you need to master these ten critical "pillars" of ad management.

1. Calculating customer lifetime value (LTV)
2. Deciding on a bid strategy
3. Setting your bids
4. Split testing your ads
5. Pausing unprofitable ad groups and campaigns
6. Eliminating "zombie" ad groups that never get any views
7. Expanding profitable campaigns with new ad groups
8. Refining targeting on existing ad groups and campaigns
9. Setting geographic bid and device bid modifiers
10. Resolving Google Ads Policy compliance issues

Like the pillars in a building, these ten pillars will support the profitability of your account.

Once you read this chapter and implement the action steps, you'll be a pro at performing all of these critical tasks.

Why You MUST Calculate Your Customer Lifetime Value

Many marketers refer to your Customer Lifetime Value, or LTV, as the "master number" for online advertising. **Knowing your LTV and continually taking steps to increase it will be the ultimate key to success with any online advertising channel.**

If you don't calculate your LTV, chances are that you will never be successful with online advertising. You may lack the confidence to bid aggressively enough, so you miss out on many potentially profitable sales. Or even worse, you may bid too aggressively — leading to you running large ad campaigns at a loss.

But once you know your LTV, you'll have a huge advantage over other advertisers. You'll be like the seeing man in the land of the blind. While everyone else is making a guess at what they should be bidding, each of your bids will be optimally set with scientific, calculated precision.

This section is about to get a little bit complicated and math-y, but stick with me here. This is really important stuff and it's worth learning to make your campaigns profitable. Your bidding strategy you're about to learn in this chapter will be based on your LTV, so it's very important to get it right.

How To Calculate Customer Lifetime Value

Your LTV is defined as **the average amount of gross profit your business makes for each customer.** "Gross profit" is the amount of money your business makes from a sale after subtracting the costs of the product or service you're selling.

If you're selling a digital product with no cost, and the average customer buys 3 products for $100, your LTV would be $300

But let's say that you're selling shoes. The average customer buys 3 pairs for $100, but each pair costs you $50 to buy wholesale. In this case, your LTV is $150 ($300 - $150 in product costs).

Note that everything outside your product costs and costs of fulfilling your product is not counted in this calculation.

Whether you are spending $100 or $1 million on things like your office, software, employees, etc. it should not affect your LTV or your strategy for bidding on ads.

This is because if you make more sales "fixed costs" like this will not increase. However, "variable costs," such as the cost of your product, will increase in proportion to the sales you're making.

If you have a brand new business, you will not be able to calculate your LTV until you've been selling at least three months. Bid conservatively until then, and at that point revisit this chapter and calculate your LTV once you have some sales.

There are two main ways to calculate LTV — a quick and dirty way to get started with, and the sophisticated way that is preferred by top marketers.

There is also a third, technologically advanced way to calculate LTV used by large companies that I'll show you as well.

Calculating LTV The Quick & Dirty Way

Getting a rough estimate of your LTV can be pretty simple.

Just divide the gross profit you made in the last 12 months by the number of new customers you acquired.

Let's say that in the last 12 months you made $1 million in revenue, and you had $500,000 in product costs. You acquired 1,000 new customers.

Your "quick and dirty" LTV would be $500 per customer ($500,000 in gross profit divided by 1,000 customers). This will be the number you base your bid strategy off of.

If you are just getting started and you don't have sophisticated Customer Relationship Management (CRM) software, use this method to start off.

Calculating LTV The Sophisticated, Better Way

While the quick and dirty method will work fine to start a small scale campaign, there are a few problems with it.

First, it's not exact. Some of your revenue for the year will come from customers you acquired in the previous year. And many customers you acquired towards the end of the year will not have realized their full value, and will make purchases in the future that don't get included.

Second, it's not specific to YouTube. **Most advertisers find that customers they acquire from YouTube have a significantly higher LTV than customers they acquire from other traffic sources.**

If you are looking at the overall LTV for your business rather than your YouTube LTV, you could be significantly underestimating how profitable your campaigns are.

So that's why when you start your YouTube campaigns, you should start a spreadsheet to calculate your YouTube Customer LTV.

I highly recommend outsourcing this task or delegating it to virtual assistant, since it's boring and time consuming work. Fortunately, you can easily hire someone in the Philippines or Colombia to do this for you for less than $100.

What you want to do is track the first 100 customers you acquire from YouTube.

Make a column in each spreadsheet for each one of your products. Then, code the spreadsheet to add in the right amount of gross profit for every product.

This sounds complicated, but it's not. You can use the template in this chapter's bonus resources as a starting point. Just fill in your own products and gross profit numbers.

To get the spreadsheet started, ask your Virtual Assistant to check your CRM or shopping cart software to see what your YouTube customers have bought. To do this, you'll need to use a **tracking link** on all of your videos that tells your software the sale came from YouTube.

She will just have to put down the quantity of each product they purchased, and the spreadsheet will calculate the right amount of gross profit for them.

To get a rough idea of your YouTube Customer LTV, you'll need to track this "cohort" of 100 people for at least three months.

Once you've tracked them for three months, you'll have a conservative estimate of what your LTV is.

Your LTV will likely be significantly higher than this when everything is said and done. Some customers will keep subscriptions active longer than 3 months. Customers you acquired years ago will continue to place new purchases.

While this number isn't your final LTV, it represents a conservative minimum estimate. You'll know that you can spend at least this amount to acquire a customer. In three months, you'll break even, and every sale you make after that will be profit.

Have your assistant update your LTV spreadsheet once per month for 12 months. Once you've gone a full 12 months, you'll have an EXCELLENT picture of your YouTube customer value. It'll be much more precise than the quick and dirty method, and specific to your YouTube advertising campaigns.

To make sure your LTV numbers always stay current, start a new spreadsheet after 12 months and repeat this process. And if you have a larger business and can do this with more than 100 customers (say, 500 or 1000) that is even better.

Software: The Ultimate Way To Calculate LTV

Making a spreadsheet like this will put you many levels above most marketers. But the ultimate way to calculate LTV that all of the world's top marketers are using to calculate LTV is software.

If you have an enterprise-level CRM, it's possible (with some development work) to get your software to calculate LTV for you. This is way better than having a VA do it in a spreadsheet for a few reasons…

First of all, even the most reliable person will sometimes make human errors. Software eliminates this source of inaccuracy, making your LTV more precise.

Software can also calculate your LTV from more than 100 customers. If you're running a large business that gets more than 1,000 new customers a month this could be very important.

Software can also continually re-calculate your LTV every single day, making sure it never gets outdated or inaccurate over time.

If you run a large business, talk with your development team about setting up your CRM to calculate LTV for you. And if you're not there yet, keep this option in mind for the future when your business is bigger.

Unfortunately, there is not any good inexpensive software I've seen that calculates LTV for you. So, this is currently only possible for large businesses using Salesforce or a similar CRM.

Most businesses should use the Quick & Dirty Method or Spreadsheet Method to get started.

So, go assign someone on your team to calculate your LTV for you. If you don't have anyone on your team who can do this, hire a virtual assistant overseas.

Once you have your LTV, you're now ready to decide on your bidding strategy.

Question: How Much Should You Spend On Advertising?

Answer: As much as you possibly can!

Many business owners foolishly believe that advertising is a cost to be minimized, like office supplies or taxes.

However, if you are investing a dollar and making two dollars back, advertising is not truly a cost. It is the best possible investment you can make, and you should be looking to plow as much money into this investment as you possibly can.

Let's say you had a chance to buy a stock for $1,000...and in six months, you could get $3,000 back.

Would you complain try and minimize the "expense," and buy less of this stock? Of course not! You'd buy as much as you possibly could, since it's very likely to be a good investment.

Since YouTube advertising can produce similar returns, you should look at it the same way.

Now, the trick is knowing how much you "possibly can" spend while still making a solid profit margin. Spend too little, and you'll leave money on the table. Spend too much, and your advertising losses will bleed you dry.

And that's why it's so critical you're using a proven bidding strategy.

The Conservative Strategy: Bid 80% Of Immediate Revenue

If you're just starting off with online advertising or if you're afraid to lose money, this is the place to start. With this strategy, you'll be setting your bids to target a 20% IMMEDIATE profit on the first sale that you make to the customer.

This means that if you're setting your bids right and turning off unprofitable ad groups, you CANNOT lose money in the long term. You are making a profit right from the first sale, and everything that comes after this is gravy.

Bidding this conservatively does have a downside though: you will never be able to scale your campaigns beyond a certain point. It's going to be very tough to compete against sophisticated marketers who are bidding more aggressively, and they will usually out-bid you in the ad auction.

I know that for people new to online advertising, spending 80% of the revenue you get from your first sale doesn't sound "conservative." But you need to adopt a new mentality if you want to be successful with online advertising.

Keep in mind that without the advertising, you would not have gotten the sale in the first place.

While you'll only be keeping 20% of the profit from the first sale, it's far better than the 0% you'd be getting without the advertising. And if you run your business well, you'll make double or triple what you make on the first sale over the customer's lifetime. These additional sales will be pure profit with no additional advertising cost.

And you can make hundreds of times more sales with a dialed in advertising campaign than you can by relying on weak organic traffic strategies.

Of course, it would be nice if we could make thousands of sales while making a 50% of 70% immediate profit. But it's simply not possible to do this at scale in the modern Google Ads competitive environment.

And even if you are running a campaign with a profit margin this fat, you will almost certainly make far more profit overall if you bid more aggressively.

It's much better to make a 20% profit on 1,000 sales than an 80% profit on 10 sales.

Because of this, 80% of immediate revenue is the absolute most conservative bidding strategy I recommend anybody use. And while this is a good place for small advertisers to start, you'll almost certainly make more profit by moving to a more aggressive strategy in the future.

The Moderate Strategy: Bid 100% Of Immediate Revenue
The moderate strategy is the best strategy for small advertisers who do not yet have a precise LTV.

If you are spending less than $10,000 a month on online advertising and you used the quick and dirty method to calculate your LTV, this is where I recommend you start.

With this strategy, you'll be acquiring as many customers as possible while "breaking even" on the first sale, or spending 100% of the immediate revenue you get from customers.

This means that you are guaranteed a profit even if your LTV calculation is a little off. If your customers stay on a subscription for a month, or buy one additional product after the first sale you'll already be in the money.

This strategy is also easier on your cash flow than more aggressive strategies. Your advertising will be self-financing, and you won't need to front money to acquire customers that will take a month or two to become profitable.

To make this and the more aggressive bid strategies work, it's critical that you're always working on ways to increase the back-end sales for your business. Here are a few ideas you could consider to do this if you're first starting off:

- Attach a monthly membership to each sale, so you can make an almost-guaranteed profit on the subscription revenue

- Improve your email marketing. Sell more of your own products, and sell other businesses' products for a commission

- Improve your remarketing ad campaigns (I'll show you how to do this later)

- Create more products for your customers to buy, and promote them through remarketing and email campaigns

- Start upselling your customers to buy more products on the phone

Business that employ even a few of these strategies usually make 2-3x their initial sale in back-end revenue. So, if you're doing at least a few of the things above, you should get to profits with this strategy very quickly.

The Aggressive Strategy: Spend 50% Of Your LTV To Acquire A Customer

The aggressive strategy is the best strategy for businesses who are spending more than $10,000 a month on online advertising, and who have precisely calculated LTV through the Spreadsheet Method or Software Method.

With this strategy, you'll be spending MUCH MORE than the immediate revenue you get to acquire customers.

This is the most profitable advertising strategy for businesses that know their numbers. Even though you'll have a front-end "loss," the amount of advertising you'll be able to buy will be exponentially increased. And this means the number of customers you acquire will go through the roof too.

It's important to understand that bidding 50% more aggressively won't just get you 50% more customers. Many times, it'll get you 500% or 1000% more customers.

This is because Google Ads is an auction where the most competitive bid wins. If you can outbid the competition, Google naturally gives you the lion's share of the traffic since you're their most profitable customer.

So, this strategy can be VERY powerful when done right. Many advertisers have used it to annihilate their advertising competition, and to completely dominate their markets.

What you want to do is to big as aggressively as you can, while still leaving yourself a fat profit margin and margin for error.

Let's say I had a business where I calculated my LTV is $300, and on average I was making $100 in immediate revenue per customer, between the initial sale I made and any upsells made right afterwards.

In this case, I would set my bids to 150% of the immediate revenue I make (or to "go negative" 50% of the first sale.) That means I'm spending $150 on average to acquire orders from new customers that average $100. I'd be very confident in doing this, since I'm really only spending half of the total gross profit I'll make from the customer.

Even if I significantly overestimated my LTV, I'll still be making a profit and I won't be at any risk of losing money. And if I can make $150 in profit from thousands of customers that money will add up really quick.

If you want to use this strategy, **set your bids so you're spending about half of your LTV on acquiring a customer.** While it's harder on your cash flow to do this, in the long run you'll make much more profit than someone bidding more conservatively.

Many top advertisers bid even more aggressively than this, spending 60-80% of their LTV to acquire a customer.

I would not recommend bidding this aggressively unless you are a large company with data scientists on staff who can make sure your LTV is precisely correct and always updated. But for large corporations who know their numbers on this level, ultra-aggressive bidding like this can be very profitable.

But What If You're Broke?

Bidding more aggressively makes sense in the long term — IF you have the cash in your bank account to finance acquiring customers at a front end loss. But if you're low on cash, you might be worried that you'll run out of money before you make your money back from these customers.

And this is definitely understandable. If you're concerned about running out of cash, I recommend starting off bidding conservatively, and to gradually step your bids up over time.

This way you can start making small-scale profits right now.

Later, you can use those profits to fund a more aggressive bidding strategy.

I also believe that this is one of the rare times in business where it makes sense to take out a loan.

If you've calculated your LTV with the spreadsheet method —
and you've been meticulous with your calculations — the
numbers will generally hold pretty closely and you're almost
guaranteed a profit in the long term. And since you know you'll
break even and have enough money to pay the loan within 1-2
months, the interest expense is not a big concern.

The ideal way to do this is to set up a business line of credit
and to have it ready to use if you might need it for advertising
campaigns.

You can also do it the way I did years ago when I was broke
— put your ad spend on a credit card once your numbers
clearly show it's profitable. This is riskier because credit card
interest rates are much higher.

However, if your numbers are ironclad and they show you will
make a profit within 1-2 months from the advertising, you'll
only pay a minimal amount of interest and there's little risk you
won't be able to pay the bill.

I know it can sound risky and scary to finance advertising
campaigns with debt. But the risk is much lower than you think
if your LTV projections are correct. And bidding just a little
more aggressively could get you 5x, 10x, or maybe even 20x
more sales than you're making right now.

Reasons Why You Should Bid More Aggressively Than You Think

I know we've spent a lot of time talking about bid strategy, but
I'm doing this because it's a very important decision. We're
going to get into the nitty-gritty of what to click on in Google
Ads in a minute. But it's important you get this all-important
decision right first. Otherwise, you'll just be efficiently
implementing a bad strategy.

So, here's the last thing I'll say about bid strategy...

Many advertisers could be making double or triple the profits with a better bid strategy, and most small advertisers are bidding far too conservatively on their ads.

Here are some arguments in favor of a more aggressive bid strategy you should consider before you make your decision:

- While Google's tracking is good, it's not perfect. It's likely that 5-10% of your sales are not tracking because users switched devices without being signed into their Google account, or did something else which made it impossible to track the sale back to your ad.

  Because of this, your true ROI from advertising is likely a little higher than it appears in your Google Ads stats.

- **The more you advertise, the more data you accumulate.** And data is very valuable because you'll be using it to make improvements to your targeting and ad creative.

  The more data you have, the more ads and targeting options you can split test. This means your campaigns will improve and scale up faster.

- **If you are using Social Response Marketing, your advertising will be building your channel and your brand.** The more you spend on advertising, the more subscribers you'll acquire and the more engagement your channel will get.

You'll also be building the value of your brand. If someone has seen a video from you on YouTube they liked, they'll be far more receptive to your advertising when they see it on other platforms.

- **The more you spend, the better your support from Google will be**. While your ad spend isn't the only factor in the quality of support you'll get, it is the most important factor. If you're not spending much, you'll have to call in to the customer support line and deal with low-level reps in India if you have a problem.

  But if you're spending a lot, you'll get your own Ad Rep who will help you improve your campaigns. She'll also help you with any Policy compliance problems that might come up. And once you're REALLY spending a lot, Google will assign an entire team of American reps to help you grow your account.

- **If your goal is to sell your business, spending more aggressively on advertising will probably maximize your payout.** Investors mainly value companies on a multiple of their yearly profits. But there are other factors they consider as well.

  Higher revenue, a larger customer database, a bigger social media presence, and a more recognized brand will all get you a better valuation if you ultimately sell your business. If that's your goal, it's especially important that you're bidding as aggressively as you can while still making a profit.

Conversion Value vs. All Conversion Value

You may have noticed that there are two sets of conversion metrics in Google Ads — one based on "Conversions" and the other one based on "All Conversions."

What's the difference between these two metrics, and which one should you use?

"All conversions" and its associated metrics track EVERY conversion you've set up in Google Ads. It also tracks what Google calls "special conversion sources." These are cross-device conversions, and other conversions that are tracked in an unconventional way by Google.

For most small advertisers, these metrics will be the same and it won't matter which one you use. But the distinction becomes important for larger advertisers with complex conversions or multiple unrelated product lines.

Let's say you're running ads for a client who tracks these conversions:

- Leads
- Checkout page impressions
- Sales

In this case, it'll be important to set up this campaign to only optimize for lead conversions. And you should use the **Conversions** metrics —— not the "All Conversions" metrics — when looking at these campaigns.

If you use "All Conversions," your checkout page impression conversions will drastically inflate your conversion numbers and it won't accurately represent your cost per lead. Using "Conversions" will give you an accurate cost per lead number, and take out any extraneous conversions you're tracking.

So, to sum up what you should use…

Use the "All Conversions" metrics if you are just tracking leads and sales, and if you do not have multiple product lines you're advertising.

Use "Conversions" if you have any conversions BESIDES leads and sales that you're tracking, or if you have multiple product lines with different customer bases.

How To Set Your Bids With CPA Bidding

Now that we've got that out of the way, let's talk about how to set your bids.

Your bid strategy will be the basis for all of the bid calculations you make in your account.

Here's how you'll do this on CPA (cost per action, or automated) campaigns, the main type of campaign you'll be using in your account.

Once you've set up your columns according to the Universal Column Formula, they'll look like this

You'll be using the metric called "Value/Conversions" (or "Value/All Conversions" for some advertisers) to set your bid.

If you've set up your conversions like I recommend, your Value/Conversions number will basically be **the amount of revenue you make from each lead.**

This is because for most advertisers who collect leads and take online sales, over 95% of your conversions will be lead conversions. That's because it almost always takes a large amount of leads to make one sale.

If you're not collecting leads now, don't worry. I'm going to show you a few easy ways to get started collecting leads (without lowering your immediate sales) later in this book.

Let's say an ad group has spent $500 over the last 30 days. You see that your Value/Conv. (gross profit per lead) is $10.

You will then set your bid using this formula:

Your Bid Multiplier (determined by your bidding strategy)
x
Value/Conv. (for that ad group)

Let's say you're following the moderate bid strategy. In this case it's really simple — you set your bid to a $10 CPA (1 x $10).

Let's say that you decided your strategy is to bid 120% of your immediate revenue. In this case, your bid will be $12 (1.2 * $10).

If you're bidding conservatively, you'd set your bids to $8 (.8 x $10).

You get the idea. Your bid strategy determines your bid multiplier number. **And your bid is just your value/conversion, adjusted upwards or downwards depending on your bid strategy.**

In the past, you had to do hundreds of arithmetic equations like this to set your bids this way. **But fortunately, using a Google Ads feature called "Custom Columns," you can now actually get Google Ads to calculate your bids for you.**

To see a video walkthrough of how to set this Custom Column up, make sure to check out this chapter's bonus video:

15StepsBonuses.com/CampaignManagement

Since we're covering many important tasks within Google Ads, this bonus video will be especially important to watch. Make sure you take advantage of it!

How To Bid For Low-Spending Ad Groups

How much should you spend on an ad group before adjusting the bid?

I recommend spending at least 2x the price of your initial product on the ad group before setting your bid, and at least $50 for low-priced products.

Let's say that your product costs $100. If an ad group has spent more than $200 in the past 30 days, you'll have enough information to set your bid based on the ad group data. But if an ad group hasn't spent $200 yet, you don't have enough information to set an accurate bid.

For these low-spending ad groups, simply use the average "Value/All Conversions" number for your campaign overall. And if it's a new campaign, use the "Value/All Conversions" number for your entire Google Ads account.

If you're totally new to Google Ads, just make a reasonable, conservative guess at what a lead is worth to start off with. Once you get enough campaign and ad group data, you can then adjust your bids based on that.

Doing this will give you a reasonable starting point for new ad groups, and you'll quickly be able to adjust to a more optimal bid once you have some data.

How To Set Your Bids With CPV Bidding

Most of your campaigns will be CPA campaigns, but you still need to bid on Video Discovery campaigns on a CPV (cost per view) basis. eCommerce advertisers using TrueView For Shopping campaigns will also need to use CPV bidding.

Here is the formula I recommend using to set bids on these campaigns:

Average Cost Per View x Conversion Value/Cost x Your Bid Multiplier

The formula looks a little more complex. But it's ultimately the same idea as setting your CPA bids.

As of the time of this writing, you cannot get Google Ads to calculate CPV for you using Custom Columns.

However, it's likely that this feature will eventually be added and you'll be able to do this soon.

In the meantime, I recommend hiring a virtual assistant to set your CPV bids for you if you're doing a lot of Video Discovery or TrueView For Shopping advertising. You'll just need to train them on how to set the right columns in Google Ads, and how to set their bids using your formula and a calculator.

While this work is tedious and time-consuming, it's easily learned by a VA working overseas. And it's easily worth the tiny amount you'll pay them to do this.

If your ad group has spent more than $200 in the last 30 days, use your ad group data to set your CPV bid.

For low-spending CPV ad groups, you'll do the same thing as you do for low-spending CPA ad groups. Set your bid using the campaign data if the ad group has spent less than $200 in the last 30 days. If it's a new campaign, use the account data.

And if it's a new account, just make a reasonable guess.

For those of you who are new to online advertising, I know this bidding process can seem complex and intimidating at first.

But don't worry — once you get used to the process, it'll be quick and simple to do.

And you should also keep in mind that once you learn the process, it's easy to train someone else to do it. I haven't personally set any bids in years – I just give someone on my team these instructions and set up systems to make sure they're not messing anything up. Soon you will be doing this too.

If you want a full step-by-step walkthrough of how to set your bids, be sure to check out the bonus video. It walks you through how to do everything, and I update it each time things change in Google Ads.

15StepsBonuses.com/CampaignManagement

How To Split Test Your Ads

Now that you know how to set your bids, let's talk about how to split test your ads.

If you recall, **split testing is the process of running two ads against the same targeting and seeing which one performs better.** And you've already learned the Three Level Split Testing system for continually improving your creative.

We'll briefly recap what you learned here and give you some more details. And you can also watch this chapter's bonus video to get a step-by-step walkthrough.

Remember, with the Three Level Split Testing system:

- You test based on ROI for ads that have spent enough (2x the price of the first product you're selling the customer, and at least $50)

- You test based on cost per lead for ads that have gotten at least five leads

- You test based on cost per click for ads that have gotten at least 30 clicks

You already knew this, but here's an interesting question we didn't discuss before…

What should you do if you have MULTIPLE profitable ads?

Should you keep all of them — or just the most profitable one?

Let's say you have an ad group that looks like this, with all ads spending more than $200 in the last 30 days:

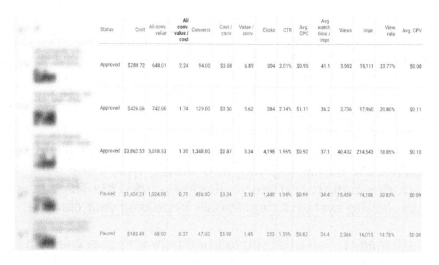

Status	Cost	All conv. value	All conv. value / cost	Conversi	Cost / conv.	Value / conv.	Clicks	CTR	Avg. CPC	Avg. watch time / impr.	Views	Impr.	View rate	Avg. CPV
Approved	$289.72	648.01	2.24	94.00	$3.08	6.89	304	2.01%	$0.95	41.1	3,592	15,111	23.77%	$0.08
Approved	$426.06	742.00	1.74	129.00	$3.30	5.62	384	2.14%	$1.11	36.2	3,736	17,960	20.80%	$0.11
Approved	$3,862.53	5,018.53	1.30	1,348.00	$2.87	3.34	4,198	1.96%	$0.92	37.1	40,432	214,543	18.85%	$0.10
Paused	$1,424.21	1,024.00	0.72	426.00	$3.34	2.10	1,440	1.94%	$0.99	34.4	15,439	74,106	20.83%	$0.09
Paused	$183.49	68.00	0.37	47.00	$3.90	1.45	223	1.39%	$0.82	24.4	2,366	16,013	14.78%	$0.08

An example of what to do when you have multiple profitable ads. You can see I kept all three of the ads above the ROI threshold of 1.0 in this account. And I paused the two ads at the bottom below the ROI threshold.

For situations like this, you should keep ALL of your profitable ads. This means keeping every ad which is above your ROI threshold for your bid strategy.

If you're following a conservative bid strategy, this means only keeping ads which have Conversion Value/Cost (or All Conversion Value/Cost for this account) higher than 1.2.

When you do this, you'll make a 20% immediate profit on the ad. This is about equivalent to bidding 80% of your immediate first-order revenue.

If you're following the moderate strategy, you keep all ads with Conv. Value/Cost above 1.

And if you're following an aggressive bid strategy where you're bidding 50% of your calculated LTV, you'll pause any ad that falls below the threshold you calculate.

Let's say your LTV is $200, and on average you make $80 on your first sale between the initial sale and upsells you offer to the customer right after they buy.

You want to spend on average $100 to acquire a new customer.

Your ROI threshold would then be $80 divided by $100, or .8. That means you keep every ad with Conversion Value/Cost above .8, since it's getting you customers at less than your target cost.

But why should you keep ALL of the profitable ads, instead of just the most profitable one?

It's because all ads eventually saturate or "wear out" over time. This is especially true for high spending advertisers using a very tight form of targeting like a remarketing list. By showing your customers more ads, you'll increase their lifespan and long-term profitability.

Let's walk through a few different split testing scenarios, so you can see how this all comes together.

Scenario 1: All Ads Spent More Than 2x Your First Sale Price, And At Least $50

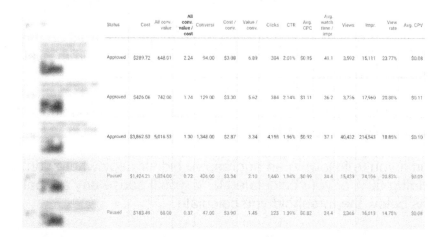

Status	Cost	All conv. value	All conv. value / cost	Conversi	Cost / conv.	Value / conv.	Clicks	CTR	Avg. CPC	Avg. watch time / impr.	Views	Impr.	View rate	Avg. CPV
Approved	$289.72	648.01	2.24	94.00	$3.08	6.89	304	2.01%	$0.95	41.1	3,592	15,111	23.77%	$0.08
Approved	$426.06	742.00	1.74	129.00	$3.30	5.62	384	2.14%	$1.11	36.2	3,756	17,960	20.80%	$0.11
Approved	$3,862.53	5,016.53	1.30	1,348.00	$2.87	3.34	4198	1.96%	$0.92	37.1	40,432	214,543	18.85%	$0.10
Paused	$1,424.21	1,024.00	0.72	426.00	$3.34	2.10	1,440	1.94%	$0.99	34.4	15,439	74,166	20.83%	$0.09
Paused	$183.49	68.00	0.37	47.00	$3.90	1.45	223	1.39%	$0.82	24.4	2,366	16,013	14.75%	$0.08

The scenario we just looked at is also an example of ROI split testing in action. Since all ads spent more than 2x the initial sale price, I simply pause out all ads below the ROI threshold (All Conversion Value / Cost < 1.0 in this account)

This is the simplest split testing situation, and the most common one for high-spending advertisers.

All you do is keep every ad above your ROI threshold, and pause out every ad below your ROI threshold.

Let's say you're following the moderate bidding strategy, and your ROI threshold is 1.0. And let's say you have three ads, with these All Conversion Value/Cost numbers: .6, 1.1, and 1.5. All of these ads have spend enough for ROI split testing.

You keep the ones with ROI above 1 as your "control" ads. Then you pause the ad with All Conversion Value/Cost of .6, since it's below your ROI threshold.

After doing this, you'll need to add some new ads into your ad group to keep the testing going. **When using the Three Level Split Testing System, I recommend having two new "experimental" ads in each ad group, and an unlimited number of proven "control" ads.**

This means if you have five proven "control" ads, you keep them all and then add two ads that you've never tested against this targeting before as your new "experimental" ads.

Scenario 2: Some Ads Spent More Than $200. Some Ads Did Not But Got More Than Five Leads

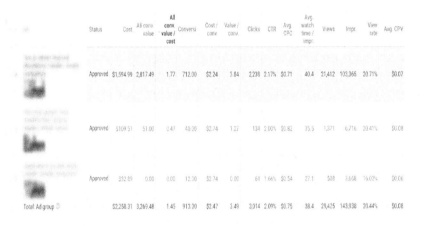

	Status	Cost	All conv. value	All conv. value / cost	Conversi	Cost / conv.	Value / conv.	Clicks	CTR	Avg. CPC	Avg. watch time / impr.	Views	Impr.	View rate	Avg. CPV
	Approved	$1,594.99	2,817.49	1.77	712.00	$2.24	3.84	2,238	2.17%	$0.71	40.4	21,412	103,365	20.71%	$0.07
	Approved	$109.51	51.00	0.47	40.00	$2.74	1.27	134	2.00%	$0.82	35.5	1,371	6,716	20.41%	$0.08
	Approved	$332.89	0.00	0.00	12.00	$2.74	0.00	61	1.66%	$0.54	27.1	588	3,668	16.03%	$0.06
Total: Ad group		$2,258.31	3,269.48	1.45	913.00	$2.47	3.49	3,014	2.09%	$0.75	38.4	29,425	143,938	20.44%	$0.08

An example of cost per lead split-testing in action. You can see I kept the top ad since it's above the ROI threshold of 1.0. I paused the bottom two ads since they're below the ad group average cost per conversion of $2.47 (which is the cost per lead.)

In this scenario, you'll split test the ads which spent more than $200 based on ROI. And you'll split test the remainder based on cost per lead.

For the ads that spent more than $200, you pause it if it's below your ROI threshold. Same thing as before.

For the other ads, you'll be testing based on the cost per lead.

Look at the average cost per lead for your ad group.

If your ad's cost per lead is above the average, pause it out. Replace it with a new experimental ad.

Most of the time you should be pausing ads which have a cost per lead above the ad group's average. However, if you believe the ad group is spending enough where you'll soon have enough ROI data, you may just want to wait a week, and then do split testing based on ROI.

Scenario 3: Some Ads Got More Than Five Leads (Or Can Be Tested On ROI), And Some Did Not But Got More Than 30 Clicks

If your campaign is spending more than $100/day, then you don't need this step. At this level you're better off just doing all your split testing based on ROI and cost per lead metrics.

But if you're running a small campaign spending less than $100/day, it can take a really long time to get enough data to test even based on lead cost. For these small campaigns, it's helpful to add in the extra step of cost per click split testing.

This will allow you to make meaningful improvements to ads even after spending just $20-$30.

Let's say you have an ad group that looks like this:

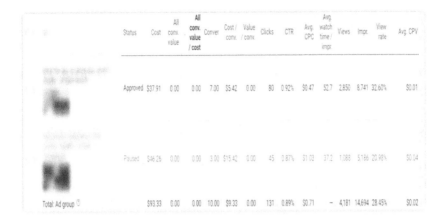

Status	Cost	All conv. value	All conv. value / cost	Conver	Cost / conv.	Value / conv.	Clicks	CTR	Avg. CPC	Avg. watch time / impr.	Views	Impr.	View rate	Avg. CPV
Approved	$37.91	0.00	0.00	7.00	$5.42	0.00	80	0.92%	$0.47	52.7	2,850	8,741	32.60%	$0.01
Paused	$46.26	0.00	0.00	3.00	$15.42	0.00	45	0.87%	$1.03	37.2	1,088	5,186	20.98%	$0.04
Total: Ad group	$93.33	0.00	0.00	10.00	$9.33	0.00	131	0.89%	$0.71	–	4,181	14,694	28.45%	$0.02

An example of Cost Per Click split testing in action. I paused the bottom ad because it's gotten more than 30 clicks, and it's Avg. CPC is higher than the ad group's average CPC. This should only be done in small campaigns spending less than $100 per day.

You can see the top ad got more than five leads. So, to determine whether we'll keep it, we compare the cost per conversion (which represents cost per lead) to the ad group average.

Since the cost per conversion is $5.42, substantially less than the ad group average, we keep the top ad.

But what about the bottom ad? It hasn't yet gotten five leads. If I was running large campaigns, I'd just leave it and do nothing regardless of what the average CPC is.

But let's say this is a small campaign that spends less than $100/day. In that case, I would pause the bottom ad like I have above. That's because it has an average CPC of $1.03, much more than the ad group average of $0.71. Since it's costing much more to get people to our website with this ad it's less likely to be one of our best converting ones.

After this, you've paused your ads, you'll need to put more experimental videos into this ad group to keep the testing going. So, you pick two new ads to test and add them into your ad group.

Why You Should Pause Ads One Week, And Delete Them The Next

I recommend split testing your campaigns once per week.

But the first time you go through your campaigns, DO NOT delete the ads which don't pass your split testing criteria. Instead, just pause them.

Why is this necessary? It's because unprofitable ads can later become profitable when conversions are attributed to them later.

And if you delete your ads right away, you'll be deleting many ads which later become viable.

That's why I recommend PAUSING your ads the first week they do not pass your split testing criteria.

If they improve during the week they are paused and are now a winner, re-enable the ads.

If they do not improve after a week, I recommend deleting the ads to reduce clutter.

How To Automate The Split Testing Process

I recommend that you do split testing manually for at least a few weeks so you understand how the process works. But once you understand it, it's now possible to set up automated rules in Google Ads that will do some of the hard work of split testing for you.

To learn how to do this, check out the bonus video:

15StepsBonuses.com/CampaignManagement

Pausing Unprofitable Ad Groups

Even if you do a great job choosing your targeting, there will be many times where your ideas just don't work.

In fact, you will probably have far more unprofitable ad groups than profitable ones. But this isn't a problem as long as you catch your "losing" ad groups and ads early and then pause them out.

By cutting your losing ad groups off early and letting your winners run, you can direct the majority of your spend into winning ad groups and make a great ROI overall.

I recommend you do this: creating an automated rule to **pause any ad group which meets these criteria:**

- The ad group has spent more than 2x your initial sale price (more than $50 for very cheap products)

- The ad group is more than 20%, (or .2) below your ROI threshold.

For example, if your ROI threshold is 1.0 (breaking even on the first sale), you'd set your automated rule to pause out any ads below .8.

For ad groups which are close to your ROI threshold, you should look at them and see if there are improvements you can make to get the ad group profitable before pausing it out.

By changing the creative or removing unprofitable targeting, you may be able to get the ad group over the top.

Again, be sure to check out the bonus video for step-by-step directions on how to do this.

Eliminating "Zombie" Ad Groups

As you expand your campaigns, you'll eventually have many ad groups that you've created which spend nothing or which spend next to nothing.

These ad groups are like the zombies in a horror movies. They're not really "alive" and making you money, but they're also not losing you enough money to pause out according to our normal rules. They're just slowly sucking up your precious time and focus.

Like zombies, one or two of them isn't a big deal. But if your account is infested with hundreds of them, it will eventually lead to serious ad management mistakes.

It's important to either get these "zombie" ad groups to spend, or to eliminate them from your account. If you don't, your account will eventually become cluttered with non-spending ad groups and it'll take too much time to manage.

You'll also be more likely to miss important data in your spending ad groups if many zombie ad groups are distracting you.

That's why once each week, I recommend **increasing your CPA or CPV bid by 30% for any ad groups that have spent less than $50 in the past 30 days.** This will get most of these ad groups to start spending eventually, and you'll be able to see if they are profitable.

When you aggressively increase your bid like this, most of the ad groups that start spending will lose money. But that's OK! You can then pause them out, and focus your spend on the select few ad groups that are profitable.

It doesn't matter if 9 out of 10 ad groups you fail and are paused out when you increase your bids like this. Your losses on these ad groups will be limited to a few hundred dollars each.

But one profitable ad group could bring you thousands, or even hundreds of thousands of dollars in revenue.

Increasing your bids by 30% per week will get most of your zombie ad groups to spend. But some ad groups will NEVER spend anything, no matter how much you increase your bid.

This could be because there's no inventory available for that targeting, or because Google's algorithm believes it's very unlikely your ads will convert with your chosen targeting.

Because of this, **I recommend pausing out any ad groups where the CPA bid is greater than 3x the average Cost/Conversion for your Google Ads account overall.**

Let's say the average Cost/Conversion for your account was $20. This means that you'd pause out any ad groups with a CPA bid of $60 that have not spent at least $50 in the past 30 days.

This might sound complicated, but you can set up simple automated rules in Google Ads that do both of these procedures for you.

Watch the bonus video at

15StepsBonuses.com/CampaignSetup to learn how to set up these rules.

Expanding Profitable Campaigns With New Ad Groups

This will be one of the most important things you'll be doing to grow your account.

When you've got a profitable campaign, you MUST regularly expand it with new ad groups. If you don't, your campaign will gradually decline over time as your old profitable ad groups slowly die out and are paused.

But if you get in the habit of regularly expanding your campaigns with new ad groups, there's no reason for your campaigns to ever decline. If you get good at expanding your campaigns the right way, your campaign will produce steadily increasing profits for years.

The targeting you pick for these new ad groups will be a critically important decision. So, you need a proven system for choosing the targeting for these new ad groups.

There are three ways you can generate ideas for new ad groups:

- **Existing profitable targeting** — Let's say you have one ad group that's wildly profitable targeting the Mercedes-Benz In-Market Audience. In this case, it would also make sense to try ad groups targeting other similar European luxury car buyers, like the BMW and Audi In-Market Audiences.

- **The "Where Your Ads Appeared" Section Of The Placements Report** — By looking at this report, you can see the YouTube channels that actually showed your ad. When you see channels that made you conversions, you can target content similar to that channel.

  Let's say you were going through this report, and you saw that many of your conversions came from chiropractors' YouTube channels. You could then target chiropractor-related keywords to get more of this traffic. You could also target the names of the channels you want your ads to appear on as keywords.

- **Google Analytics** — Google Analytics can be a great source of targeting ideas to test in your campaigns. The process for doing this is a little too complex to go through here, but I walk you through it in the campaign management tutorial

15StepsBonuses.com/CampaignManagement

So, here's the step-by-step process for expanding a profitable campaign.

First, decide how many new ad groups you want to make.

Next, go through and brainstorm at least twice that many targeting ideas.

Refine your ideas, and pick the best ones to make into ad groups. Then go through and make the ad groups with the targeting you've chosen, or assign your assistant to do this for you.

I recommend outsourcing the process of creating new ad groups to a Virtual Assistant once you understand how to do it yourself. This way, you'll just have to come up with the targeting ideas. You can get someone else to actually make the ad groups very cheaply and easily, and this will save you hours of time every week.

Once you have a skilled Google Ads agency or employee working for you, the process can be even easier. You just need to identify the type of ad group you want, and someone else can do the brainstorming and make them for you.

For example, when I see a bunch of sales coming in from entrepreneurship channels, I don't bother to find a bunch of these channels to target, or to brainstorm entrepreneurship-related keywords. I just assign my CMO to do this for me. All I have to do is tell him how many ad groups of each type I want and include a screenshot of the data I'm looking at. He'll then choose the targeting for the ad groups and exactly like if I'd made them myself.

So, don't get discouraged if making new ad groups is time consuming for you at first. Once you understand the process you can easily delegate ad groups creation to a VA, and when your business grows bigger you delegate the brainstorming part too.

Refining Targeting On Existing Ad Groups And Campaigns

In your campaigns you'll have many "borderline" ad groups. These are ad groups that are almost profitable, but not quite.

To try and get these ad groups over the top, you should review the ad group targeting and try to "refine" it by taking out any unprofitable targeting.

Let's say that you're advertising a product for seniors. You notice that in one high-spending ad group, your 65+ age group is getting great ROI. But your 55-64 age group is losing money like crazy.

By pausing the 55-64 demographic, and keeping only the profitable 65+ demographic, you can probably make this ad group profitable. You'll be reducing the traffic you can get by half, but this is far better than just pausing out the ad group altogether and losing everything.

Setting Device Bid Adjustments

Google Ads allows you to set "bid adjustments" so you can bid different amounts for conversions from different devices. **I recommend always running campaigns for all devices together using this function, and never making campaigns that target phones, tablets, or computers individually.**

How do you know where you should set these bid adjustments?

Let's say you're seeing a situation like this:

☐ Device	Level	Added to	Bid adj.	Cost	All conv. value	All conv. value / cost	All conv.	Cost / all conv.	Value / all conv.
☐ Computers	Campaign	instream | keyword | FU | 35-65+, UA | GEO TIER 1	+46%	$5,534.28	8,939.07	1.62	2,225.00	$2.49	4.02
☐ Mobile phones	Campaign	instream | keyword | FU | 35-65+, UA | GEO TIER 1	-1%	$55,844.15	66,054.27	1.18	24,299.00	$2.30	2.72
☐ Tablets	Campaign	instream | keyword | FU | 35-65+, UA | GEO TIER 1	-44%	$4,737.52	4,545.51	0.96	2,492.00	$1.90	1.82
☐ TV screens	Campaign	instream | keyword | FU | 35-65+, UA | GEO TIER 1	—	$0.00	0.00	—	0.00	—	—
Total: C... ⓘ				$66,115.95	79,538.85	1.20	29,016.00	$2.28	2.74

An example of how bid adjustments should be set. To calculate the tablet bid modifier, I divided its Value/all conv. (4.02) by the campaign's average Value/all conv. (2.74). This gives me a bid adjustment number of 1.46, which is equivalent to a 46% positive bid adjustment.

You can see here that tablets are producing conversions valued at [X], compared to the ad group average value/conversion of [Y]

What I recommend doing is setting your bids to [X] / [Y]. This will account for the difference in the value of the leads these two devices are producing.

I recommend waiting at least two weeks, and until the campaign has spent at least $5,000, before making any changes to your bid adjustments.

This will ensure that you have enough data to make a good decision. Many times, initial differences in lead value from different devices will be reduced over time. So, waiting a bit will ensure you're not setting these bid modifiers incorrectly based on a few early fluke sales.

Setting Geographic Bid Modifiers

You'll set your geographic bid modifiers (bid modifiers for the different countries, states, or cities you're advertising in) the same way as you set your device bid modifiers.

- Set geographic bid modifiers for any location that has spent at least $500. You can easily see these locations by setting a filter in Google Ads.

- Set the bid modifier using the same formula as device bid modifiers:

  [Value / Conv. For Location] / [Average Value / Conv. For Campaign]

Let's say that leads you get from the U.S. are worth $20 to you, but leads you're getting from Canada are worth $10.

You'd set your bid modifiers to -50%, since your Canadian leads are half as valuable.

This process will ensure you're bidding the right amount for leads from different geographic locations, even if those leads have different values.

Geographically Expanding Your Campaigns

If you have a profitable campaign, it makes sense to expand its geographic scope in addition to your targeting.

Let's say you're running a local campaign for your martial arts school. You start by targeting everyone in a 10 mile radius around your school — and your campaign starts making great profits.

The next step would be to try targeting anyone within 20 miles of your school (but outside your original 10 mile radius.)

To test this out with minimal risk, I recommend adding a -75% bid modifier for this "outer circle" radius around your school. If it's profitable on a small scale, you can gradually make your bid modifiers less and less negative over time.

Here's another scenario to consider...

Let's say that you're an online merchant, and you can sell products in any country.

If you have a campaign that's done well in the US, it makes sense to test out other similar wealthy English speaking countries. For example, Canada, Australia, and the UK. Add these countries into your campaigns at a -75% bid modifier, and you can test them out with little risk.

You can also try targeting countries that you've gotten sales from before without spending money on advertising. You can find out which countries your customers are located in from your CRM software, or from Google Analytics.

Resolving Policy Compliance Issues

All advertisers will occasionally have to deal with Google Ads policy issues. And if you're in a high-risk category for Google, like dietary supplements or firearms accessories, you are much more likely to have these types of issues.

It can sometimes be frustrating when Google disapproves your ads or gives you site violations when you're a legitimate business selling products that help customers.

But in my experience, Google is great with working with you to make the changes they need, and you can almost always overcome these issues if you know how.

Here are a few tips for preventing compliance issues:

- Make sure to familiarize yourself with the Google Ads Policies before running your campaigns. While most of the policies are vaguely written, they'll at least help you get an idea of what type of ads might cause problems with Google.

- Make sure to have a **Privacy Policy page, a Contact Us page, and a Legal Disclaimer page on your site.** While few customers will actually go to these pages, Google requires them and they may suspend your site if you don't have them.

- The most common reason why ads are disapproved is for **Misrepresentation.** This is basically making a marketing claim that Google considers unrealistic.

  Since there is no hard definition of what is unrealistic and what's not, this can be one of the most frustrating disapprovals to get.

To avoid this, **make sure you are not making any hyperbolic-sounding claims, or quantitative claims (claims with numbers in them) which Google may think sound unrealistic.**

For example, let's say you've invented a system that allows all of your customers to make $30,000 in 30 days.

Even if it works every time, you cannot say customers will make "$30,000 in 30 days" with your system or your ads will be disapproved. It sounds unrealistic to Google, and they'll suspend your ads even if you can prove this claim is true.

You also can't say "you'll make mountains of cash shockingly fast!" This sounds hyperbolic and will trigger disapprovals even if it's completely true.

You can talk about results customers will get with more moderated language which seems more realistic to Google. Saying that your customers can achieve financial freedom, that they can build a profitable business, and they can build a great side income would all be safe options.

- The text on your page will be the most heavily scrutinized part of it. **Be especially careful to avoid aggressive marketing claims in your text.** You can make claims a little more aggressively in your video, but you should still avoid hyperbolic language or numerical claims like "make $30,000 in 30 days."

- **If you are including an attached monthly subscription with your product, make sure your subscription terms are clearly disclosed.** The user should be clearly presented with the billing terms when they check out. They also need to give "affirmative consent" by checking a checkbox next to the billing terms to show they understand.

If your ads are disapproved, here's the process I recommend you follow:

First, see if it's an issue that can just easily be resolved by fixing the ad. For example, if you have a Video Discovery ad disapproved for punctuation, you can just fix the incorrect punctuation in your ad copy and re-submit the ad.

This works for simple disapprovals, but most disapprovals will require more work than this to overcome.

If you get a disapproval for Misrepresentation or some other issue that is not easily resolved by changing your ad, call into the Google support hotline at **1-866-2-GOOGLE.** You'll get to talk with someone who can help you resolve the issue and get your ads back up.

If you have a Google Ads rep, call them directly first before calling into the Google hotline. Your rep can advocate on your behalf with the Policy team, and help you to get your ads re-approved.

Once you've called the hotline or talked with your rep, Google may ask you to make some changes to your ads or website to get back on. They'll also initiate an email support thread that you can reply to.

Make the changes to your site, and email them as soon as possible to let them know it's done. **It also helps to call in to the hotline or your rep in addition to this, to ensure they're making re-approving your ads a priority.**

If your ads aren't re-approved right away, **follow up daily by phone and email until your ads are re-approved.** Make sure you're courteous to the support agents helping you, and make sure to tell them how much you appreciate their help.

But you should also make sure to make it clear that this site violation or ad disapproval is really hurting you and your business, that you've made all the changes that Google requested, and that you'd really appreciate them making this a priority and fixing their mistake as soon as possible.

If you're running a legitimate business and you take the precautions I mentioned before, Policy issues should be rare for you. And when they do happen, you'll be able to quickly resolve most Policy issues with this process.

Making It All Come Together: Your Weekly Campaign Management Schedule

The best bodybuilders have an established routine for when they do what exercise. On Monday they'll work their chest, on Tuesdays their legs, on Wednesdays their back, etc.

The best Google Ads managers also have an established schedule and routine for when they do each task. This ensures the important stuff gets done regularly. It also prevents work from piling up in your account, so you only need to spend a small amount of time per day.

I recommend dividing your campaigns into groups that represent a manageable amount of work to go through in a day.

You'll do almost all your changes to a campaign on a set day each week, and avoid making any other changes most of the time during the remainder of the week. **This will prevent making changes too frequently to your CPA campaigns, which will give them time to learn and optimize.**

Here are the procedures I recommend doing once per week for each campaign:

Weekly Procedures:

- **Setting Bids**
- **Split Testing Ads**
- **Pausing Unprofitable Ad Groups & Campaigns**
- **Eliminating "Zombie" Ad Groups**
- **Expanding profitable campaigns with new ad groups**
- **Refining targeting on existing ad groups and campaigns**
- **Setting geographic bid and device bid modifiers**

Here are the procedures I recommend doing once per month:

Monthly Procedures:

- **Set device bid modifiers**
- **Set geographic bid modifiers**
- **Geographically expanding profitable campaigns**

Let's say that you're running a small Google Ads campaign.

Here's an example of what a good Google Ads schedule would look like for you:

Monday: Perform all weekly procedures for cold traffic InStream Campaigns (all InStream campaigns besides remarketing campaigns)

Wednesday: Perform all weekly procedures for cold traffic Video Discovery Campaigns (all Video Discovery campaigns besides remarketing campaigns)

Friday: Perform all weekly procedures for InStream and Video Discovery remarketing campaigns

1st Monday Of Each Month: Perform Monthly Procedures On All Campaigns

If you are running very large Google Ads campaigns, you can divide your campaigns into five "chunks" of similar campaigns. Here's what my ad management schedule looks like for a client who I run Google Ads campaigns for which are much larger than my own, and which go beyond YouTube Ads:

Monday: InStream cold traffic campaign weekly procedures
Tuesday: Video Discovery and TrueView For Shopping Weekly Procedures
Wednesday: Image ad campaign weekly procedures
Thursday: Search ad campaign weekly procedures
Friday: YouTube remarketing campaigns weekly procedures

1st Monday Of Each Month: Perform Monthly Procedures On All Campaigns

Sticking to a regular schedule for each client like this has been a huge part of my success with Google Ads. And you don't need to spend a ton of time managing your ads when following a schedule like this. You just need to consistently do a little bit each day.

You can divide the days up however you think makes most sense for you. But like a great bodybuilder, make sure to always do your procedures on their assigned day.

If you can do this, you will be successful with YouTube ads.

This System Will Make Hiring Someone To Manage Your Ads Easy

You can manage small campaigns with less than two hours a week of work. But as your campaigns become larger and more profitable, they'll take more time to manage.

If your campaigns get REALLY huge, they'll be so much work to manage that it'll be a full-time job. Or like some of my clients, it'll be a full time job for many different employees and agencies.

But don't worry! You're not doomed to more and more work as your campaigns grow.

In Step 15, I'm going to show you how you can eventually hire an agency or employee to manage your ads for you.

And this will be much easier to do now that you have my system. You can use it to train the guy managing your ads.

When you understand the system yourself, your chances of success when hiring someone to manage ads for you are drastically increased. You'll know who to hire, when to fire someone, what changes to ask them to make. It'll be easy to tell if they're doing a good job, and you'll know exactly what you need to do to support them.

So, don't worry! You'll eventually be able to get someone doing the bulk of the work for you using this system. You just have to understand it yourself first in order to be able to delegate it later.

The End Of The Beginning

Managing Google Ads accounts is an incredibly valuable skill. If you can do it right, you can make millions of dollars with very little time spent. **But like any other valuable skill, it takes time to truly master.**

If you're new to Google Ads, I know that this is a ton of stuff to learn all at once. If you don't feel confident you can do all the procedures I describe after reading this chapter, don't worry!

You just need to understand the ideas behind the procedures as the first step. And this book is a great vehicle for me to teach you these ideas.

But to really learn how to do these procedures, you'll need a step-by-step video walkthrough. And that's why it's so important that you watch the free Campaign Management tutorial that comes with this book:

15StepsBonuses.com/CampaignManagement

Especially if you're new to Google Ads, be sure to take advantage of that tutorial.

These campaign management procedures will give you a big advantage over most other advertisers.

But I recommend that you eventually go beyond these fundamental skills, and eventually invest in an advanced level course to take your campaign management skills to the next level.

That's why I'm offering 40% off my best advanced ad management course to anyone who buys this book. To take advantage of this discount and to learn more about the course, go to:

15StepsBonuses.com/YouTubeBlackBelt

Your Action Steps From This Chapter:

1. Watch the tutorial at
15StepsBonuses.com/CampaignSetup. Seriously, do it if
you haven't already. There's a reason why I keep
repeating myself and pounding you over the head with this
URL. This book is great for understanding the ideas behind
campaign management, but if you're new to Google Ads,
you need a video walkthrough to get the mechanics.

2. Create your ad management schedule. I recommend using
one similar to my three day schedule above if you're just
starting off. If you're already running large campaigns and
managing Google Ads campaigns outside of YouTube, you
can use the five day schedule I laid out above.

Schedule uninterruptible time in your calendar to manage
your campaigns on the days you've chosen.

3. Begin managing your campaigns, and stick to your
schedule as consistently as you can.

Step 11: Take Your Creative To The Next Level With Advanced Ad Formulas

You can get started making money from YouTube advertising by just making ads that stick to the simple "Master Formula" I gave you in Step 5. But you'll make far more profit — and you'll get your audience to love you much more — if you know how to write copy and produce ads like a pro.

This chapter will show you advanced copywriting and video production strategies that you can use to take your game to the next level.

Why You Need To Go Beyond The Master Formula

The "Master Formula" is the best way to get started with writing ads. It's a simple, effective, universal formula that I've used to create many winning ads.

But eventually, you'll need to move beyond this single ad formula if you want to get to the highest levels of YouTube Marketing success.

That's because if you write EVERY ad your business uses the Master Formula, your audience will eventually start to get bored. This is especially true for people on your remarketing lists who are seeing your ads over and over again.

Using a variety of ad formulas also increases your chances of producing an ultra-profitable mega-hit ad. And once you've got some experience writing YouTube ads under your belt, you'll really benefit from "swinging for the fences" like this.

Not only this, but you'll be able to tailor your approach more precisely to your product and target customer.

This is where the fun part really begins. You're about to unleash your creativity — and you're about to get paid shockingly well for it. So, get excited!

The Media Appearance Formula

Although digital media is quickly replacing TV, TV media still has tremendous credibility in the eyes of most people.

Most people see journalists as trustworthy guardians of truth.

While this may seem laughable to those of us familiar with the news industry, it is nonetheless the perception that most people have.

If someone sees a YouTube commercial for a product, they're naturally skeptical of the advertiser's promises until they see some kind of proof. But if someone sees a business featured on the TV news, that business has an entirely different type of stature.

When a prospect sees you featured on TV, he'll assume you're both trustworthy and popular. And he'll be much more receptive to any sales message you have for him later.

And getting media appearances is MUCH easier than you think.

Many local news stations are financially struggling. In fact, most of them are on the brink of bankruptcy because of the transition to internet media. Because of this, they're looking for any possible way to bring in revenue.

And this can work to your advantage...

Many local news stations will be willing to sell you a sponsored segment at an off-peak time very inexpensively. And buying these sponsored segments can be a great investment for YouTube advertisers.

Many business owners think that media appearances are a waste of time and money, because they typically produce very few sales directly from TV. And this is true. But there is a way you can make big profits off media appearances without needing to make sales from them directly.

What you want to do is to get a video of your sponsored news segment, and the rights to edit it and use it in your ads. Most news programs will gladly give you this when you're a sponsor.

You'll usually get a clip that's 5-10 minutes long. **To make this clip an effective YouTube ad, you'll need to edit it down aggressively to a 2-3 minute clip.**

Remove the parts that don't support your sales message. Edit it down to just the high points, and ideally a call to action at the end. You should also re-order the content if it helps your video make more sense as an ad.

I've made many winning ads for my own companies and for clients by doing this. Many of them were edited from appearances on small local news stations that we bought for $1,000 - $2,000.

If you get a profitable ad out of a local news station appearance, I recommend that you scale up and start trying to get national media.

To do this, I recommend hiring a publicist on a per-hit basis, meaning that they only get paid if they secure a media appearance for you. They can send out the clips of you on local news shows to show you're interesting and featured by other media. And if they're able to get you a national media appearance, it could revolutionize your business.

Not only do media appearances make great commercials, they can also **tremendously improve the performance of your sales video.** So, you'll be getting two opportunities to get profit-increasing marketing material out of each appearance. And I'm going to show you exactly how to boost the performance of your sales video with a media clip soon.

You'll have to pay significantly more for national media appearances than for local news. But I've gotten some HUGE advertising wins by investing in national media, and they could take your campaigns to the stratosphere as well. These media appearances will also massively enhance your brand.

When using this formula, it's critical that you review the footage closely and give your editor very specific directions for cutting it. Since there is no script for this type of ad, the editing is everything.

So, make sure to be very involved in the process, and to use the best possible video editor you can afford.

The Pure Content Formula

In markets where the customer is VERY interested in learning, a promise of content can itself be the most effective Skip Stopper.

In markets where you're selling advice (health advice, dating advice, parenting advice, business advice...etc.) this formula tends to work especially well. It also works well for products that are complex and which require knowledge to understand, like nutritional supplements, cosmetics, and software.

This formula is also great for people selling complex services, like business consultants, lawyers, doctors, and accountants.

A great example of this formula in action is Brendan Burchard's Six Keys To Motivation ad. Check out this chapter's bonus video page if you haven't seen it yet: **15StepsBonuses.com/AdvancedCreative**

One of our best known ads I made for SixPackAbs.com also used this formula, and gave the user five tips for getting six pack abs in a similar way. And many other advertisers have successfully used this same formula.

The Pure Content Formula can be powerful — but you can't just give them any content. **Your content needs to be Conditioning Content that primes them to buy.**

What you want to do is give the user a few quick tips or keys to achieving the result they want. **These should not be specific tactics to use, but rather a general solution they'll need to learn more about.** Once you've shown them what the general solution is, they'll later buy from you since you're the best provider of this solution.

For example, in Brendan's commercial, he tells you that the keys to motivation are Ambition, Expectancy, Focus, etc. He tells you the elements of motivation you'll need, but not HOW to develop Ambition, Expectancy, and all the rest.

Later, he presents his book as the solution to develop these traits.

Our ad taught viewers that the keys to getting six pack abs were intermittent fasting, time under tension training, and other general fitness concepts. Then we presented our product as the best way to learn HOW to do these things.

For the viewer, just learning that intermittent fasting was the most effective way to get six pack abs – and seeing the proof – was very valuable. But it still leaves a huge need for our product, since they don't know exactly how to implement this technique.

These are just two examples, but there are many other mega-successful YouTube ads that have used the Pure Content formula as well.

You can use this skeleton outline to create a Pure Content ad. Start by pasting these bullet points into your document, and fill in your content for each section beneath them.

- **The Big Promise, which also acts as your Skip Stopper**
- **The Conditioning Content**
  - **3-7 Quick Tips That Fulfill Your Big Promise.**
  - **These tips should be general solutions, not specific tactics**
- **The First Call To Action**
- **More Details About Why They Should Click**
- **The Final Call To Action**

To save you the work of re-typing all of this out, I've put together a Google Doc with all of the skeleton outlines in this chapter. You can get it on this chapter's bonus page:

15StepsBonuses.com/AdvancedCreative

To turn your skeleton outlines into an ads, fill in the sections of the outline with your Big Promise, your Conditioning Content, etc. Use Brendan's ad as a model, and create a similar ad for your market.

The Quiz CTA Formula

If you have a quiz funnel, I highly recommend making a few ads that use this formula. It's simple and incredibly effective when combined with a high-converting quiz.

It works because it takes advantage of quiz funnels' biggest strength: **the ability to give the user a solution designed just for them.**

When using this formula, you won't be directly attacking other businesses in your market. In fact, you'll acknowledge that most business owners in your industry are good people who genuinely want to help their customers — which is true in almost every market.

But you'll also point out that despite this, most people in your market aren't yet getting their desired results. This is also true in almost every market.

So why do most customers not get results, if most business owners are genuinely trying to help them?

The biggest reason for this is that most businesses are selling generic, one-size-fits-all solutions.

These are usually better than nothing. But customers will get MUCH better results if they get a CUSTOMIZED solution to their problem. A solution designed specifically for them, which is ideal for their needs, goals, and individual situation.

And that's where your quiz comes in...

In your ad, you'll present your quiz as the perfect tool to use to determine what the best solution for them is. And you'll show them why getting the personalized recommendations your quiz creates is the key to getting the benefits they want. Here's the Quiz CTA Formula:

- **Skip Stopper**
    - Here's why most people [TRYING TO GET A BENEFIT] aren't getting [THE BENEFITS THEY WANT].

- **Conditioning Content**
    - It's not because businesses selling [YOUR PRODUCT TYPE] are scammers. Most of them are genuinely good people who want to help.

    - But the reason why people aren't getting [THE BENEFITS THEY WANT] is that there is no one single solution to everyone's problems.

        - Explain why the same solution doesn't work for everybody in your industry– everyone has different goals, different challenges, different lifestyles, different talents, etc.

- **The First Call To Action**
    - That's why I created my quiz. In less than a minute, it can show you the best solution to get [THE BENEFITS THEY WANT]

- **More details about why they should take your quiz**
    - Tell them more about the quiz and what they'll learn from taking it

- **The Final Call To Action**
    - Tell them to go to your website and take the quiz again.

Let's say you're in the skin care market, and you're selling an acne reduction system. The first part of your script would go something like this…

Why do most people who buy acne products never see any improvement in their skin?

It's not because acne products don't work. Most of them work very well for certain people. But the problem is that everyone's skin is different. You don't know exactly what the problem with your skin is that's causing your acne — it could be excess oil, dead skin cells, pH imbalance, or one of many other issues. If you don't know your specific skin type, finding the right solution will be impossible. And if you just buy a product without knowing your skin type, chances are that you're treating the wrong problem.

And that's why I created the Skin Type Quiz...

–

Apply this formula to your quiz funnel, and watch leads and sales from your quiz start rolling in.

The Interview Formula

The simplest, fastest, and cheapest way to film commercials is with a single person. **But commercials with two people in them are more visually interesting. And sometimes they produce far more sales than monologue commercials.**

By making your commercial an interview, it'll seem more like a conversation and less like someone reading a script. And you can also get your interviewer to "socially proof" you. They can let the viewer know that you're a trusted authority, and agree that what you're teaching in the video is correct.

It's much more effective to have someone else talk about your credibility, rather than having to brag about yourself. And this makes it much more likely the viewer will believe that you're an expert.

Here's the formula to use when making an interview commercial:

Roles for this commercial:

The Spokesperson — The face of the brand. Can be you or your main on-camera talent. Their responses can either be scripted or outlined.

The Interviewer — An attractive and well-spoken actor/actress hired to introduce the spokesperson and to ask them scripted questions.

Here's your skeleton outline:

- **The Skip Stopper & Believable Promise**
  - The interviewer delivers the Skip Stopper & Believable Promise while looking straight into the camera

- **The Accomplishment Introduction**
  - The interviewer introduces the spokesperson, and talks them up as an expert in their field

- **The Conditioning Content**
  - The interviewer asks questions designed to elicit the Conditioning Content from the spokesperson.

  - The interviewer socially proofs the spokesperson throughout the video by agreeing with and amplifying their responses

- **The First Call To Action**

- o The spokesperson tells the viewer to go to your website

- **More Details About Your Website**
  - o The interviewer asks "What else will people learn from your video/quiz?"

  - o The spokesperson gives more details about why people should go to their website

- **The Final Call To Action**
  - o The interviewer urges the person to go to your site

Let's say that a client hired me to help them market a course on real estate investing. Since most of the customers in this market are male, I would pick a physically attractive and well-spoken woman to interview the brand's spokesman.

I'd have her start off the commercial like this…

–

INTERVIEWER: If you're interested in real estate investing, you need to watch this short video right now. Because in the next few minutes, we're going you can make passive income from real estate without needing to risk any of your own money.

*My guest today is Jack Smith, author of the best-selling book **How To Buy Real Estate With No Money Down**. Jack's been featured on numerous different TV shows, and he's known as the king of creative real estate financing. He also has over twenty thousand people who follow his YouTube channel to learn his real estate investing advice.*

Thanks for joining us today Jack! It's really an honor to be talking with you today.

JACK: Thanks for inviting me! It's great to be on the show.

INTERVIEWER: So, tell me...how can it be possible for someone to buy a property even if they don't have any money to invest?

[JACK EXPLAINS HOW YOU CAN BUY REAL ESTATE WITHOUT PUTTING ANY OF YOUR OWN MONEY DOWN BY FINDING GREAT DEALS, AND RECRUITING AN INVESTOR TO FUND THE DOWN PAYMENT]

–

The interviewer would then affirm and amplify Jack's response, saying things like "that's a great idea!" or "I can see how that would work."

After this, they'll ask more scripted questions to elicit more of the Conditioning Content from Jack.

Get the creative gears in your head churning, and think about how you can take advantage of this formula in your own business.

One last tip for doing interview commercials before we move onto the next formula...

Doing a three camera shoot will tremendously enhance the look of your interview commercial, and is highly recommended if you can afford it. If you don't have the equipment right now, it can be worth hiring a videographer with their own equipment to film this for you.

The Free Stuff Formula

Giving away a free item like an ebook, a video course, or a sample-sized product can be a powerful lead generation strategy. **But the biggest mistake marketers make when using this strategy is "overselling" their free item.**

Overselling free items backfires because it makes the customer believe there's a "catch." People will be wary of claiming your free item. It seems like if you were really giving away a valuable gift for free, you wouldn't be selling so hard.

It usually doesn't make sense to have a call to action RIGHT AWAY in the video before you've spent a minute or two building up to it. But for sales processes that begin with free stuff, this can work very well.

What you want to do is to begin the commercial acting surprised the prospect has not yet gotten your free item. You then give an immediate call to action for anyone who's willing to sign up right now. And then you give more details about why they need to download your free item.

The formula looks like this:

- **Skip Stopper**
  - ○ **Spokesperson runs up to the camera and acts shocked they have not yet claimed their free item**

- **Immediate CTA**
  - ○ **Spokesperson tells the prospect to go claim their free item, and that they have a limited time to do so. A graphical CTA stays on screen for the rest of the video**

- **More details about the free item**
  - ○ **The spokesperson explains more in depth why they need this free item, and its key benefits**

- **Final CTA**

–

One market where the "free stuff" lead generation is common is the survivalist or "prepper" market. These are people who buy products to prepare for natural disasters, government collapse, war, and other doomsday scenarios. Because leads in this market are very valuable, many prepper supply companies will give away a free item to get a customer on their email list.

If I were making a commercial in the prepper market, I'd start it off like this:

[SPOKESMAN RUNS UP TO CAMERA AND WAVES HIS ARMS DRAMATICALLY]

Whoa, whoa, whoa. Hold on one second. Have you really not claimed your free survival lighter yet?

[SPOKESPERSON SHOWS THE LIGHTER]

This lighter is made from solid steel, and it works even after being submerged completely underwater. And it produces a flame twice as hot as regular lighters so you can start a fire even in damp conditions.

I've got 342 of these lighters left to give away for free — and once they're gone, they're gone. To claim yours, click "Claim Now" below.

—

After this, I'd have the spokesman talk for another minute or two, telling the prospect more details about why they need to get their lighter and visually demonstrating its best features. I'd also have the spokesman talk about how the lighter could save their family if one of the apocalypse scenarios they're worried about happens. After this, they would deliver one final call to action.

If you are giving away a physical item, you can incentivize people to take action by limiting your giveaways to a certain quantity. If you're giving away a digital product, like an ebook or app, you can say that it's only free until a certain deadline.

If you have a free item people want, it's easy to generate quality leads cheaply using this formula. **But the biggest key to getting this formula to work will be maximizing these leads, so it's worth the cost of generating them.**

This means doing solid email marketing and making sure to maximize the value of every name on your list. It will also help tremendously if you can contact these leads by phone, to add another source of revenue that will offset your advertising costs.

And of course, you'll need to have your remarketing campaigns dialed in as well.

So, make sure you pay close attention to the advanced remarketing tactics I'm going to teach you in the next few chapters!

The Testimonial Montage Formula

The testimonial montage formula has been one of my most consistent winners in remarketing campaigns. It's great because it leverages the trust and credibility other YouTubers have with their audience for your benefit.

Because the audience already knows and loves them, their endorsement will carry more weight than a regular paid spokesperson. This formula also allows you to harness other YouTubers' creativity to put together a great ad, cheaply and with minimal hassles.

Here's how to use it…

First, you'll need to buy a few sponsored videos from YouTubers. The best way to do this is with **FameBit.com**.

There are many influential YouTubers out there who are willing to make sponsored videos for you super cheaply. But in the past, the problem was that it was too big of a hassle to do many small sponsored deals. Although it was easy to make a great ROI on a $200 sponsorship, each one of these took hours to put together and it wasn't practical to do at scale.

And that's why I'm SO grateful that YouTube created FameBit.

FameBit makes it quick and easy to buy sponsored videos from small YouTubers. You can post your offer and get as many small sponsorships as you want with just a few minutes of work.

You can make money from these videos directly, and there are many businesses built on sponsoring influencers. **But the ultimate way to make money from sponsoring small channels is to cut these videos into ads.**

What you want to do is to post an offer for a sponsored video on FameBit, and buy 3-5 sponsored videos. You can do this for as little as $200 per sponsorship if your budget is low, or you can spend more to get sponsorships on bigger channels.

And of course, I'm not leaving it up to you to figure out the mechanics of how to do this. This chapter's bonus video walks you through exactly how to buy sponsorships on FameBit:

<u>15StepsBonuses.com/AdvancedCreative</u>

Once you've got your sponsored videos, aggressively edit them down in the same way I recommended for a media appearance. Each one should only be 30-60 seconds long once they're edited.

Try and find an attention-getting moment from one of the sponsored videos you can use as a Skip Stopper. Put the testimonial containing your Skip Stopper first, then order the remaining testimonials from best to worst.
The formula looks like this:

- **Skip Stopper**
  - ○ **Cut an attention-getting moment from one of the sponsored videos. Make this moment the first thing the viewer sees in your commercial**

- **First Testimonial**
  - ○ **The testimonial the Skip Stopper came from**
  - ○ **A graphical call to action comes on screen here after the Skip Stopper and stays on screen for the rest of the video**

- **Second Testimonial**
  - ○ **The best testimonial outside the one already used**

- **Third Testimonial**

Ideally, you'll have more than three sponsored videos to choose from. That way, you can be selective and only use the best ones.

When using this formula, there is no verbal call to action since it's tough to get YouTubers to explicitly pitch your website like this. Instead, you'll be using a graphical CTA that starts right after the Skip Stopper.

When using this Formula, you're relying on the YouTubers you sponsor to do the selling for you. So, it's really important that you make this a win/win for them, so they're happy to keep working with you.

Now, here's a very important thing you'll need to make sure you do before using this formula...

Get a signed video release from each YouTuber giving you permission to edit their video into an ad!

Most YouTubers will be happy to do this as part of a sponsorship, but there needs to be something in it for them too. Since you're not paying them extra for this, the best way to do this will be to give exposure to their channel.

That's why for each YouTuber in the video, you should have a text graphic at the bottom with the name of their channel.

This will send some subscribers their way, so being in the ad is a win/win for them. It also helps you to establish that these are real influencers and not just hired actors.

You should also link to each channel whose sponsored video appears in your ad in the description for your commercial.

If your ad is successful, you'll be able to buy millions of views and get them a ton of exposure. And if you can do this, YouTubers will be happy to give you the rights to use their sponsored video in an ad for no additional cost.

You profit and their channel grows — a win/win for everybody.

The Question Timer Formula

The Question Timer Formula hooks the viewer's attention by asking an intriguing question, and then promising to reveal the answer when a timer counts down to zero. It gets incredibly high view rates because it gets people curious about the answer, and it also promises it in a short, definite time frame.

Here's the formula:

- **Ask A Skip Stopping Question, And Promise The Answer In X Seconds**
  - ○ **Ask an intriguing, thought-provoking question**
  - ○ **Tell them "I'll reveal the answer in just 30 seconds" (can also be 60 seconds, or 90 seconds)**
  - ○ **A countdown timer appears on screen when you make this promise**

- **Now, before I reveal the answer…**
  - ○ **Begin your Conditioning Content, and build up to the answer as the timer counts down**

- **Reveal the answer**
  - ○ **Show them the answer and proof that what you're saying is true**
  - ○ **Explain why the answer you revealed shows they need to get the solution on your website**

- **First Call To Action**

- **More details about why they should go to your website**

- **Final Call To Action**

–

Here's an example of a commercial I put together for a client in the skin care industry using this formula.

What's the easiest way for women over 50 to look younger? I'll reveal the answer in just thirty seconds.

[COUNTDOWN TIMER STARTS]

Most women our age have tried EVERYTHING to look younger. We dye our hair, we take collagen supplements, and we spend a fortune on makeup and anti-wrinkle creams for our face. But if you're anything like me, you're not completely satisfied with the results.

That's because most of us are missing the one thing that's actually the biggest giveaway of our age. And if we address this one thing, we can immediately start looking years younger.

So, what is this one thing that makes all the difference in our appearance?

[TIMER GOES OFF WITH A BELL SOUNDS EFFECT]
The answer is...your NECK!

–

After this, the spokeswoman showed how loose, sagging neck skin can make a woman look old — even when her makeup and hair are expertly done. And she shows many instances of older women who have improved their look significantly by firming their neck skin.

Once we got the prospect to accept that firming her neck was the best way to look younger, it was easy to get them to buy my client's skin firming cream later. It's one of the only creams designed specifically for neck skin, and they have hundreds of amazing before and after pictures from the cream that no other company can match.

This commercial was the most profitable ad my client had ever made, and it drastically outperformed the commercials her previous agency had made for her.

The key to making this formula work is asking the right question. The question you ask is everything for this kind of commercial, so think about it a lot before writing your script.

You need a question that will pique the viewer's curiosity and induce them to watch the ad. The question also needs to have a surprising answer that only intrigues them more when they hear it. And this answer needs to smoothly lead into them seeing your product as the best solution.

Choose the right question, and this formula can make you huge profits.

The Deep Indoctrination Series

The Deep Indoctrination Series is a series of ads intended to be used in a Designed Ad Sequence Campaign. This is an advanced type of video remarketing campaign that you'll learn how to create in the next chapter.

In this type of campaign, your customers will see ads in a predefined sequence. They won't just see whatever random ad Google thinks is most likely to convert.

The Deep Indoctrination Series can produce incredible ROI, especially when targeted to remarketing audiences. And it will build your brand and YouTube engagement far beyond what a non-sequential advertising strategy could do.

Here's the outline for the sequence of videos:

- **Video 1: Top Mistakes**
  - Shows the user the mistakes they're making which are causing their pain, and preventing them from getting the benefits they want. This video also gets them to commit to watching the rest of the series

- **Videos 2-5: Conditioning Content**

- Conditioning Content videos which instill beliefs in the prospect that will later cause him to believe your product is the best solution

- These videos are pure content and are not ads

- **Videos 6-8: Content Based Commercials**
    - Commercials written using the Pure Content Formula or which are your most content heavy

    - These are ads, and contain multiple calls to action like any other ad

- **Videos 9-11: Hard Pitch Commercials**
    - The prospect is offered a special deal which they can only get for a limited time, and only through these commercials

    - These commercials are very short and sell the product directly since the viewer has already seen many ads before getting to this point.

The Deep Indoctrination series is especially effective when used in an industry that requires a lot of trust for someone to buy from you. The application of this I'm proudest of was an ad series I created for a client who's a financial advisor.

The product we were advertising showed entrepreneurs how to save money on taxes. While it was very effective, the problem was that for many entrepreneurs taxes weren't a "pain point." They weren't aware it was even possible to legally pay far less tax than most business owners do, so they weren't seriously looking for a solution.

So, my client and I created this Deep Indoctrination series to educate them…

- **Top Mistakes**

- Video 1: The Top Five Tax Mistakes Entrepreneurs Make That Cost Them Thousands Every Year

- **Conditioning Content**
  - Video 2: How To Cut Your Tax Rates IN HALF With A Captive Insurance Company

  - Video 3: How To Save $10,000 A Year In Taxes By Renting Your House To Yourself

  - Video 4: How To ELIMINATE Taxes By Moving To Puerto Rico

  - Video 5: How To Ensure You Never Get In Trouble With The IRS When Taking Aggressive Deductions

- **Content Based Commercials**
  - Video 5: My Top Five Tips To Save Money On Taxes (a commercial made with the Pure Content Formula)

  - Video 6: Saving Taxes In The News! (a commercial my client made using the Media Appearance Formula)

  - Video 7: An interview with my most successful student (a commercial made with the Interview Formula that was also a testimonial)

- **Short Hard Pitch Commercials**
  - Video 8: Get A FREE Tax Savings Consultation (LIMITED TIME OFFER)

  - Video 9: How I Can Save You Thousands In Taxes In Our Free Consultation

- o **Video 10: Last Chance To Claim Your Free Tax Consultation!**

This series was a ton of work to create. But ultimately it was worth it because it got my clients leads at a 57% lower cost than his old regular remarketing campaign did, while also generating more than three times as many leads.

If you're selling a very expensive product, or something that requires the customer to trust you a lot, you should seriously consider a Deep Indoctrination sequence.

When To Write Without A Formula

Your experience with YouTube advertising should dictate how you use these ad formulas.

When you're a beginner, you should stick to the simple Master Formula and not worry about complex techniques. Wax on, wax off.

When you're an intermediate advertiser, you should pick from the advanced formulas. You can use more complicated techniques, but you still need to stick to what's proven.

But when you've reached mastery, you will have internalized the principles behind the formulas. At this point you can write free-form with no predetermined formula. In fact, you can create your own formulas based on these internalized principles.

Once you've internalized the principles and developed a "feel" for what will work, your ad creative will get even better.

And this is the ultimate goal of learning all of these formulas.

Like a martial arts black belt who's trained for years, you'll develop a "feel" and an instinct for what will work over time. And once you do, your YouTube ads will be unstoppable.

Your Action Steps From This Chapter:

1. Choose the five advanced formulas in this chapter that you think will work best for your business

2. Script a new batch of five ads. Each one should use one of the advanced formulas, and should be written from one of the structures above.

    (The only exception will be media/testimonial ads, since these ads have no script and they just rely on skillful editing.)

3. Film your five ads

4. Edit your five ads, and upload them to YouTube

5. Add your five new ads to your Ad Bank, and start testing them in Google Ads

Step 12: Expand Your Campaigns With My 13 Advanced Google Ads Strategies

Keyword targeting and remarketing are great to create your first campaigns. And the Targeting Ladder is a simple, effective strategy for scaling these first campaigns up.

You can make money with just these fundamental skills alone. But there are more advanced tactics that you can use within your Google Ads account to drastically scale your campaigns up, increase ROI, and grow your channel's engagement.

These are the skills that YouTube's highest spending advertisers are using, but which no so-called 'YouTube Experts' are talking about.

This chapter will teach you thirteen advanced ad strategies I've personally used to make millions of dollars.

Why You Need Google Ads Ninja Skills

If you know how to create basic Google Ads campaigns — and you can manage them well — you're already far beyond the average advertiser. And these skills will be more than enough to start making a small scale profit. So, congratulate yourself for making it this far!

But once you congratulate yourself, I also want you to realize that there's an entirely different level of Google Ads "ninja skills" the top marketers in the game have. Guys who have been doing this for decades and who have spent millions of dollars on YouTube ads go far beyond the basics and have some seriously incredible advanced strategies.

Like a black belt in martial arts, it almost seems magical if you don't know what they're doing. Google Ads ninjas can pull profit out of seemingly doomed campaigns. And if they have a small profitable campaign, they can scale it up to do mind-blowing numbers.

But like martial arts black belts, what they're doing is not really magic. Their "ninja skills" are just advanced strategies that most advertisers don't know about.

I've consulted with many "ninja" level marketers, and I've personally overseen many millions of dollars in YouTube ad spend myself. So, in this chapter, I want to show you some of the best advanced Google Ads strategies I've learned over the years. These strategies will take you far beyond the basics, and up to the "ninja" level of Google Ads skills.

Another VERY IMPORTANT Bonus Video

This book is intended to help you understand the principles behind each strategy. But with all Google Ads specific strategies, the step-by-step mechanics of what to click on to execute the strategy will change in the future.

To learn how to implement this chapter's strategy, make sure to watch the free video walkthrough I posted at 15StepsBonuses.com/AdvancedStrategies. You can watch my screen as I execute all the strategies above, and you'll learn exactly how they all work.

The bonus video will show you exactly what to click on in Google Ads to use the strategies I'm describing. And it's always updated with each new release of the Google Ads interface.

The Profitable Survey Strategy

If done right, surveys can provide you with incredibly valuable information that you can mine for ad targeting ideas. **The problem is that almost all marketers are doing surveys wrong in two important ways.**

The first way marketers are messing up is **seeing surveys only as a way to collect information, and not as a way to make money directly.** This is a big mistake. When done right, surveys can get collect information for you AND directly make a profit.

This was the biggest reason why I personally didn't do enough surveys before I learned this strategy. We'd send surveys to our email list, but I'd always hate "wasting" an email on a survey.

After all, if you have a large email list, you can make $10,000-$20,000 per email you send. I always felt like by sending a survey, I was flushing real, guaranteed cash down the drain — only to get abstract data that I wasn't sure how to use.

The Profitable Survey Strategy changes all of that.

What you want to do is send a survey to your customer email list, **but to make it an undercover sales promotion.**

Don't announce that it's a sales promotion in the email. Instead, just tell them you need their help and ask them to take your survey for a free gift.

Send out your survey, and once they take it, **give them 10% off one of your products as a "thank you" once they've completed the survey.**

I was shocked by how well this strategy worked for me, and for my clients as well. If done right, this type of email can make MORE money than the average email you send, and it'll produce great email list engagement as well. It'll be perceived as a "give" from your customers. If you had just sent a "10% OFF!!!" pitch email, it would not be seen this way.

This technique will give you the freedom to survey your email list often without losing any money.

The second way that most marketers mess up their surveys is by **asking questions only about their product or service.**

They ask the customer what product features they want, what problems they're trying to solve, what benefits they want from the product, what price they'd be willing to pay, etc.

All these can be valuable things to know and could help you improve your product and website marketing. **But I've found the MOST valuable information you can get from a survey is information that helps you improve your ad targeting.**

If you know what features a customer wants, maybe it'll help you improve your product or marketing...or maybe not. It's tough to tell. I've never seen a noticeable effect on sales or customer satisfaction from doing this kind of survey.

On the other hand, if you know what YouTube channels your customers are watching, you can plug this information into your Google Ads account. This means you can start measurably making real money from your survey data within a few days.

Here are the questions that I recommend asking your customer when using the Profitable Survey Strategy:

1. **What types of YouTube videos do you watch most often?**
2. **What YouTube channels do you regularly watch?**

3. **Across every type of product, what brands are your favorites?**
4. **Which websites do you visit most often?**
5. **What is your gender?**
6. **What is your age?**
7. **What city, state, and country do you live in?**

These questions will generate a goldmine of Google Ads targeting ideas for you.

When you know what types of content your customers are most interested in, and what channels they're watching, you can use this to generate ideas for keyword targeting.

If many of your customers are interested in videos on the same topic, you can also target that topic in Google Ads.

When you know what brands are your customers' favorites, you can use this information to choose the best In-Market Audiences of buyers to target your ads to. For example — if many of your customers love the PlayStation and Xbox brands, you can target the Video Games In-Market audience.

Knowing what websites your customer visits will help you to build custom affinity audiences. If you find many of your customers visit espn.com, you can build a custom affinity audience targeting espn.com and other similar sports news sites.

Gender and age will show you which demographics to target if you don't yet have this data in your account. It can also give you ideas for new demographics to start selling to.

And knowing your customers' geographic location can help you with the Local Sniper strategy, a strategy I'll review later in this chapter.

I recommend using **SurveyMonkey** for your surveys. They're inexpensive, simple, and their surveys work great.

When setting up your surveys, make sure that you set up all of your questions as **open-ended responses, not multiple choice responses.** This will allow your customers to respond without you feeding them pre-set, limiting choices.

Most marketers don't use open-ended written responses because it's impossible to go through hundreds of responses. But with SurveyMonkey, you can do a "text analysis" on open-ended responses to find the most common words used.

For example, if the most common word used in response to "What YouTube Channels Do You Watch?" is "PewDiePie," SurveyMonkey will scan your responses and tell you this.

The only questions which should NOT be open-ended are gender and age. Make these multiple choice, since they're discrete options in Google Ads and there aren't infinite options for customers to choose from.

To sum it up, you'll be sending out a survey to an email list of your customers — and you'll be making a profit on it. The goal of this survey will be to collect information that will improve your ad targeting, leading to even more profit.

The Combination Targeting Strategy

To keep the Targeting Ladder simple, I've focused on using only a single targeting type per ad group. **But you can actually combine multiple targeting types together to create "combination targeting."**

I don't recommend Google Ads beginners use this strategy because it'll make things too complex and confusing. And even for veterans, most of your ad groups should use a single targeting type.

But when combination targeting can really help you is when **you have a broad, scalable form of targeting which is almost profitable, but not quite there.**

One way you can use this technique is to expand your remarketing campaigns.

Most marketers can make a profit advertising to anyone who's been to their sales page in the past 30 days. But most marketers cannot make a profit on anyone who has been to their website in the past year (365 days.)

The 365 day audience is twelve times bigger. But it contains many people who might have forgotten about your business or who may no longer be interested.

Does this mean the remarketing list is worthless? No!

You just need to identify the most valuable segment of the remarketing list, and use combination targeting to hit that segment.

Let's say that you know that your most profitable demographic is women aged 35-54. In that case, it would make sense to try an ad group which is targeted to BOTH the 365 day remarketing list, AND ALSO to women 35-54.

You do this by adding the 365 day remarketing audience to your ad group targeting, then excluding all ages and genders outside of women 35-54.

Or let's say that you're selling a financial product, and the Finance topic is very profitable to you. **You could then target your ad group to people in your large remarketing list AND the Finance Topic.** This will show your ads to anyone who's visited your site in the past year ONLY when they're viewing videos about finance.

They're familiar with your business, AND they're watching videos about Finance right now. This makes them much more likely to buy from you than someone who's just on your remarketing list alone.

You can use this strategy for any targeting type, not just remarketing lists. If you have an affinity audience or any other broad form of targeting that's borderline profitable, this could help you take the ad group over the top rather than giving up on it.

One important note about combination targeting before we move on to the next strategy…

When you're using combination targeting, **it's important to know that you cannot combine two audiences together.** If you target two audiences (say an affinity audience and an in-market audience) you will show ads to users in EITHER audience, not users in BOTH audiences.

You can combine any other targeting types besides two audiences though — just make sure to watch out for this tricky aspect of Google Ads.

The Customer Match Remarketing Strategy

Customer Match remarketing is when you remarket to people on your email list. For businesses with large email lists, it can be incredibly lucrative.

Not every advertiser is eligible for Customer Match remarketing, but the requirements are easily achievable over time. At the time of this writing, you need:

- A good history of policy compliance.
- A good payment history.
- At least 90 days history in Google Ads.
- More than $50,000 total lifetime spend

If you meet the criteria, you're eligible now! And if not, you'll be there soon as long as you keep advertising and avoid policy or payment problems.

To use Customer Match remarketing, you'll first need to upload your email lists to Google Ads. This chapter's bonus video will show you how to do that:

15StepsBonuses.com/AdvancedStrategies

While it's called "Customer Match," you can actually upload any type of email list to remarket to — not just customer lists.

If you've gathered a list of prospects from a quiz funnel, for example, you can remarket to all of these prospects with Customer Match remarketing.

I recommend segmenting your list into these segments before uploading it:

- **Your customer email list (no matter when they bought or last opened an email)**

- **Your list of prospects (people who have opted in, but not yet bought) who have opened an email in the past 30 days**

- **Your list of prospects who HAVE NOT opened an email in the past 30 days**

This will divide your email list into warm, medium, and cold segments.

If you're advertising multiple brands, you can upload these lists for each brand you are advertising.

Once you've uploaded these lists, I recommend adding them to your Instream and Video Discovery remarketing campaigns.

These lists are also great to use with the other advanced strategies you'll learn later in this chapter, and with the brand advertising strategies you'll learn in Chapter 14.

My 3 Advanced Ad Sequence Campaign Strategies

Remarketing is a powerful tool — but it has some disadvantages.

The biggest disadvantage is that the customer sees the same ad over and over again with most remarketing campaigns .

After a while, the ad loses its effectiveness and starts to annoy the customer. You've probably experienced this yourself with advertisers who repetitively remarket to you over and over again with the same ad.

Here's another disadvantage of most remarketing campaigns...

In standard remarketing campaigns, there is no order to the ads that will show up. Google will just show the ad it think is most likely to perform well, even if it doesn't make sense in the context of the other videos the customer has watched.

This was a huge problem that was annoying a lot of YouTube viewers, and losing advertisers a lot of money. Fortunately, Google created a solution to this problem called **Ad Sequence** campaigns.

With an Ad Sequence campaign, you can show a series of ads to your prospect in a pre-defined order. This is a VERY powerful feature in remarketing campaigns, because it reduces problems with people seeing the same ad repeatedly.

It also allows you to educate your customers on a deeper level about why they should buy from your business.

There are three different strategies that you can use with Sequential Remarketing campaigns: **a Product Launch Adaptation, an Engagement Based Sequence, and a Sequential By Design campaign.**

The Product Launch Ad Sequence Strategy

If you've done successful product launches in the past that involved video content, the **Product Launch Adaptation** will be the best strategy to start with.

If you're not familiar with product launches, they're events marketers run where they start selling a new product, or do a big sales promotion on an existing product. They typically consist of about a week's worth of free videos educating the customer, and other free giveaways to entice people to follow the emails and videos.

At the end of the promotion, the marketer will offer a compelling reason for them to buy right away, This could be a discount, a free gift with their purchase, or a limited time window to buy.

There are many marketers who spend hundreds of hours planning a brilliant product launch, and who make millions when they launch the product to their email list. But they typically don't make anything from the videos once the launch is over.

The Launch Adaptation Strategy makes these videos evergreen, so you can keep making money off this valuable content and marketing perpetually.

Here's how you do this:

Create an Ad Sequence campaign with your Product Launch videos. Watch the bonus video to learn the mechanics of how to do this.

For the first videos in your sequence, **use your product launch videos in the order that you sent them out to your email list.**

Once you've put all your launch content videos in, put in the final video you used to tell customers the launch is now open and they can buy.

You'll essentially be putting YouTube prospects through your full product launch through these ads. If your launch was successful, chances are this ad campaign will work well too.

But that's not the end of your profits with this strategy

Add a series of five regular ads after your launch videos. Use your best performing, most profitable ads first, and your lowest performing ads last in the sequence.

These videos will pull in more sales who did not buy from the initial launch, but who were ready to buy later.

To start with, I recommend targeting your new Ad Sequence remarketing campaign to **people who have visited the Shopping Cart for the product you're selling, and customers for your other products besides the one you're selling.**

These are the most valuable people to advertise to, and the ones who get the heaviest remarketing. You'll benefit the most from showing these ultra-valuable lists a more varied, sophisticated remarketing campaign.

It's very important that you run your Ad Sequence campaign for a minimum of 30 days before assessing the results.

The first few weeks of an Ad Sequence campaign will always look terrible because most people are just watching the content videos and haven't seen the ads yet. But after 30 days, you'll have a full picture of what ROI looks like once more people have gone through the full sequence.

Run both your sequential and regular remarketing campaigns to these lists for 30 days. After 30 days, see which one got better ROI. If your sequential campaign outperformed, then keep that one...and make a new, bigger sequential remarketing campaign.

Your new campaign should target a bigger remarketing list, like your prospect email list, people who have visited your website in the past 30 days, or people who have watched one of your YouTube videos in the past 7 days.

Follow the same approach, and it's likely you can improve your ROI on these broader remarketing lists using Ad Sequence Campaigns as well.

And of course, it's fine if you don't know what to click on in Google Ads to do this right now. These campaigns are actually very simple to set up.

The tutorial at **15StepsBonuses.com/AdvancedStrategies** walks you through the mechanics.

The Engagement Based Ad Sequence Strategy

If you've got a highly engaged YouTube community and strong video content, the **Engagement Based Ad Sequence** will be perfect for you.

This is remarketing campaign which is not designed in advance, but which is created from existing content videos based on YouTube engagement metrics.

You start an Engagement Based Ad Sequence by advertising the videos that your community loves the most. And once they've seen your best video content, they'll be MUCH more receptive to your ads.

You'll be using **YouTube Analytics** to determine what your most engaged videos are. Watch the bonus video for a walkthrough of how to access YouTube Analytics, and how to get these engagement numbers.

What you want to do to make a sequence that looks like this:

- 5 Content Videos
- 3 Content Based Commercials
- 5 Regular Ads

For the Content Videos, you'll be using the five most engaged videos on your YouTube channel right now. The simplest way to do this is to use the five videos on your channel with the most organic views (views that did not come from advertising.)

You put your most viewed video first, followed by the second most viewed, and so on in descending order. If this is your first time making an Ad Sequence campaign, start this way to keep things simple.

I've also seen success creating ad sequences based on the five most liked videos on a channel, the five most shared videos on a channel, and the five videos on a channel with the highest total watch time. Later on, you should experiment with these options as well.

Once you've added your content videos, the next step is to **add three content based commercials.**

To do this, go through your commercials and find the three that teach the viewers the most, and which are the most like your regular content videos. Commercials written with the **Pure Content Formula** you learned in the last chapter will be ideal for this.

These commercials will help to make a smooth, gradual transition between your content and the ads that will come later in the sequence.

Order these content based commercials from the commercial that's made you the most revenue overall to the one that's made you the least.

Finally, put in five regular ads at the end of this sequence.

These should be the five ads that have produced the most revenue for you in the past 30 days (besides the ads you already used as your Content Based Commercials.)

Put these ads in descending order by revenue. Your highest revenue producing ad should be first. Your fifth highest revenue producing ad should be last.

Run your campaign for 30 days, and see if it beats your regular remarketing campaign's ROI. If it does, pause your other campaign, let the Ad Sequence take over, and enjoy the extra profits.

The Designed Ad Sequence Strategy

I recommend that you start with one of the two options above if you haven't yet made a profit with an Ad Sequence campaign. You can create either one with no new videos required, and often they'll work very well.

But the ultimate way to create an Ad Sequence campaign is the **Designed Ad Sequence Strategy.**

A Designed Ad Sequence is a series of ads planned as ad sequence from the start. It requires considerably more time and effort than the other two Ad Sequence strategies. But it usually produces FAR better results than campaigns made with existing videos.

And remember the **Deep Indoctrination Series** formula you learned in the last chapter? It's perfectly designed to create an Ad Sequence like this.

Here are the ads you'll be using for a Designed Ad Sequence:

- 5 Content Videos
- 3 Content Based Commercials
- 3 Short Hard Pitch Commercials, advertising a limited time deal

With a designed Ad Sequence, the key to success is making a killer first video that gets users to commit to watching the rest of the sequence.

After knocking their socks off with your best content, you tell them that you'll be showing the other content videos like this instead of the annoying ads they usually get. Tell them to make sure to watch out for them, and to watch them all the way through, since there is no other way to access these videos.

In each subsequent step, tease what they'll see in the next video. This will get them looking forward to it and will enhance the effectiveness of your ad sequence. You also want to keep reminding them that if they skip any of these videos, there is no other way to access them. They will NEVER see the video they're watching again unless they watch it right now.

This keeps your view rate incredibly high, which lowers your ad costs and improves your ROI.

Your first content based commercial should have a very soft pitch, just briefly mentioning at the end to go to your website to learn more. Your second and third content based commercial should gradually transition to a more standard, less gentle call to action.

By the time the viewer has watched five content videos and three content based commercials, they're much more receptive you directly selling your product.

So, in the final three ads of this sequence, you'll put ads giving the viewer an exclusive offer which they can only get through these ads. These ads should explicitly sell your product and promote your exclusive offer.

You can offer them a small discount on your product, a free gift with their order, or a buy one get one free deal. Basically, you just need to sweeten the deal so you can aggressively pitch your offer in the later part of this sequence without it coming off as pushy. You also want to give your customers to buy immediately, now, from this ad in front of them since it's the only way to get the deal.

Transition the ads gradually, so the first regular ad is still fairly content based. This is the biggest advantage of the Designed Ad Sequence. You can smoothly and gradually transition from content to pitch, bypassing all of your prospect's resistance to being sold to.

Your final ad will be a pure pitch — just notify them that this is the absolute last opportunity to get the offer, remind them of the benefits of taking advantage, and tell them that if they don't respond to this ad, they've lost the opportunity forever.

It would normally be a huge mistake to explicitly pitch your product like this in an ad. **However, because this ad ONLY shows to people who have already seen many other content videos and ads, it works in this type of campaign.**

If you've got a Designed Ad Sequence that's killing it on your remarketing lists, **scale up your results by moving it to cold traffic.**

Use the same approach to test out the campaign. Use the targeting in the ad group that's made you the most revenue in the most 30 days, and run this concurrently with your Ad Sequence. See if you can beat your ROI, and pause the other ad group if you do.

This strategy has produced some truly incredible profits for me. I encourage you to try it out!

The TrueView For Shopping Strategy

This is a killer strategy for advertising an eCommerce store that I briefly touched on before. **With this strategy you'll be creating a TrueView For Shopping Campaign, and designing ad creative specifically for that campaign.**

If you recall, **TrueView For Shopping campaigns are campaigns that advertise your eCommerce store using a dynamically generated "feed" of your products.** Rather than showing a call to action for a single product, the prospect sees multiple different products next to their ad.

Google chooses the products it believes your prospect will be most likely to buy. The algorithm makes this decision based on which pages on your site they've visited, their browsing and purchasing behavior on other sites, and many other factors like the prospect's age, gender, and geographic location.

Nobody knows exactly how the TrueView for Shopping algorithm works. But the fact is that it does work — and it works like a motherfucker.

EVERY eCommerce client I have ever ran remarketing campaigns for has outperformed their regular remarketing campaigns with TrueView For Shopping.

Many eCommerce advertisers even use Shopping campaigns as their ONLY video campaign type. It's that powerful, and if you have a Shopify store, you've got to take advantage of it.

While these campaigns are a powerful tool, they do also have a few drawbacks.

First, you cannot use CPA bidding. You'll need to bid the old fashioned way, with cost per view (CPV) bidding. This is a significant disadvantage, but it's easily outweighed by the huge benefits of these campaigns.

Second, **you need to make sure that the ad creative you are using makes sense no matter which products your customer sees.**

There are two keys to doing this:

First, you need to restrict your product feed for this campaign to only one category of products on your site.

Then, you need to create ads that make sense to advertise any product in that category.

Let's say that you have an online shoe store that sells sneakers, boots, and high heels.

If you create a campaign advertising ONE pair of sneakers on your site, this ad won't make sense when the user sees it. It's unlikely the product you're advertising will show up in their ad, and they may not even know how to get to the product you're advertising if they do click.

That's why when using TrueView for Shopping campaigns, **you want to make videos which promote a category of products on your site rather than an individual product.** This way the ad always makes sense no matter what products show up in your prospect's feed.

Let's say I was advertising the sneaker category. I would make an ad where the Conditioning Content taught customers how to buy stylish sneakers that look great, last forever, and which have a reasonable price.

While being educated, they'd also be indoctrinated with the beliefs that will later help them see why our store is the best.

And at the end of the ad, I'd tell them to click one of the PRODUCTS below to learn more about the sneakers on our store.

By designing your ad specifically for Shopping campaigns like this you'll get far better results – especially if you're advertising a large eCommerce store with hundreds of products.

If you run a small eCommerce store, you can test this idea out with your existing ads before committing to filming new videos.

Let's say I run a low-carb food store for people on the ketogenic diet. And I've got a commercial working like gangbusters advertising one of the ten types of zero carb bread I sell on my website.

If I restrict my campaign to only zero-carb breads, the call to action for the commercial will make more sense. The user is likely to see the product I'm advertising, and if they don't, they can probably get to it quickly from another zero carb bread page. Absolute worst case if they can't figure it out, they'll see another very similar product.

So, if you're skeptical of these newfangled data feed campaigns, test out a campaign like this and see if it works for you. If it does, you can probably make MUCH more profit by making new ads that are designed specifically for Shopping campaigns.

The eCommerce/Funnel Hybrid Strategy

If you're using sales funnels, you might have been burning up with envy reading the previous section. But I've got some good news!

The eCommerce/Funnel hybrid strategy allows funnel marketers to access TrueView For Shopping campaigns, and provides many other benefits as well.

Most businesses selling using sales funnels start with a single product. Then you add in a few upsells to support your sales funnel.

Later, you launch new sales funnels, and new upsells for those funnels. Soon, you have 10-15 different products, and it gets hard for customers to know how to find the lesser known ones.

If that describes your business, this funnel will be perfect for you.

What you want to do is create a simple Shopify store for your products. If you have fewer than 30 products, this can be done very quickly and inexpensively. You can spend more to upgrade the store later, but you just need a basic store to get started.

Once you've done that, you just need to upload your stores product feed to Google, and BAM! You can now use the TrueView For Shopping strategy without having to give up your other campaigns.

The eCommerce/Funnel Hybrid Strategy has many other benefits as well…

If you have repeat customers, you're annoying them by making them go through sales funnels to buy products they've already bought before. A sales process is necessary for a new prospect, but repeat buyers often just need a convenient way to add the products they know and love to their shopping cart.

This means that you will get more sales from your existing customers, and you will have a higher customer LTV.

And I've already spent many pages harping on how important this "Master Number" is for your advertising.

Having an eCommerce store also drastically alters the way the Google Policy team perceives you. You'll be perceived as a more trustworthy business - even if 99% of your sales come from funnels — and you'll be less likely to have Ad Policy compliance problems.

Finally, having an eCommerce store increases the value of your brand compared to using funnels alone. You'll get a higher valuation if you eventually sell your company. If you run your company long term, building a strong brand will give your company longevity and make all your ads more effective.

The Image Ad Remarketing Strategy

Video remarketing campaigns are great, but they only have so much reach. **You can double your sales from remarketing campaigns by adding image ads into the mix.**

That's because YouTube ads serve mostly on YouTube itself.

Some campaign types can serve on other sites, but they can only serve on videos.

Of course, this is a huge amount of ad inventory. **But there's also another whole universe of ad inventory for image ads on the Google Display Network.**

If you're not familiar with them, image ads are ads which contain an image with text next to it advertising a product.

Most image ads are now created in a responsive format, meaning that you upload one set of images and copy and Google can adjust it to fit any ad size.

Most exciting of all, **you can now use videos in your image ads.** This will give you a significant advantage if you're a YouTube advertiser, since most advertisers who focus on image ads typically have laughably poor video ads.

Here's how to take advantage of this strategy.

First, create a new image ad remarketing campaign.

Reproduce all of the campaign settings, ad groups, and ad group targeting from your existing video remarketing campaign.

Then instead of video ads, add one image ad into each ad group.

You'll only need one ad because each image ad is actually a set of many different creatives. You can upload multiple different images, videos, headlines, and body copy variations.

Google will test the different combinations, and serve the one it thinks is most likely to get sales for you.

I've made millions in easy profits using this strategy, and many other businesses have as well.

So why does the Image Ad Remarketing Strategy work so well?

Many advertisers struggle to get image ads to work because it's hard to convince someone to buy your product — or even to watch your sales video — using just an image and text.

Image ads are far more competitive than YouTube ads, and the vast majority of advertisers who start image ad campaigns lose their shirt.

But if someone has already seen many video ads and visited your site, it's a lot easier. Your image ad just has to give them the final nudge to buy a product they were already considering.

Try this strategy out first on your most tightly targeted remarketing lists, like your customer lists or people who have visited your shopping cart. If it works, expand it out into broader, larger remarketing lists.

Even if you specialize mainly in YouTube marketing, you should still be able to make image ad remarketing campaigns work. And if they work well for you, you may want to think about expanding your image ad campaigns to cold traffic!

The Search Maximization Strategy

The Search Maximization Strategy will kill it for you if you currently run large search campaigns, and if you are in a market where search clicks are very expensive.

One of my agency's clients is a personal injury attorney. When I first saw his Search campaigns, I almost couldn't believe it.

He was paying upwards of ONE HUNDRED DOLLARS PER CLICK — and he was actually making a profit from it!

That's because for personal injury attorneys, prospects are very rare but very valuable. They have to have gotten some type of injury recently, and they usually need to be in the law firm's city. But a single case can produce hundreds of thousands of dollars in revenue for the firm. This is why the search click costs in this industry are so insane — this type of click is actually worth that much.

I saw that my client, after investing $100+ to get a single person to his website, was not remarketing to them at all. **And I saw a big opportunity to maximize these ultra-valuable prospects.**

First, we set up a remarketing campaign targeted to prospects coming from search. You can do this using Google Analytics.

It's easy to do, and the bonus video walks you through the mechanics of doing this.

Next, we showed them an Ad Sequence of five video ads we created specifically for these search prospects.

The result? My video remarketing campaign more than doubled the leads my client was getting from Google Ads. And his cost per lead from Google Ads went down by 37%!

That's because rather than paying $100+ per click, we were paying just a few pennies per view. The additional advertising cost was minimal, but the additional sales the campaign produced were huge.

If you're running large search campaigns — or if you're paying more than $5 per click for search ads — this strategy will be perfect for you. You'll be maximizing the value of these incredibly expensive search clicks by getting them back to your website for a fraction of the cost of the original click.

The Local Sniper Strategy

The Local Sniper Strategy is when you combine very tight geographic targeting with another broad form of targeting. It works best when you're trying to attract a very specific type of valuable customer, or if you have data that shows you where your advertising is most profitable.

One example of the Local Sniper Strategy was a campaign I'm running for a financial advisor. He ONLY works with clients with a net worth over $1 million dollars, and he's built a very successful business with this strategy.

When we first met, he didn't think that YouTube marketing could work for him. After all, 99.9% of the people on YouTube wouldn't have enough net worth to become one of his clients.

I proposed that we start by restricting our targeting to the 100 wealthiest zip codes in the US. Since we'd only be targeting the top .002% highest wealth areas in the country, we were very likely to find clients with the type of net worth he needed.

To further increase our chances of finding a good prospect, I told him we'd also use other forms of targeting. But since we were targeting such a small geographic area, we would keep this secondary targeting broad. This way we we'd be advertising to people in extremely wealthy areas who also showed interest in investing and retirement, or who were in his ideal target demographic.

He took me up on it, and hired me to make the campaign. And he acquired six new clients in a single year!

Since each client will be worth hundreds of thousands of dollars in revenue to him over their lifetime, he was VERY happy with this. And since our targeting so was tight, the ad spend was minimal — so it was almost all profit.

You can use the Local Sniper Strategy this way if you're targeting a very specific type of customer.

You can use it to target the 100 wealthiest zip codes in your country if you sell a product only the rich can afford.

Or let's say you sell a high fashion product and you know that most of your customers come from large, wealthy metropolises. You could use this strategy to only target fashion hubs like Los Angeles, New York, and San Francisco.

If you run an eCommerce store that sells baseball hats, you could make a locally targeted campaign for each team's hat.

Then you could combine this with other broad forms of targeting, like demographics and affinity audiences.

Let's say that you run a large company that uses advanced CRM software to manage your business. And you're able to run an analysis showing you the 500 most profitable zip codes for your advertising.

Targeting these zip codes with other broad forms of targeting would be another great application of the Local Sniper Strategy.

The possibilities are endless. **So, consider creative geographic targeting possibilities in addition to regular targeting, and you could create some great opportunities for yourself.**

The Designed For Demographic Strategy

If you want to make profits on a large scale, your goal should be to ascend the Targeting Ladder until your ads can be profitable with very broad targeting. **And if you're ambitious, your ultimate goal will be to get your ads profitable with demographic targeting alone.**

Any advertiser who can do this will rake in millions of dollars in profit.

Of course, this is much easier said than done. But one way you can make reaching the top of the Targeting Ladder much easier is by using the **Designed For Demographic Strategy.**

This is when you explicitly design a product ONLY for one specific demographic group. Not only should your product be exclusively for people in this demographic, you should emphasize this in your marketing and actively tell everyone outside the demographic NOT to buy from you.

An example of this was a product I created at my last company, Abs After 40. By its nature it only appeals to men over 40. The product is designed only with this group in mind, the marketing emphasizes this repeatedly. It's even in the name of the product itself. And using the Designed For Demographic strategy with this brand gave us a big advantage in getting demographic targeting to work.

The best Designed For Demographic ads use at least two demographic targeting factors. This is because even when combining two different targeting factors, like age and gender, you'll still be targeting hundreds of millions of people.

Age/gender combinations are the most common way of using the Designed For Demographic Strategy. But here are a few other examples of how you can use it:

- **Products marketed towards mothers or fathers.** By targeting users who are both female and a parent, you'll be reaching your target audience very efficiently. And the same thing goes for fathers.

- **Products marketed towards wealthy men or wealthy women.** You can target the top 10% highest income demographic combined with a gender.

- **Products marketed towards wealthy non-parents.** You can target the top 10% highest income combined with the "Not A Parent" demographic. This is great targeting for many "status symbol" type luxury products, since this is the demographic group with the most disposable income.

The Ladder Hopping Strategy

The Targeting Ladder works great as a general rule of thumb. When you're a beginner, you should stick to it strictly to keep things simple.

But once you're advanced, **it makes sense to sometimes go outside the Targeting Ladder when the situation justifies it.**

And once you're familiar with all of the different Google Ads targeting options, you'll be able to recognize these situations.

Let's say you're selling a cookbook. Of course, you should start with tightly targeted keywords — but you should also consider the "Cooking & Recipes" topic right from the beginning. It normally doesn't make sense to use topic targeting right away, but in this case it does because there's a topic that's perfectly designed for your product.

Or let's say you're advertising a salon. Because there is an affinity audience called "Frequently Visited Salons" ideally targeted for your business, you should start with this affinity audience from day 1 of running your campaigns.

Or let's say you're a wedding planner. In this case, it makes a lot of sense to target the "Getting Married Soon" life event even when you're just starting off.

If there is a perfect targeting option for your business higher up the ladder, you should skip straight to that option in these situations.

Most of the time this will not apply, and the Targeting Ladder will be the best way to expand your campaigns. But once you're an expert in all the different targeting options, be on the lookout for perfect targeting options farther up the ladder as well. While these perfect opportunities are rare, they can also be very lucrative if you can find them.

How To Use These Advanced Strategies

Knowing these advanced strategies will give you a big advantage in Google Ads. But knowing them isn't enough. **It's also important to identify which strategy could make the biggest impact on your business. And you need to make implementing it your top priority!**

Not every strategy will be appropriate for your situation. And if you try and implement too many at once, you'll just end up confusing yourself.

That's why I recommend you pick ONE strategy from this chapter, and focus on getting a big win out of it.

Once you've gone through the rest of this book, you can return to this chapter and implement other strategies as well. But focusing on the one most impactful strategy you've found here will produce the most immediate results.

Your Action Steps From This Chapter:

1. Pick the ONE strategy from this chapter you think will have the biggest positive effect on your business. Highlight or underline the strategy you'll use below:

    a) The Profitable Survey Strategy
    b) The Combination Targeting Strategy
    c) The Customer Match Remarketing Strategy
    d) The Product Launch Adaptation Ad Sequence
    e) The Engagement Based Ad Sequence
    f) The Designed Ad Sequence
    g) The TrueView for Shopping Strategy
    h) The eCommerce/funnel Hybrid Strategy
    i) The Image Ad Remarketing Strategy
    j) The Search Maximization Strategy
    k) The Local Sniper Strategy
    l) The Designed For Demographic Strategy
    m) The Ladder Hopping Strategy

2. Create a campaign (or multiple campaigns) to implement this strategy in your account. After this is done, move on to the next chapter while continuing to manage your new campaigns.

3. Make your new campaign(s) the FIRST thing you check for the next 30 days in your ad management procedures. This will increase your focus on your new campaigns and help you build them into a big win.

Step 13: Learn The Top Ten Ways To Take Your YouTube Sales Website To The Next Level

You can get started making money on YouTube with just a basic sales funnel or Shopify store. But now it's time to take your profits to the next level with advanced techniques to double or triple your website's conversion rate.

This chapter will give you my ten most proven techniques to increase sales from your YouTube sales funnel or eCommerce store. Once you've got these website optimizations dialed in, building cash-generating YouTube campaigns is going become far easier for you.

Kaizen: The Japanese Secret To Improving Your Website

How can you make a web-site that reliably converts YouTube traffic into profits and loyal customers?

By using the same principle that the Japanese used to become an economic superpower after World War II – **kaizen.**

The Japanese were the pioneers in implementing kaizen. But the idea actually originated with an American named W.

Edwards Deming. Deming was a brilliant business thinker who created a system that American companies could use to make their manufacturing more efficient.

Deming tried to get companies to hire him to implement his system after World War II ended. But right after the war, American companies were on top of the world. They told him to get lost, because they were fat and happy. They didn't see any need to change anything from the status quo.

So, Deming took his system to Japan. Japan had been bombed into rubble during World War II, and its industries were completely destroyed. So Japanese corporate leaders were much more receptive to new ideas than Americans. They weren't content with the status quo – they were eagerly seeking any possible advantage that would help them rebuild.

Deming taught the Japanese his "14 Principles" for improving the quality of their manufacturing. And the most important principle he taught them was to **"Improve constantly and forever the system of production and service, to improve quality and productivity, and thus constantly decrease costs."**

Deming-advised companies would look for small ways to improve their manufacturing process every day. At the time, this was a revolutionary new mentality.

Most manufacturers wouldn't be constantly trying to improve – they would just be satisfied with whatever their current factory was producing. Their motto was "if it ain't broke, don't fix it."

They might make an improvement to their processes every year or so. But the idea of continuously making small improvements every single day was unheard of at the time.

Especially for companies that were already profitable and selling lots of product, there was not a mentality of always needing to get better.

At first, the effects of Deming-style tinkering didn't seem significant. But over time, they added up. Japan's manufacturing sector grew like gangbusters over the next few decades, and drastically outpaced the US and Europe.

This led to Japan growing from basically having no economy at all at the end of World War II, to being the wealthiest country in the world (on a per person basis) by 1980.

It wasn't good luck or something special about Japanese culture that took them from destitute to rich. **It was the fact that they learned and implemented kaizen, Deming's principle of constant and never-ending improvement.**

Why does this matter to you?

It matters because **you can use the principle of kaizen to dramatically out-perform other marketers, just like Deming and the Japanese used it to out-perform other manufacturers.**

How To Continually Improve Your Website With Kaizen

Most marketers are like American manufacturers after World War II. They're satisfied with where they're at, and they don't continually try to improve their sales website.

To get a new sales funnel or eCommerce listing working, they think they just need to come up with some brilliant marketing ideas, put them online, then watch the profits roll in!

In reality it rarely works like this.

Top marketers know that creating a mega-profitable sales process is actually a **process**. Once your website is up and running, you continually come up with ideas to improve it and to make it more profitable. You **split test** these ideas, and keep the ideas which are proven to improve your conversion.

By doing this you'll continually make small improvements to your site over time. It won't seem like a big difference at first...but over a few months they'll really add up.

If you keep this up for years, the gains you make will compound in a stupendous way.

You might think that constantly creating new marketing material and testing it will be a ton of work, and that it'll make you a slave to your business. In reality, nothing could be further from the truth. Adopting the kaizen mentality will not only make you more money, it will require you to work LESS and free up huge amounts of your time in the long run.

That's because once you adopt the kaizen mentality, your website will quickly turn into a cash-generating machine. You'll need to do the work yourself to make these improvements if your budget is limited. But once your website is profitable enough, you can hire highly paid, highly skilled people or marketing agencies to improve your website for you.

Once you get to this level, your team will continually improve your sales website for you. And once your system is established, it'll require very little work or time from you to keep it going.

You just need to put in a little work up front. If you do, you'll reap the rewards of passive income for years afterwards.

In this chapter I'm going to show you the ten most important improvements you can make to your website. By implementing these over time, you'll be giving yourself a huge advantage in YouTube marketing.

I'll start by showing you a few small, quick things you can do to immediately make a positive difference in your website conversion. And at the end, I'll also show you a few changes bigger picture changes that will take more time to implement, but which could make a HUGE difference in your business.

Implement My "Lights Out" Code To Improve Conversion

The "lights out" code is the simplest, easiest way you can get started improving your sales funnel.

Marketers have known for years that sales page which have only a video on them, and no text content, tend to convert visitors to sales at a higher rate than pages with both video and text. This is because it increases the focus on the sales video, which is the most powerful selling tool on the website.

However, having a page like this is against Google's rules – which is why you never see pages like this advertised. Not only this, but sending users to pages like this is bad for your brand. While video only pages convert, they also confuse users, make it difficult to buy, and make you seem like a scammy company.

My "lights out" script is a way to get the best of both worlds.

You can focus the user entirely on the sales video, WHILE ALSO having text and image content on your page.

Here's how it works…

When the user goes to the site, they see all the text and image content just like normal. It'll look like this:

But when they play the sales video, a script in the background dims out the rest of the page like this:

The focus is now entirely on the video. But the user also has the option to "turn the lights on" and toggle this dimming off, so they can see everything on the page like normal.

This means your website will convert like a video only website. But you also won't have problems with Google, since you have all the text content on the website that the Policy team will be looking for. And you'll be presenting a clean, trustworthy brand image to your customers.

This simple script has been one of my most consistent split test winners with YouTube traffic. Just by adding it to your site, you can increase your conversion rate by 10-30%.

That's why as my gift to you, I'm giving you the actual "lights out" code that I use in my own funnels. You can get the code and instructions for how to install it on your site here:

<u>15StepsBonuses.com/AdvancedWebsite</u>

Download that code now, and install it on your site. It will take only a few minutes, and it will probably make your advertising significantly more profitable.

In a few minutes, I'll walk you through how to split test this code on your website.

I gave this to you as the first technique so you can get a quick taste of what a HUGE impact these website optimizations can make. All you'll have to do is copy and paste a few lines of code, and you'll probably see a bump in sales right away.

Once you see these results, I know you'll be motivated to take even bigger steps to improve your site later.

Make Your Website Load Faster

A study by Akamai Technologies found that 47% of internet users expect websites to load in 2 seconds or less. This means that if your website takes more than 2 seconds to load - like most small businesses' websites do - you are losing a ton of sales.

In another study, AI healthcare software company mPulse Mobile found that their page converted at .6% when it took 5.7 seconds to load. When they improved this load time to 2.4 seconds, it shot up to 1.9%.

This means they got TRIPLE the sales with the same amount of advertising by doing nothing but making their site load faster.

There is a huge amount of research that proves how important load time is to convert prospects into customers, and even more importantly to keep customers buying from you. **But most marketers drastically underestimate its importance, because they think that getting their site to load faster is too complicated for them to figure out.**

But the truth is that there are a few very simple things that anyone can do to make their site load faster – even people like me with zero technical skills. And once you understand the basics of how to make a site load faster, you can hire a developer to do the work for you very cheaply and easily.

Here is what I've found are the most important keys to making your site load faster:

- **Upgrade your hosting.** Do you know what type of web hosting plan you have? If not, chances are that your site is on what's called **shared hosting.** This is an inexpensive hosting plan where you share a server with many other small websites.

  Because many websites are hosted on the same server, shared hosting tends to be slow and unreliable.

  Because of this I recommend NEVER using shared hosting, and immediately upgrading your hosting plan if you are on shared hosting right now.

  The best inexpensive alternative will be a **virtual private server**. This is a server where you have a certain part of it "partitioned" just for your website. This makes your site faster and more reliable. You can get a good Virtual Private Server hosting plan for just $20-$40 a month.

  If your business is doing more than $5,000 a month in revenue it will be worthwhile to get a **dedicated server.**

  This is a server that's entirely just for you. You can get one for between $80 - $400 per month depending on the quality of the server you're renting.

If you are using Clickfunnels, you will need to use their hosting and unfortunately you cannot host your funnels yourself. This hosting is OK for businesses first getting started, but eventually it will make sense to upgrade to a dedicated server.

For this reason alone, I recommend all businesses doing more than $100,000 a month in revenue consider moving away from Clickfunnels and onto their own server.

While Clickfunnels has some great features, the improvement in load time alone can justify the hassle and expense of coding your own pages once your business is making this much.

- **Use the YouTube video player.** My developers extensively tested this, and we've found that the YouTube video player serves videos the fastest and most reliably for our average user.

  This is mainly because YouTube is better at detecting the user's bandwidth and device quality and serving them the optimal sized video. It's also because the Google/YouTube content delivery network is much better than other video hosting platforms in some important countries outside the US.

  The YouTube Video Player also has some serious marketing advantages which I discussed in a previous chapter.

  It is possible to modify the YouTube video player to remove the controls, and to autoplay the video without sound. Many marketers do this because they believe it increases their conversion.

  However, my own testing has found that using the YouTube player as-is with no modifications performs best almost every time.

The reason why I believe it's worked best for me – and not for other marketers – is that I used a tested and optimized thumbnail image. Most other marketers did not think about this, and just used one of the screen capture thumbnails randomly generated by YouTube.

The thumbnail image is very important if you are using the YouTube player and not auto-playing the video.

It's what entices the user to click on the video. If it sucks, nobody will watch your sales video. If nobody watches your sales video, your website will not convert.

I recommend using the thumbnail image which has gotten the highest view rate in Video Discovery campaigns as your sales video thumbnail. You should also add text into this thumbnail image telling them to click below to play the video.

Using this approach, you'll be using an image that you know entices people to click rather than guessing at what people might click on.

- **Use Google's Pagespeed Insights Tool And Pingdom's Speed Test To Diagnose Other Issues.**

These tools are great, and they can show you an array of changes you can make to your website to get it to load faster. I've linked to both of these tools in this chapter's bonus page:

15StepsBonuses.com/AdvancedWebsite

- **Hire a developer to make these changes for you cheaply and quickly.** Unless you're a developer yourself, I DO NOT recommend trying to optimize the loading time of your website yourself. There are coders out there who do this professionally. These guys can optimize your load time far better than you can, and they'll do it very cheaply.

To hire someone to optimize your site's load time, first do both the Google and Pingdom speed tests. Then create a job ad on UpWork or a similar site for a developer to optimize your funnel pages. Give them a specific goal to hit on both tests, and a few suggestions for the most important tasks to achieve that goal.

The most impactful tasks will usually be **using WebP or another modern web image format, compressing images as much as possible, using cloud hosting for your images, and removing unnecessary scripts and CSS from your site.**

There are also many other more complex changes that they can make, but these changes are the best place to start.

If you don't understand how to do these things, that's OK! I don't either. You just need to know what they are so you can tell a developer to do them, and you need to know how to check the tests to ensure they changes have been made.

I recommend aiming for a minimum score of 80 with PageSpeed Insights, and a minimum performance grade of "B" when testing your site from the US. This will ensure your site is fast enough to convert without having to go into making any super difficult changes.

Outsourcing load time optimization of your sales page to Upwork is a great place to start. And once your business is large enough, you can have someone on your team (or a partner company) doing this constantly for all of the pages on your website.

Continually Improve Your Website With Split Testing

There are some improvements you can make to your website without needing to test them.

For example, there's no upside to having a slower website. So, you can simply install your faster page, and count on a conversion bump once it's up. No need to test.

However, most changes to your website need to be tested to ensure you're making a real improvement. This is absolutely critical. Many business owners make big changes to their website thinking they're improving it, but they're actually making their conversion rate lower.

If you don't split test changes to your site, chances are that all your hard work is actually REDUCING your sales!

The motto of salespeople is ABC – Always Be Closing.

For YouTube marketers like us, our motto should be **ABT, or Always Be Testing.** You want to be ALWAYS running some type of split test on your website. If you are not testing anything, you are missing out on the opportunity to improve your site. That means you're losing money!

If you are using Clickfunnels, there is a split testing tool built into the software that you can use. If you're advertising a non-Clickfunnels sales funnel, I recommend using **Google Optimize.** It's free, and it integrates very well with Google Analytics and Google Ads.

I highly recommend avoiding Optimizely, Visual Website Optimizer, and other split testing software outside of Google Optimize and Clickfunnels.

I've tested many different split testing platforms in the past, and I've found that many of them produce an EGREGIOUS rate of error. They're so bad that you'll think you're making your website better while you're actually making it worse.

Optimizely and Visual Website Optimizer were the worst of the worst in my test, so avoid these platforms at all costs.

To get a full breakdown of how to split test your website, check out this chapter's bonus resources:

<u>15StepsBonuses.com/AdvancedWebsite</u>

In the video there, I'll show you exactly how to perform split tests, and how to interpret the results.

Test Your Way To A Killer Sales Video

Once you've got your split testing software set up, the first thing that you should focus on improving should be your sales video. That's because it's the most important selling tool on your sales page, and it'll have a bigger impact than anything else you could test.

A dialed in sales video will also get more people to the later parts of the funnel. And this will make it faster to test your shopping cart and upsells later.

You should start with one of the easiest ways I've found to improve your sales video - **by testing shorter edits of the same video.** Especially if your sales video is longer than 20 minutes, chances are high you can beat it by skillfully cutting it down.

Here's how to do this:

First, go through your video script and cut any unnecessary parts. Remove any fluff or filler, and keep only the parts the user needs to see to move them further along in the sales process. **You should aim to cut at least a third of the content from your video for this shorter edit.**

If your video is very long (30 minutes or more) I recommend also testing an "ultra-short" edit of your video. First cut one version down to about 20 minutes, and then cut even more aggressively down to a 10 minute video.

It's important that you or another skilled marketer specify exactly which parts of the script to cut for these videos.

It's critical that you cut the right parts, and only someone with marketing knowledge can do this. But once you've picked the parts to cut, any video editor can easily follow your cutting directions.

Once you've tested a shorter edit of your video, I recommend testing a different introduction to your sales video. Since the introduction is seen by the most users, it usually has the biggest impact.

Here are a few ideas to test that have been consistent winners for my clients:

- **Media appearances.** This has been by far my most consistent winner. The key is to edit it down VERY aggressively to only the best 30-60 seconds. This will give you the credibility of appearing in the media without losing too many people before your main sales video begins.

- **An accomplishment introduction.** Having someone introduce you and brag about your accomplishments before your script begins can also increase conversion.

  You can hire an actor or actress cheaply to do this if you're just getting started, or you can ask a customer to do this for you.

- **An intro written by another copywriter.** Sometimes it's easier for someone who didn't write the video script to figure out a way to beat it. And you can hire copywriters to write these types of short intros very inexpensively.

  When hiring a copywriter, you want to structure the deal so they make most of their money ONLY if their copy beats your control. "Beating your control" means that you did a split test, and found through testing that their copy is converting at a higher rate than yours.

  I'll usually offer writers a $500 guarantee for writing the intro, and a $5000 bonus if their intro beats my control and I use it permanently.

  Since I'm only paying the $5000 if it wins, I'm always glad to pay it since I know this copy is guaranteed to make me many times this.

I also recommend **testing a quiz, opt-in page, or some other way to get leads BEFORE your sales page.** Many times, you'll find that you can collect leads without reducing your conversion at all – or sometimes even increasing it! And with the advanced follow-up strategies I'm going to teach you later, these leads will be worth serious money.

Test Your Way To A Killer Shopping Cart

Most marketers underestimate the importance of their shopping cart, and do not put enough effort into improving it. I know I was guilty of this for years. But I've since learned it's worth focusing on your cart once you've done a few tests on your sales video. Just a few simple changes could lead to thousands more in profit for you every month.

Here's the most important thing to test: a video or audio clip on your cart page. By using a video or audio clip, I've been able to MORE THAN DOUBLE the conversion of multiple clients' sales funnels.

It's by far the best way that I've found to improve shopping cart conversion, and I'm really shocked that so few businesses have caught onto this.

So, you need to test a video or audio clip on your cart page. But what should you say in your video?

First, you want to congratulate them for deciding to purchase, and affirm they made the right decision.

Next, walk them through what they'll be getting and briefly recap the benefits they'll be getting from their products. If you're offering multiple product options, explain to them why it makes sense to buy the more expensive option.

Finally, give them clear and explicit directions telling them what to do next to buy the product. And let them know how they can contact you for support if they're having problems.

The way I recommend testing this is to record a video that accomplishes the three things above. You should test this video as one split test variation on your shopping cart. And you should also test the audio clip made from this video as another variation.

I have sometimes seen an audio clip do better, and sometimes a video clip. Using this approach, you can test both audio and video while only having to film and edit once.

You should also make sure that your cart is mobile friendly, and that it works well on all devices. The key to doing this will be to regularly test your funnel out on different phones and tablets to make sure everything's working properly.

And finally, you should make sure to have a good error page for your cart. This is the page your customers will see if they attempt to buy, but their card is declined.

Most marketers neglect to make an error page, and it's costing them a ton of money!

When customers try and buy your product, the transaction doesn't go through all the time. **Usually between 20-40% of transaction attempts will decline depending on the business.**

Most people whose cards decline are legitimate customers who just made a small mistake in the checkout process. They usually typed their address in wrong, messed up a digit in the card, or are using a card that's expired or over its limit.

The majority of websites will just tell them their card declined, and they'll display an unpleasant, techie-looking looking error message. The user is coldly informed their card has been declined, with no information as to how they can fix this. This makes them feel stupid and like they failed. Many potential customers will just give up on purchasing because of this.

But there's a much better approach…

What you want to do is make a dedicated error page that will display anytime someone's transaction is declined. This page should have a different video on it that walks them through how to fix the error so they can buy from you.

Here's what you should say in your video, and in the text of your cart's error page:

Tell them there's an issue, but it'll be easy to resolve and you'll walk them through how to do it.

Then, just tell them how to double check for the most common source of decline producing errors – their name, address, card number, expiration date, CVV, etc. Tell them to try again if they find a mistake. If that doesn't work, tell them to try again with a different card. And if they're still having problems, give them directions to call or email into your support team so you can help them put the transaction through.

With a page like this, you can get many customers to buy who otherwise would have given up. And all those additional sales are pure profit, going straight to the bottom line.

Master The Art Of The Upsell

When using a sales funnel, your upsells are also super important. **A well designed upsell funnel can produce 50-100% of the revenue of the first sale, and you should work on improving your upsells until they're in this range.**

This means that if you are selling a $100 product, you should be making an average of an additional $50 per order – AT THE MINIMUM.

If you're making less than this right now, that's OK. But you should obsessively focus on improving your upsells until you get to this level. You can get there with just a few days' work on marketing improvements. And these improvements will EXPLODE your profits from your YouTube campaigns.

The most important thing to know about improving sales funnel upsells is that **your first upsell will produce the vast majority of your sales.** Because of this, you should spend at least 80% of your time and effort on improving the first upsell.

The remaining 20% of your time spent optimizing upsells can be spent on your later upsells, which are much less important.

So, here's an approach you can use to CRUSH it on the first upsell.

I learned this upsell method from my friend Justin Goff when I attended his $25,000 advanced copywriting seminar. I've personally used it to beat multiple controls, and many other top internet marketers have as well.

First, you want to make your first upsell appear to be a video only page when the user first lands on it. They should see the video only, and no other content on the page besides this and a headline telling them to watch the video.

Once you mention the price of the product, you should use a **delay script** to make the buy button and some text describing the product appear. The customer should see ONLY the video when they land on the page, and the buy button and other content should show up later.

This way you'll have a few minutes to properly frame the product you're upselling before putting a buy button in their face. It sounds like a small detail, but I've found its made a huge difference in how upsell pages like this convert.

Any developer can set up a simple delay script like this to hide the buy button until a certain number of seconds has passed. You can even copy and paste a script that will do this off many coding websites, and build the page yourself.

Your upsell video should be 15-20 minutes long – MUCH longer than upsell videos typically are. It should almost be like another sales video, but designed for someone who's already bought something from you.

The video should congratulate them on their purchase, and remind them of the benefits they're about to be getting. But then, your video should tell them how this second product is complementary and will help them get even more of the benefits they want.

Let's say that you're selling a diet program. You could start your video by reiterating all the benefits they'll get from the diet they just bought.

But then you could tell them "wouldn't it be nice if you had a way to accelerate your progress with this diet, and make losing weight faster and easier?"

Then you can show them how your weight loss supplement, or your exercise course, or another product does this.

Or let's say that you're selling software that helps used make a budget. On your first upsell, you could ask them "wouldn't it be nice if you had someone to walk you through the software, so it's easy and you ensure you're saving the most possible money?"

Then, walk them through exactly how your second product will get them those benefits.

This is the big picture strategy you can use to make a winning upsell video. But of course, to truly master creating upsell videos there are a lot more details you'll need to learn.

So, I'll leave you with one final tip, which will be the ultimate long term key to developing a great upsell sequence.

The best way to learn to make great upsell videos is to go through heavily advertised YouTube sales funnels, and to record and take notes on all of the upsell videos you see.

By doing this, you'll learn what top marketers are doing firsthand. Just by buying a cheap product, you can learn as much as you can from a $10,000 seminar – and for a fraction of the cost.

If you're really a cheapass, you can even refund the product after you've bought it. I'd recommend keeping it just for good karma though. Since you're learning from their upsell funnel, the least you can do is to send them a $20 sale in return.

Use Ad Level Testing For Shopify Stores

One major disadvantage of using Shopify is that it's very difficult to perform split tests on your website. And this is a REALLY big deal.

A skilled marketer can improve his conversion by about 30% EVERY MONTH through split testing. If he does this every month for six months, **his website will be converting 371% better than when he started.** But if you're using Shopify and you can't test at all, your website will stay the same.

This isn't acceptable. But fortunately, there's a workaround that you can use to get the benefits of split testing with Shopify.

Here's how I recommend doing this…

First, **test the three products on your store you think are most likely to convert highly to YouTube traffic.** Put a lot of effort into these pages, and make sure they have a strong sales video, and that they're well designed.

Next, make one YouTube ad for each product. You'll have three ads in total, and they should all be written and filmed with a similar style.

Then you run your campaign, and test the ads out!

Run the campaign for at least one week, and spend at least $2000 on each ad. At the end of the campaign, the product with the highest ROI is your winning product.

Focus on advertising this product on cold traffic moving forward. Keep you ads for the other products, but only use them in remarketing campaigns.

Once you've determined your highest converting product, the next step is to try and improve the conversion of your page.

With this round of testing, you'll want to create two new sales video variations to test on your website. Put these videos on two separate pages. Make the new pages "unlisted" pages on your Shopify store, so they only show up to users clicking on your YouTube ads. This will prevent cluttering your site with duplicate listings while you're testing.

You'll be advertising the same video for every variation – the same one that you used previously for this product. But for each variation, you'll be linking them to a different landing page.

Run your campaign for another week, and spend at least $2000 advertising each variation. See which page variation performs the best. The page that produces the best advertising ROI becomes your new control. You can then confidently delete the other listings from your site, and make this the new page for that product.

Once you've determined the best page, then you can test different variations of ads going to that page.

By using Google Ads to split test your store like this, you'll be leaps and bounds ahead of most Shopify store owners. Most eCommerce store owners are totally unscientific when it comes to improving their site, and as a result of this they never make any meaningful improvements to their conversion rate.

If you can steadily make small improvements to your store over time, they'll add up very quickly. Soon you'll dominate your industry and leave your competition in the dust.

Use The Best Shopify Apps & Themes

Shopify is great software, but to get the most out of it you need to be using the right **apps** and **themes**. "Themes" are designs that customize the look of your store, and "apps" are plugins to the Shopify software that add additional functionality.

Here are the most important functions that you'll need:

- **A theme that not only supports video, but emphasizes it.** Some Shopify themes do not support video at all, or make it difficult to put video on your site.

  These themes are a catastrophe for YouTube marketing and should never be used. Since you're advertising to a site full of video watchers, you MUST use video as the main selling tool on your website.

  That's why it's important to use a theme that supports using a video, and makes adding a video to a page simple and easy. But the best Shopify themes will EMPHASIZE the video in the theme, and put it front and center on every product listing page.

Ideally, your theme will support both a sales video AND product images on each page. If the theme you like does not do this, it'll be worth paying a developer to customize the theme for you to add this functionality.

- **An app that allows you to do continuity (monthly recurring orders.)** This is a MUST-HAVE for your site if you're selling any consumable product, like lotion or supplements. You can offer the user a small incentive (like 10% off) to make their order a regular monthly order. 10-20% of people will choose to do this, adding thousands in passive income from recurring orders to your business every month.

  Because competition in the Shopify App marketplace is intense, the best app for doing this will change regularly. **Check out the bonus resources page to get the app I'm currently using for Shopify Subscriptions.**

- **Apps that will let you do upsells in your shopping cart and after the sale.** Shopify's base software does not let you do upsells, and most Shopify users are foolishly neglecting to add upsells to their store. But you can add upsells – and extra revenue from every order – to your store with just a few simple apps.

  See the bonus resources page for the apps I currently recommend for shopping cart and post-sale Shopify upsells.

  15StepsBonuses.com/AdvancedWebsite

These are the most essential Shopify customizations you'll need to get started. But there are many more apps out there you can explore that will enhance your store.

You can add apps that increase sales with promotions, apps that enhance your Shopping feed for TrueView ads, apps that convert prices to users local currencies...and much more.

The incredible variety of apps available is one of the biggest advantages of Shopify, and it's important to take advantage of these apps if you're using a Shopify store.

Master Email Marketing Follow-up

Most people who go to your website will not buy on their first visit. **That's why it's so important to collect leads on your site – so you can continue to build trust and market to these people through email.**

Email is an incredibly powerful marketing tool in the hands of an expert. Skilled email marketers will commonly make double or triple their immediate sales from later sales made through email marketing. And if you can do this, it would tremendously help your YouTube advertising.

Many marketers think email marketing doesn't work anymore. But that's just because they suck at doing it. While it's gotten harder to get email delivered, it's still possible to make big profits if you're doing things right.

Here are a few guidelines to follow:

- **Focus mostly on your EMAIL DELIVERABILITY -- not your email copy.** This is the most important mindset shift you need to make if you want to be successful with email marketing.

    Most marketers obsess about their email copy, but know nothing about the process to getting their email into the customer's inbox. Their brilliant copy then just goes into the Promotions folder or Spam box, and never gets read.

There is a lot that goes into getting your email delivered at a high rate. But now that you know that this should be your focus, you'll be able to make huge improvements to your email revenue with just a few days of focused learning.

- **Make sure you are using a dedicated IP address.** Your IP address is a unique number that tells mail services like Gmail, Yahoo Mail, etc. who is sending your email. And it's super important for getting your emails delivered!

  There are two types of ESPs (software that sends your email for you.) Some will send your email from a shared IP address, and some will give you a dedicated IP address just for you.

  You want to make sure to always get a dedicated IP address (or multiple dedicated IP addresses) to send your email from even though it costs a little more. That's because if you're on a shared IP, you will have no way of improving your list engagement.

  List engagement is that determines whether your emails will be delivered or not. A shared IP service therefore dooms you to be stuck in the Promotions Gmail tab – or even worse, the spam box. But when you're doing the right things with a dedicated IP, you'll get better email deliverability and sales.

- **Keep your list engagement high.** You should aim for an open rate of at least 20% of your emails to start with. Your open rate is the ratio of people who opened your email divided by the total number of emails you sent.

If your open rate is under 20%, then simply send your email to a smaller segment of your list.

Let's say I'm mailing everyone on my list right now, and getting an open rate of 5%. Not good! If I just keep mailing with this terrible open rate, I'll eventually get stuck in the spam box permanently. And eventually even fewer people will be able to read your emails!

So what I'd do is **only mail people who have opened another email within the last 60 days.** Most ESPs can create "segments" of users on your list like this very easily.

If that didn't get me over 20%, I'd then cut it down to anyone who opened in the last 30 days...and so on, until I hit my target open rate.

It seems like you'd be reducing your sales by just mailing a tiny fraction of your list like this. But the truth is you'll get more emails delivered and you'll make more money with this high engagement approach in the long term.

That's because you'll establish a good reputation with ISPs like Gmail, Hotmail, and Yahoo Mail. And once you do, they'll put your email in the user's Primary tab more often. Once this happens, you can mail a larger segment of your list and still get good engagement metrics.

Open rate is one of the most important engagement metrics and the best one to start optimizing for. But there are other important engagement metrics you need to watch as well, like spam complaints, clicks, click-to-open ratio, and whitelists. Once you're an advanced email marketing ninja, you should make sure these metrics are optimized as well.

- **Set up an autoresponder that's also a Designed Ad Sequence.** An autoresponder is a series of emails that is automatically sent out to a subscriber after they sign up. For example, you could set up an autoresponder to send a new email every day for seven days after they subscribe.

The best autoresponders give the user Conditioning Content over the course of a few days, and follow that up with a sales promotion immediately afterwards. **And you can get double mileage out of the videos you make for your Designed Ad Sequence by also using them for an autoresponder.**

What you want to do is to send a short email each day teasing that day's video, and getting users to click to watch it.

But rather than sending them directly to YouTube, you'll want to link your email to **a simple page with the video embedded on it.** That's because you can put a link to your sales page beneath the video, and eliminate the distractions of related videos from other channels showing up in the sidebar.

I've gotten great results using Ad Sequence videos as autoresponders, and I encourage you to try this approach as well.

- **Hire someone as soon as you can to send a daily broadcast email for you.** A "broadcast" is a one-time email that's sent to a segment of your list. And the best way to maximize your list engagement and email revenue is to send a new short broadcast email every day.

This is a lot of work. It's not practical for most business owners to do this while also creating YouTube videos and optimizing their funnel. **So, I recommend hiring someone to write a daily broadcast email for you as soon as possible.**

You can hire someone to do this as cheaply as $25 per email. Even businesses just starting off should be able to recoup this cost with a few email sales. And you can even hire an email marketing agency that will manage your email marketing for a percentage of the revenue, with no money at all due up front.

The key to success when hiring a cheap writer or agency is to rely heavily on your YouTube videos for content. Most email copywriters can put together decent short sales promotion emails, but they aren't experts in your industry like you are.

By mailing to your YouTube video subscribers, you can send your users better content with far less work. You'll also be increasing the engagement your videos get, leading to more people discovering your videos on YouTube.

- **Get started now, and learn more as you go.** Just by doing the basics I outlined here, you can probably increase your sales by 30-50% vs. doing no email marketing at all. So, get started and do this now, even if you don't know anything about email marketing!

Once you're up and running, you'll want to continually learn more about email marketing over time. These guidelines are a great starting point, but you'll get the most out of email marketing once you've mastered more the more nuanced details of deliverability and structuring email sales promotions.

I encourage you to invest in your education in email marketing once you've got it making some money for you. It's just as important as your website conversion and advertising, and mastering it will help you tremendously to scale up your YouTube marketing campaigns.

Double Your Profits With Phone Sales Follow-up

Imagine if you could DOUBLE the amount of revenue and profit your ad campaigns were making – without spending a single dollar more on advertising.

And even better: imagine if you could do this without making a single change to your website or ads!

You don't have to imagine. You actually CAN do this – **by adding phone sales to your business.**

For my companies and for many of my clients, this has been the key to being able to buy YouTube advertising on a huge scale.

When you add phone sales to your business, your customer lifetime value will become much higher. And because your customer LTV is higher, you can afford more advertising.

So not only will you make more profit per customer, you'll acquire many more customers than you could without a phone team.

Most businesses aren't using phone sales because managing a large phone sales team is a big hassle. But there are ways you can get started quickly and easily. And once your sales grow to a certain point, you can easily hire a phone sales manager who will do most of the work for you.

Here are a few tips to get you started:

- **Call your declines!** If you're selling online, you have customers who are trying to buy but who were not able to check out for one reason or another. **At the bare minimum, you or someone on your team should contact people whose card declined and help them put their order through.**

  I did this myself in the early days of Six Pack Shortcuts. Even though I had zero sales skills, I was able to close thousands of dollars in revenue simply by typing customers' cards in for them, or asking them for a different card. Some customers just wanted to talk to a real person to be reassured we were a legitimate business, and they put in big orders as soon as we had a quick phone call.

  You or someone on your team can do the same thing, and get thousands of dollars a month in easy revenue from these declines – even if you're an awful salesman like me.

- **Hire ONE Killer Salesman To Call Your Customers First.** A large phone sales team can be difficult to manage. But a single star salesperson can add a ton of money to your bottom line without requiring a ton of management. Find someone who has a track record of being a star in another sales organization, and get him to join your team.

  Start him off by only having him call your customers, and seeing if there are any additional products they'd like to order. Just by doing this, you'll add thousands to your revenues and profits with very little work required on your part.

- **When you're ready to scale up, invest in a great phone sales manager.** A single sales agent can add as much a million dollars a year in revenue to your business. But to go beyond this, you'll need a team.

    It's not practical to manage a phone sales team and an online business at the same time. So to make both successful, you'll need to hire a great phone sales manager to handle most of the day-to-day work needed to run your phone team.

    A great phone sales manager can handle your hiring, setting quotas, writing scripts, distributing leads to sales agents, and the hundreds of other important things you need to do to run a great phone sales team. And if you're serious about building a large in house phone team then this will be the most important person to hire.

Adding an in-house phone sales team can be very powerful, but it's also a lot of work. But even if you don't want to do the work yourself, there's still no excuse for not doing phone sales!

There are outsourced call centers that you can work with that will handle the phone sales for you in return for a percentage of the profits.

This can be a great solution for anyone who wants to take advantage of phone sales without actually doing the work to set up an in house team. You'll need to give your call center a cut, but you'll still have a lot more money after this compared to if you didn't do phone sales at all.

Use The Best Software For Your Business

To use all of the advanced strategies in this chapter you'll need software. Your software will handle sending your emails, split testing your website, managing your customer data, and many other important tasks.

Because of this, it's important that you're using the absolute best software available for your business. But I know it's hard to tell what software is the best if you haven't spent a lot of time studying the different options.

That's why I put a complete list of my current software recommendations to execute the strategies in this chapter in bonus resources. I've spent many hours testing different software packages, and you can benefit from my experience and take the shortcut to the best products.

To get my current software recommendations – and videos walking you through all of these advanced strategies – go to:

15StepsBonuses.com/AdvancedWebsite

Your Action Steps From This Chapter:

1. If you are using a sales funnel: implement my "lights out" code on your YouTube funnel sales page.

2. If you are using an eCommerce store: Install the apps that I recommend in the bonus resources, and any other apps you think will improve your store performance.

3. Choose ONE additional strategy from this chapter to focus on implementing over the next week. Think about what would have the most impact on your business that's also realistic to get done in that timeframe.

For example, if you see a big opportunity to improve your upsells focus on this. If you're not doing email marketing and you think this would add a ton of sales to your business, make email marketing this week's focus. Whatever your biggest opportunity for improvement in, take that area of your marketing to the next level this week.

Step 14: Build A Valuable, Long-Lasting Brand With The Four Pillars Of Modern Branding

Making a direct response profit from your advertising is important. It's what keeps you in business, and allows you to fund your ad campaigns. But building a valuable brand is very important too!

A valuable brand will make people more receptive to your ads, so all of your ads will convert higher. A trusted brand also gives your company staying power, so you know your company will last for years. And if you want to sell your company one day, having a great brand will tremendously increase your payout.

This chapter will give you advanced Social Response tactics to build a great brand while making a profit from your ads at the same time.

Old-Fashioned Branding vs. Modern Branding

Most business owners appreciate the value of a strong brand. The problem is that they're trying to build their brand using old-fashioned, antiquated tactics. While these tactics worked to build many iconic brands in the past, they're no longer effective in the social media era.

Before the social media era, branding was mostly based on "getting your name out there." The thinking was that the more people recognize your brand name, the more likely people were to buy your products.

So, business owners spent tons of money on TV commercials, radio spots, billboards, etc. that "got their name out there." If studies showed more people recognized their brand after they ran the campaign, they considered it a success.

This approach worked in the 1900s to build legacy brands like Coca-Cola, Nike, and Budweiser. **But every business that's tried this approach to build a new brand after the year 2000 with traditional brand advertising has catastrophically failed.**

Think about it. Can you name a single NEW brand that's been built in the last twenty years using traditional "get your name out there" brand advertising?

You can't, because there aren't any.

The reason for this is that since the 1980s, people have been saturation bombed with this type of advertising across many different mediums. So many companies "got their name out there" that this technique stopped being effective.

But there have been MANY new, valuable brands built in the last twenty years. **They just weren't built with traditional broadcast brand advertising. These brands were built with a modern approach that's designed to work in our social media dominated world.**

Tesla: The Best Example Of Modern Brand Building

By far the most valuable brand built from scratch in the past twenty years is Tesla. And it's important to note they built their brand by doing no traditional brand advertising whatsoever.

Tesla only spends a tiny amount on brand marketing compared to other companies their size. Yet, their brand is growing in value faster than any other company founded in the last twenty years.

So, what is driving Tesla's success?

Of course, the quality of their products and the fact that many people support their mission of fighting climate change is one part of it. But there are many other car manufacturers who make electric cars just as good as Tesla's who have no following at all.

The reason why Tesla dominates the electric car industry — and other companies with great products are shut out — is because of Tesla's huge social media following.

For example, on YouTube alone Tesla has **more than a million subscribers.** And they've got dozens of videos with more than a million views.

And this is really only the tip of the iceberg. **In addition to their own channel, Tesla has millions of people TALKING about them on social media.**

Many people discover Tesla through videos on YouTube.

There are millions of views on videos of Teslas doing things like self-driving or using Ludicrous Mode.

Many people discover Tesla through social media videos like these. **And Tesla's popularity on social media - both on its own channel and with other channels talking about them — is the true source of their brand's strength.**

People who are engaged with the Tesla brand already are very receptive to its advertising. They've got such a rabid fan base that they got 325,000 people to pre-order their Model 3 within 24 hours of the car being launched.

Obviously, we'd all love to have such a valuable brand. But the question is, HOW do you build social media engagement like this is you don't have world-changing products like Tesla, or charisma like Elon Musk?

The answer is by using a new and different type of brand advertising called **Modern Branding.**

The Four Pillars Of Modern Branding

I've spent years thinking about this question and experimenting with different branding strategies. And what I've concluded is that building a valuable brand comes down to building these four "pillars" that will support your branding.

So, here's what I recommend you to build a brand in the social media era:

1. **Avoid brand-damaging business tactics**

2. **Have a brand advertising budget that makes sense given the size of your company**

3. **Estimate how much each subscriber is worth to your business as accurately as you can**

4. **Run brand advertising campaigns whose main goal is to grow your YouTube channel's subscriber base**

I'll walk you why each pillar is important, and how to use each to build your brand.

Pillar 1: Avoid Brand Damaging Business Tactics

For the most part, what's good for your brand will also make the most immediate sales. **However, some marketing tactics can produce great immediate sales, but will hurt your business in the long term.**

For example, let's say that you deceptively signed someone up for a monthly membership on your site, and they didn't clearly understand the billing terms.

On a direct response basis, you'd probably show that this funnel was more profitable than one that didn't contain this deceptive monthly charge. But this is one of those rare cases where the numbers can deceive you.

That's because using tactics like this will cause long-term problems for your business. Even if tactics like this make you far more money immediately, they won't be worth the damage they do to your brand.

When your customers see your sneaky monthly charge, they'll feel tricked and they won't buy from you again. They'll tell other people about their bad experience. And they may even complain to Google or YouTube and get your ad campaigns shut down.

Because of this, it's important to establish from the start that certain tactics are unacceptable in your business regardless of how profitable they might seem in the short term. Besides deceptively signing someone up for a monthly membership, here are a few other examples of this:

- Sending users to a website that converts well, but which is a frustrating user experience

- Expressing an opinion on a controversial political or religious topic that will alienate many of your customers

- Using false scarcity or discounts. For example, telling a user they can only get a deal in the next five minutes when it's really available forever

- Allowing your phone sales team to charge customers who did not clearly and explicitly consent to the order

- Offering an unconditional money-back guarantee policy, and then hassling people who want to get a refund

Basically, anytime you deceive your customer or mistreat them it'll damage your brand in some way — even if it makes you an immediate profit. You might not feel the effect right away, but mistreating customers will eventually come back to haunt you.

To avoid this, I recommend writing out "brand guidelines" that define the brand-damaging things that nobody in your company is allowed to do. Making this clear will avoid most problems from the beginning.

What To Do If You Screw Up

Even if you have good intentions and clear brand guidelines, you still aren't going to be perfect. No business is, and occasionally you are going to do something that pisses some of your customers off.

Because of this, it's also important to consider customer feedback on social media and to respond to it.

The clearest example of this is with your ads themselves. Since users can "vote" on an ad through liking or disliking it, you'll immediately see how they emotionally react to it in addition to how many people bought.

I recommend enabling likes and dislikes on ALL of your ads, and taking down any ad which gets over 50% dislikes.

Now, it's important to note that users only have the ability to like or dislike a commercial when it's shown as a Video Discovery ad. For InStream ads, your customers will not be able to like or dislike your ads most of the time. And this is why you should do a small amount of Video Discovery advertising on EVERY commercial you make.

If your budget is limited, just spend a dollar per day on each ad in Video Discovery campaigns. Even this tiny spend will give you enough user feedback to judge whether an ad is brand damaging within a few weeks.

This feedback is very important, because it allows you to catch any mistakes you make early – before they alienate many customers.

A very high dislike ratio indicates that something in your ad is pissing a lot of people off. It's not worth running a brand-damaging ad like this, since there are many ways you could make the same amount of profit while building your brand.

Even if you're making a million dollars a day from the ad, you can probably make just as much — or more — if you re-work the ad in a more customer friendly way.

You can't measure feedback on your website and products as closely. But you should monitor talk about them on social media, and if any brand-damaging issues come up you should respond to them.

For example, let's say that you see many people on social media are complaining that your sales video is long and annoying. And let's say that this video is converting very well for you — putting you in a bind.

You can't just take the video down a put up a shorter one, because you'll probably get a fraction of the sales and go out of business.

But you can make it a priority to test shorter videos that are a better user experience. Given time and focus, you can probably find something that converts just as well or better — and which is better for your brand.

Pillar 2: Have A Brand Advertising Budget That Makes Sense Given The Size Of Your Company

You need to spend the right amount on branding. Too much and you'll go broke before you start to see the benefits of your brand advertising. Too little, and you'll be squandering an opportunity to build a valuable asset.

So how do you know the right amount to spend?

First of all, I recommend that businesses **have a brand advertising budget of ZERO until they reach $50,000 in monthly revenue.** You should still have brand guidelines, since it doesn't cost you anything to avoid brand-damaging business practices. But in the very early stages of a business, you need to focus on making a direct response profit first and foremost.

That's because learning how to make a direct response profit from advertising is hard enough, and adding branding to the mix when you're an advertising neophyte will make it too complicated.

There are other important reasons to avoid branding in the early stages of your business as well.

Before you're making $50,000 a month in revenue, you need to re-invest every dollar into getting you more immediate sales. Until you've built up a large enough customer base and cash reserve to be confident your business will last at least another five years, getting to this point needs to be your priority.

But once you are making at least $50,000 a month in sales, investing in branding is worthwhile. A business this size will probably last for years longer, justifying an investment in brand building. Not only this, at $50,000/month you're approaching the size where you may even be able to sell your business.

Spending a small amount in improving your brand is clearly a good investment at this point, even if it takes a year or two to start paying off.

But how much should you spend on brand advertising?

There is no mathematically correct answer to this question like there is with direct response advertising. But over the years of doing it, I've come up with a good rule of thumb that's worked very well for me and for my clients.

It's called **The 1% Branding Solution.**

The 1% Branding Solution

Once you're making more than $50,000 per month, you should set your brand advertising budget to 1% of your revenue. **This means that you'll start by spending just $500 a month on your branding campaign.**

Even with a very small budget like this, you can significantly improve your customers' perception of your brand. It doesn't cost much to reach your customers, since they're only a tiny fraction of the people you're advertising to. And you can really do a lot to improve your company's image when you show them the right brand-enhancing videos.

But it gets even better than this…

When you're following my approach, **your branding ads will also make some revenue for you on a direct response basis.** While they may not be as profitable as your regular campaigns, they also won't be a total loss.

Well-run branding campaigns usually make about 75% of what's spent on them back on a direct response basis. **This means that if you're spending 1% of your revenue on branding, you are really only spending .25% of your revenue after subtracting the sales these campaigns directly made within a few days.**

Is it worth .25% of your revenue to make your customers and most engaged fans more responsive to every other ad you run? Is it worth .25% of your revenue to massively grow your YouTube subscribers, and to dramatically spike the engagement on your channel?

I think so. And even if you're a hardcore direct response marketing dogmatist, I think you'll agree.

But let's say you're ultra-cheap, and you're not even willing to spend 1% of your revenue on brand advertising. **In that case, start with a branding budget of .1% of your revenue.** If you're making $50,000 a month in revenue, surely you can spare a mere FIFTY BUCKS to try this branding thing out.

I think you'll be pleased with the results if you try this on even a miniscule scale. And you'll quickly see why spending the full 1% makes sense.

Pillar 3: Estimate Subscriber Value To Quantify Your Branding

The reason why most internet marketers are opposed to brand advertising is that they don't think there's any way to know if their campaigns are actually working or not.

With traditional branding campaigns, you run the campaigns and hope for the best. There's no way to know what impact it had on sales, or if it had any impact at all. Big companies do things like run "brand lift" studies. But in my opinion, these traditional ways of measuring branding are total horseshit.

Using Modern Branding, you CAN measure your campaign's performance. And you can split-test and improve your campaign over time, just like you would with a direct response campaign.

Here's how it's done…

Your advertising campaigns will generate sales, but they'll also generate engagement and YouTube subscribers. In our traditional direct response campaigns, we value the sales fully but we assume the subscribers we acquire are worth nothing at all.

In a sense, this is a safe, conservative approach. **But it's also completely wrong.**

YouTube subscribers are not worthless — they are obviously extremely valuable. Subscribers produce revenue directly from the videos they watch. Even more importantly, having a large subscriber base helps other people discover your channel organically. And the more subscribers you have, the easier it will be to make your ad campaigns profitable.

This gives us an easy and effective way to measure the performance of our branding campaigns.

You can run an effective branding campaign EXACTLY the same as you run your regular campaigns, but with one exception: you assign a value to every subscriber you acquire, and count this equally with sales you make directly from your ads.

Here's how this works...

Let's say that you've estimated that each YouTube subscriber is worth fifty cents to your business. And your ROI threshold is to break even (achieve ROI of 1.0) on an immediate direct response basis.

Let's say that you spent $200 on an ad, and only made $150 in revenue back directly. In your regular campaigns you'd declare this ad unprofitable, and turn it off. It's ROI is .75 — below your threshold. Therefore, you'd pause out the ad and stop running it.

But let's say that this ad also generated **two hundred YouTube subscribers for your channel.**

If this ad was in a Modern Branding campaign, you'd evaluate it differently. You'd value the 200 YouTube subscribers you acquired at $100, bringing the total amount you made from this ad to $250 ($150 direct sales + $100 subscriber value.)

In a Modern Branding campaign, you would then consider this ad profitable — and you'd keep running it.

Running your campaigns this way is FAR superior to unmeasured "spray and pray" brand advertising for a few reasons...

First, you know which ads are working and which ads aren't. You have real metrics that tell you what an ad is doing for your brand, and you can take the direct sales into account as well.

This means that you'll be able to improve your campaign rapidly over time, unlike old-fashioned "spray and pray" broadcast branding campaigns.

Second, managing the campaigns is simple. You have ONE branding metric you're looking at — subscribers. This makes sense because subscribers are the most important part of building your brand on YouTube. You run your branding campaigns exactly like your other campaigns, except that you take the value of the subscribers your ads acquire into account.

And finally, running this type of branding campaign is far easier on your cash flow than an old-fashioned branding campaign. Since you are taking direct sales into account — not just brand effects — you'll tend to run branding ads that make at least decent sales directly.

This means you'll recoup most of what you spend on your branding campaigns in direct response sales. After taking these sales into account, your brand advertising campaigns will cost you almost nothing.

How To Estimate Subscriber Value

We all know that YouTube subscribers are worth SOMETHING. But the question is, how much exactly is a subscriber worth to your business?

There is no way to know this precisely. **But making a conservative educated guess will be far better than assuming they're worth zero — which is clearly wrong.**

Here are a few ways you can estimate how much subscribers are worth to you.

The "Buy 1 Million Subscribers" Thought Exercise

Even if you have no social media presence whatsoever, you can use this exercise to get a rough estimate of what subscribers are worth to you.

Let's say that you could just straight up BUY 1 million subscribers. Real, engaged subscribers who will watch, like and share your videos - not bots or people from the third world.

How much would you be willing to pay for 1 million real, engaged subscribers in your target market?

Personally, I would be willing to pay a million dollars for a million subscribers if I could just buy them. That's because I know that I can make far more than one dollar per subscriber on my channel.

So how much would you be willing to pay?

Before you decide, consider all of the ways subscribers can help your business:

- Most subscribers will watch many of your videos. Once you have a large subscriber base, you'll make a significant amount of revenue even from your unadvertised videos.

- People who subscribe to your channel and regularly watch your videos are a valuable remarketing list. You'll make more money showing ads to this list, on top of the sales you'll make from your unadvertised content videos.

- The more subscribers you have, the better Google Ads will treat you. You'll get better support, and you'll be far less likely to have problems with Policy if you're popular on YouTube. Nobody is more on board the Modern Branding train than Google, and they view your YouTube subscriber base as an important measure of how trustworthy your business is.

- If you run ads for other businesses on your channel (sponsored videos), getting more subscribers will grow this source of revenue.

- **Most importantly, subscribers are a business asset that grows in compound fashion over time.** This compound growth will explode your subscriber base within a few years. It's very similar to how financial assets earn compound interest, except the process happens much faster.

  Your subscribers help you get more subscribers, which in turn help you get more. Because of the strong "rich get richer" effect with YouTube subscribers, they're worth even more to your business than what they generate in sales directly.

Thinking about all of the above, estimate how much you'd be willing to pay per subscriber.

Then, to get a VERY conservative number to use in your branding campaigns, divide what you think subscribers are worth by 10.

Let's say you think each subscriber is worth a dollar. You're probably right, and they're probably worth even more than this. But to be conservative — and to be absolutely sure you don't lose money on your branding campaigns — you'll start by valuing your subscribers at a mere 10 cents each.

If you can get a subscriber for ten cents, it's virtually certain that you'll make a profit on this over the lifetime of your business.

As your branding campaign develops, you'll be able to estimate your subscriber value more precisely. When you do, you'll be able to confidently spend more for each subscriber you acquire.

If you have no idea what subscribers will be worth to you, I recommend estimating each subscriber is worth 10 cents. If you can acquire subscribers for ten cents or less ANY business should be able to make a long term profit on that.

You can start with this ultra-conservative estimate, and gradually increase it over time once you're able to use one of the more accurate methods below.

The 10% Of YouTube Revenue Estimate

If you already have an established YouTube channel and ad campaigns — but you can't track exactly how much you're making from unadvertised organic videos — this will be the best method for you to use.

To get a conservative estimate of what your subscribers are worth, **attribute 10% of the revenue you've made from YouTube to your subscribers, both from advertising and unadvertised videos.**

In my opinion this is a very conservative estimate, since even very ad-driven channels clearly owe more than 10% of their revenue to their subscriber base.

Let's say that you have a 10,000 YouTube subscribers, and you made $50,000 in revenue from YouTube over the lifetime of your business. So, you've made five dollars in YouTube revenue for every subscriber you have.

In this case, you'd estimate each subscriber is worth 50 cents (5 dollars per subscriber divided by 10).

Again, they are probably worth much more. But the purpose of this exercise is to get a conservative number that will clearly make sense for you so you can confidently get started with brand advertising. You know that you can get a subscriber for less than this amount it'll be a good long term investment. And you can always increase your subscriber value estimate later, once your branding campaigns have proved their worth.

I recommend putting a tracking link on each of your unadvertised videos so you can track the revenue you're making from these videos more exactly. You'll then be able to use the most accurate way of assessing your subscriber value…

The Directly Tracked Sales Calculation

The best and most accurate way to estimate your subscriber value is to calculate how much revenue your unadvertised organic videos have made. To do this, you'll need a tracking link in the description of each unadvertised video.

Let's say that you have 500,000 subscribers. Over the lifetime of your business, your unadvertised videos have made $500,000 in directly tracked sales.

In this case, you're making $1 per subscriber from unadvertised videos alone. And this doesn't count any revenue you made from running ads for other businesses on these videos.

In this case, it clearly makes sense to value your subscribers at $1.

That's because you have data showing you that subscribers have produced that much directly tracked revenue for your business. Not every sale on unadvertised videos comes from subscribers, but most of them do. And even the unsubscribed viewers who buy from these videos never would have found them if not for your subscriber base.

You know that you're probably making much more than $1 per subscriber, because subscribers are adding value to your business in many other ways besides directly tracked revenue.

You'll make more money remarketing to your subscribers and engaged viewers. Your subscribers will organically grow your channel, sending more subscribers and sales your way without you having to spend money on advertising.

And most important of all, your subscribers help keep your all-important Google Ads account safe. Especially if you're in a niche that has a lot of Policy compliance problems, like supplements or sex toys, this can really be invaluable.

If you are using this calculated method, you will usually have a higher estimate of subscriber value than if you are using a rough estimate method. And that's by design. The more information you have about the revenue your subscribers are producing, the more confident you can be in spending to acquire them.

How To Choose Branding Campaign Creative

Choosing the best ads for most campaigns is pretty straightforward. You just stick to the Three Level Split Testing system. This means you'll usually run the ads which are getting the best ROI, or the lowest cost per lead.

But how do you know what creative is best for your branding campaigns?

First of all, you should not be using any video that was designed to be an ad in these campaigns. The goal is to build your brand beyond what your regular campaigns are doing. If you use the same ads then you'll just be running a redundant direct response campaign, defeating the purpose of what we're doing.

Instead, use YouTube Analytics to determine which videos have generated the most engagement from your audience. Then advertise those videos!

To get a full video walkthrough of how to find your most engaged videos with YouTube Analytics, check out this chapter's bonus resources:

15StepsBonuses.com/Branding

What I recommend is advertising your most engaged video in each of the five most important engagement categories over the last 30 days:

- Your most viewed video
- Your video with the highest average view duration
- Your video with the most likes
- Your video with the most comments
- Your video with the most shares

If one video is the top video in two categories, use the second most engaged video in one category so you're always advertising five videos.

For example, if your most liked video is also your most shared video, use your second most shared video instead to get five unique videos to advertise.

How To Set Up Your Branding Columns

Your branding columns should be the same as your regular columns, **but with the addition of these engagement columns on the far right:**

- **Earned subscribers**
- **Earned likes**
- **Earned shares**
- **Earned views**

You will only be using the subscribers column to make your advertising decisions, but you'll be able to see other engagement data and take this into account.

The far right of your columns should look like this:

Earned subscribers	Earned likes	Earned shares	Earned views

For Modern Branding campaigns, add these columns directly to the right of all the Universal Columns you usually use. These metrics will show you how much engagement your ads are producing.

How To Create Your Branding Campaign

When you have your columns and creative set, you're ready to make your branding campaigns!

I recommend creating both a Video Discovery and an InStream campaign. Most of the time, Video Discovery campaigns will get you cheaper engagement. But InStream ads can also work well, especially to very engaged remarketing lists.

In each campaign, I recommend starting with just one ad group: **your customers who have already bought something from you.** This can be a website generated list coming from people who have hit your product's "thank you" page. Or if you've been approved for customer match, you can upload your customers emails directly to make this list.

Set a frequency cap of 2 impressions per user per week. A frequency cap will limit how often someone will see your ads. The strict cap of two impressions per user per week is so your branding campaign will not totally crowd out your direct response campaigns — that way you don't lose any immediate sales.

Set a high bid in each ad group to ensure you're buying as much traffic as you can. I recommend a starting bid of $2 per view for Video Discovery campaigns, and $0.50 per view for InStream campaigns.

Now, run your campaign for a week!

If you have an older, established business with a huge customer database then you can probably spend your entire branding budget on customers. And that's great! Your existing customers are the most likely to buy from you again, so their perception of your brand is the most important.

Most businesses will not be able to spend their entire branding budget only on customers. So, I recommend expanding your campaigns with one ad group per week, progressively targeting less and less engaged remarketing lists, until you've spent your branding budget.

Here's the order you should create your ad groups in until you're spending your entire branding budget:

- Your highest spending customers

- All of your other customers, outside the highest spending ones

- People who have visited one of your shopping cart or checkout pages

- People who are on your email list, but who have not bought something (if you're approved for Customer Match remarketing)

- People who have engaged with one of your YouTube videos in any way (anyone who has subscribed to your channel, added one of your videos to a playlist, liked one of your videos, or commented on one of your videos.)

- People who have visited your website, but who have not yet visited a shopping cart or checkout page

All businesses can eventually spend their entire branding budget by expanding into these larger lists. Usually, you can spend the entire budget just on customers, shopping cart viewers, and prospects on your email list.

And again, make sure to check out this chapter's bonus video for a full walkthrough on the mechanics of creating branding campaigns.

How To Manage Your Branding Campaigns

You'll manage your branding campaign exactly the same as your regular campaigns, but with two important exceptions.

First, you'll be adding the value of the subscribers you gained to your directly tracked conversion value.

Let's say that your ROI threshold is 1.0, and your subscriber value estimate is 10 cents.

And let's you're seeing this that one of your ads has spent $200 and made you $150 back, for an All Conversion Value / Cost (ROI) number of .75.

In a regular campaign, you'd say DAMMIT! This ad lost money. Then you'd angrily turn it off.

But this is a Modern Branding campaign — so you consider the value of the subscribers you've acquired as well.

You see that this ad has earned you five hundred subscribers!

You calculate this is worth $50 to you ($.10 x 500), and add this to your directly tracked conversion value of $150. This means that with subscriber value included, your ad made you $200!

This means that it's meeting your ROI threshold of 1.0 when subscriber value is included. And this means you SHOULD keep this ad if it's in a Modern Branding campaign.

Use this procedure to know which ads to pause out for your ads once per week. Pause any ad that's spent more than $200, and which is below your ROI threshold when subscriber value is added in.

How To Add New Videos To Your Campaign

In your Modern Branding campaigns, you should pause the ads that don't meet your ROI threshold (when subscriber value is included) once per week. But to save time and simplify things, you should only add new creative to your campaign once per month.

Once every month, go through your YouTube videos and re-calculate your five most engaged videos (one for each category) over the past 30 days.

You should add five unique, NEW videos to your campaign every month. If the most engaged video in a category has already been used — or is the top in another category — use the second or third most engaged video in that category instead.

This is important to do for two reasons:

First, if you just use your most engaged videos without changing them, you'll just be advertising the same old videos forever. This is because your branding campaign will itself generate a lot of engagement, and your unadvertised videos won't be able to compete.

And second, keep in mind people on your remarketing lists will be seeing these ads VERY frequently. It's important to keep the ads fresh so they don't get annoyed watching the same video over and over again.

What To Do If One Of Your Modern Branding Videos Makes A Direct Profit

Modern Branding campaigns have an awesome side effect: **you'll occasionally discover that some of your organic unadvertised videos are more directly profitable than your ads — without even counting the value of the subscribers you acquire!**

If you run your branding campaign for long enough and test enough videos, it's inevitable you'll eventually get a happy surprise like this. It's nearly impossible to predict which videos they will be in advance, and I've been shocked multiple times by videos that made a profit I never expected to.

Let's say you're running a branding campaign, and you see a video has spent $200 and made you $250 in sales. Again, let's assume your ROI threshold is 1.0.

This video is profitable on a direct response basis – and it's gaining you subscribers at a higher rate than a straight-up ad.

So, when you discover an organic video like this, start using it in your regular direct response remarketing campaigns!

Many times, you'll find these content videos continue to be more directly profitable than your ads — especially on highly engaged remarketing lists.

If you get the video profitable on less engaged remarketing lists (like people who have visited your website in the past 60 days) you could have a monster hit on your hands! It's time to get excited.

Add your video to a few cold traffic ad groups, and see if it keeps performing. And keep scaling it up as long as it's more directly profitable than your straight-up ads.

I've used this method to create many multi-million dollar hit ads from content videos that were never intended to be advertised. And if you run Modern Branding campaigns long enough, I guarantee you'll eventually get some surprise direct response hits like this.

Full Disclosure: This Is A Simplified Version Of The Branding System I Actually Use

If you use this Modern Branding system, you'll be leaps and bounds above other advertisers.

While direct response advertisers focus only on the profit they make that day and don't invest in the future, you'll be gradually investing in your brand over time. Over time, this means you will make bigger profits, and you'll get a bigger exit if you eventually sell your business.

On the other hand, old-fashioned brand advertisers will be squandering their money with the unmeasured "spray and pray" approach to branding.

But you'll be using a proven, scientific method to improve your brand over time based on the most important branding metric — YouTube subscribers.

Unless you've been through one of my advanced training courses, I recommend you stick to this simple branding system. But I should disclose that the branding system in this book is a simplified version of the Modern Branding campaigns I run myself.

The ultimate way to run a Modern Branding campaign — and the way I personally use — is to estimate a value for ALL engagement metrics, not just subscribers.

With my large corporate clients, our modern branding campaigns assign a smaller value to each subscriber than what I recommend above. **But each like, playlist addition, earned view, and share is assigned an estimated value as well!**

These engagements are valuable, even if they're not nearly as valuable as subscribers. And the best branding systems accurately account for their value.

Running this type of advanced Modern Branding campaign requires a trained Data Analyst to calculate the engagement value of each ad, and to handle the pausing of ads for you.

It is not practical to run a campaign like this yourself, and most advertisers should not attempt it. **Because of this, I only recommend this advanced branding system to large companies with a skilled Data Analyst on staff, or large advertising agencies with a skilled Data Analyst.**

So, get started with the simplified Modern Branding system I just taught you, because it's certainly complicated enough for small companies. But if you get good results, consider creating a system to value all engagement metrics once you're running a large company.

Your Action Steps From This Chapter:

1. Create your brand guidelines. This should not be a wishy-washy, vague mission statement like "Don't be evil." It should be a very specific list of brand-damaging activities that are prohibited in your company, regardless of how immediately profitable they are. Create your brand guidelines now. If you have employees, make sure they're familiar with the brand guidelines too.

2. Review all of your ads, and stop advertising any ads which have more dislikes than likes. Make sure the ad has at least 100 likes and dislikes total before pulling it, so you don't pull an ad that has 2 dislikes and 1 like.

3. Check your revenue for the past 30 days.

   If you made less than $50,000, don't start a branding campaign yet. Make a note to remember to start one once you have your first $50k month, and move on to the next chapter.

   If you've made more than $50,000 in the last 30 days, it's time to start your branding campaign! Follow the steps below before moving on to the last chapter.

4. Calculate your branding budget. This should be 1% of your monthly revenue for the past 30 days. You can also use 1% of your average monthly revenue for the past year if the last month was an unusually high or low revenue month.

5. Estimate your value per subscriber.

If you can track sales from you unadvertised videos separately, estimate your subscriber value as **Your Total Lifetime Revenue From Unadvertised Video / Your Total Subscribers.**

If you can't track sales from your unadvertised videos separately but you already have a YouTube presence, estimate your subscriber value to be **Your Total Lifetime Revenue From All Of YouTube / Your Total Subscribers x 10%**

If you have no YouTube presence, do the "Buy 1 million subscribers" thought exercise. Estimate your subscriber value to be **10% of the amount you think they're actually worth.**

If you have no clue what a million subscribers would be worth for you, start with the ultra-conservative assumption that each subscriber is worth a mere ten cents. Re-calculate using one of the more precise methods above in six months.

6. Create your branding columns, and save them in Adwords. These will be the same as your regular columns, but with **earned subscribers, earned likes, earned shares, earned playlist additions, and earned videos added to the far right.**

7. Create your Video Discovery and InStream branding campaigns

8. Create your first ad group in each campaign advertising to customers

9. Schedule a weekly time to manage your branding campaigns (just like your other campaigns), and a monthly day to add new creative to your campaigns.

10. Use YouTube Analytics to find your most engaged videos and add them to every ad group in your branding campaigns. Repeat this process once per month.

11. Expand your campaigns with one new ad group per week until you're spending your entire branding budget. Expand your campaign with new targeting in the order I recommend above.

12. Check in on your campaigns once each week. Set your bids and pause creative just like you would in a regular campaign, except take subscriber value into account.

13. Once you understand this system, delegate the management of these campaigns to an employee or ad agency. Since the way you choose new creative and pause ads is very formulaic, it will be easy for someone else to learn.

Step 15: Find The Perfect People To Help You Scale Up Your Campaigns

Congratulations! You've almost finished the book! And you now have a high level understanding of how YouTube marketing works.

While all business owners need a basic understanding of YouTube ads, it doesn't make sense for most business owners to manage their YouTube campaigns themselves.

That's why as soon as you can, you should hire someone who specializes in YouTube advertising to help you scale your campaigns up.

This chapter will show you how you can hire the right in-house person or advertising agency to manage your ads. This is the ultimate key to YouTube success, since you'll need a skilled team to make profits on a large scale.

Why You Should Not Manage Your Own YouTube Ads

It might seem strange that after spending hundreds of pages and dozens of videos teaching you the ins and outs of YouTube marketing, I'm now telling you that you need to hire someone else to run your ads for you.

But if you think about it, you'll see why this makes sense once you're running big campaigns.

First of all, you need to have a good understanding of YouTube advertising in order to effectively hire and manage someone to do it for you. Most business owners don't understand the principles behind successful YouTube campaigns, so it's impossible for them to make a good decision when hiring an agency or employee.

For example, let's say you don't know what a Skip Stopper is.

You'll never get good results hiring an agency or in-house employee, because you'll have no idea how to tell good YouTube ads from shitty ones.

That's why I recommend everyone who reads this book and get at least a little experience running ads themselves, rather than skipping straight to hiring someone. And it's why I stressed the importance of doing all the action steps in the previous chapters so heavily.

Now that you know the fundamentals of YouTube marketing, it'll be easy to hire someone to scale your campaigns up.

You'll know exactly what to look for when you're hiring, how to evaluate results, and how to improve your campaigns over time.

In the next few pages I'm going to show you how to determine what your personal Core Strength is. This is your unique talent where you can add more value to your business than anyone else can, and it should be where you focus as much of your time as possible.

If YouTube is not your Core Strength, then it makes a lot of sense to outsource or delegate these campaigns as much as you can.

Someone who specializes in YouTube advertising exclusively and who is managing YouTube campaigns all day can probably do a much better job than you can. And they'll be freeing your time up to work on your Core Strength, which is the best way for you to contribute value to your business.

Even if YouTube advertising is your Core Strength, then you'll still need to hire people or agencies to expand your campaigns beyond a certain point. You can only manage so much yourself, even if you're spending all day on YouTube marketing.

I'm personally laser-focused on YouTube marketing — but I still used the techniques in this chapter to hire eleven different employees and six different agencies to help me with my YouTube campaigns. So even if you obsess about YouTube ads all day like I do, you still need to know this stuff.

If YouTube marketing is your Core Strength you'll always be personally involved with your campaigns. But in the future, you'll be more like a general directing your advertising army – not a foot soldier who's doing the grunt work yourself. So, you'll also be using what you learn in this chapter, just in a different way.

The first step to tackling this final YouTube marketing challenge will be identifying your Core Strength.

The Theory Of Core Strength

The Theory Of Core Strength will help you not just with your YouTube campaigns, but with all aspects of your business.

If you're like most business owners, you're handling a ton of different things for your business. You might spend some of your time on writing copy, some on doing meetings with your team, some on your taxes, and some time on creating your product.

The Theory Of Core Strength states that there is ONE of these activities you are doing for your business that is more valuable than any of the rest. And the more you can focus your personal time on this ONE core strength, the more successful your business will be.

You determine your Core Strength by thinking about what you are doing that's the most valuable to your business, and what you are doing what would be difficult or impossible to outsource.

For example, let's say that you're the on-camera talent and spokesperson for your company. If you are, it would probably be difficult or impossible to get another spokesperson who is as good as you. Since you're the owner of the company, nobody else is going to care about your products or sell them like you do.

Because of this, if you are the on-camera spokesperson for your brand yourself, this is probably your core strength. And it should be what you focus on as much as possible.

Or let's say that you run a software company, and your main competitive advantage is that your product is technically better than the competition. In this case, your Core Strength is probably managing your development team, since it would be very hard to find someone who can do this as well as you're currently doing it.

If you're doing multiple important things for your business, it might take you a little while to identify which one of them is the MOST valuable. But it's important that you do.

You only have so much time in a day. If you try and do everything, you will just end up a slave to your business. Over time, you'll get burned out and you'll start the company you created. **So, it's critical you use your precious personal time in the best possible way if you want to build a successful company.**

Is Your Core Strength YouTube Marketing?

I would personally consider YouTube marketing my core strength. I spend most of every day I work focused on it, and I have for more than nine years now. I also run an advertising agency that specializes in YouTube marketing, which handles only this aspect of the business for many clients.

If you're like me and you run a YouTube marketing agency, YouTube is probably your core strength too.

But if you run a regular business – or an unspecialized, all-purpose ad agency – how can you tell if your core strength is YouTube ads?

Here are a few easy ways:

- **Can you spend the MAJORITY of every workday on YouTube marketing?** If you can't, then you'd be better served by hiring a specialist who can.

- **Do you ENJOY YouTube advertising more than any other aspect of your business?** If not, there are many people who do.

- **Are you MAKING MORE MONEY PER HOUR from the time you're investing in YouTube advertising vs. every other aspect of your business?** If not, you'll make more money by focusing on a higher value per hour task.

- **Would it be MORE DIFFICULT TO OUTSOURCE YouTube marketing than any other important task you're in-house right now?** If not, you should take advantage of this and hire someone to free up your time.

If your answer to all of these questions is YES, then YouTube advertising is your Core Strength. **This means that you should hire employees to manage your YouTube advertising so you can personally hire and supervise them.**

But for the majority of you, you've answered NO to at least one of the questions above. This means YouTube advertising is not your Core Strength. **This means that you should hire a YouTube marketing agency, so you can get someone managing your campaigns who is hyper-focused on YouTube.**

If you found out YouTube marketing is NOT your Core Strength, this is actually great news! Because it means you have a way to scale up your YouTube campaigns while focusing on tasks that are more enjoyable to you and more valuable to your business.

How To Hire Employees To Manage Your YouTube Ads

If YouTube advertising IS your Core Strength, then it may make sense for you to expand your campaigns by hiring in-house employees that you personally manage. For example, if you run a YouTube-focused ad agency this is clearly the approach that makes sense.

While hiring employees comes with many hassles, there are some advantages to it…

First of all, hiring someone as an employee can sometimes allow you to lock down great talent that you couldn't get any other way. If someone has a proven track record of making money on YouTube for years, this could be really important.

Second, some business owners are simply more comfortable working with employees regardless of the financial disadvantages. This is especially true for older business owners in their sixties and seventies, who grew up during an era where outsourcing was uncommon.

And finally, hiring an employee will give you greater day-to-day control over your YouTube advertising campaigns. If you don't mind spending most of each day on YouTube advertising — and you're sure it's your core strength — this control will help you to get better results. This is the biggest reason why I've mostly used my own employees to manage my campaigns in the past.

The advantages of employees usually outweighed the disadvantages for me in my previous companies. And for other YouTube-obsessed business owners who have good HR systems, it could make sense too. But hiring employees may not be the right strategy for everyone.

Because if you've hired employees before, you know what hiring employees also comes with many disadvantages...

The Disadvantages Of Hiring Employees

I had more than a hundred W-2 employees working from my office for my last company. I've also hired many agencies and contractors, so I got to know the advantages and disadvantages of both very well.

Here are just some of the disadvantages that come with hiring employees...

- **Hiring employees is very time consuming.** To get a quality candidate, you need to write a job ad, post it on many sites, go through hundreds of resumes, do multiple rounds of interviews, and eventually design a compensation package and offer for your chosen candidate. Sometimes even when you do everything right it doesn't work, and you have to fire the person and start again.

  This means you'll either have to hire an HR manager, or you'll have to spend many hours of your personal time sorting through resumes and doing interviews.

- **Training and managing employees is time consuming and not enjoyable for most people.** You'll need to spend at least an hour a day training a new hire for the first thirty days, and meet with them at least once a week permanently after this.

- **Firing underperforming employees is difficult.** For example, I once hired an ad manager who performed terribly and who wasn't making any profit for the company six months after she'd been hired. We were about to fire her, but then we learned that she was pregnant and due to give birth in a few months. I knew she needed the money badly and I couldn't bring myself to fire her because of this.

  We ended up keeping her on the payroll for almost two additional years, where she cost us far more in salary than her campaigns were making for the company. It's never as easy to fire underperforming employees as you think because of situations like this.

- **In a small business, you may not be able to get someone to specialize in YouTube ads exclusively.** More likely, you'll just have one person to manage your online advertising generally. Because they're dividing their time between many different platforms, they won't be as good at YouTube marketing as a YouTube specialist.

- **Hiring W-2 employees costs you a boatload of money in taxes.** Right off the bat you'll need to pay payroll taxes, which costs you and your employee about 20% of their salary in total. You'll also need to pay unemployment insurance (usually around 3% of their salary), and some states have additional employment taxes on top of this.

  This means that for every dollar an employee costs you, they're only receiving about 75 cents. This alone is a huge reason why you should minimize the number of W-2 employees you hire.

- **If you have more than 50 employees and you're in the United States, you must provide your employees with health insurance by law.** Many other countries have similar laws mandating large businesses provide health insurance for their employees. And this insurance can get very expensive.

  Even worse, if you have younger employees, they won't value this insurance you're forced to provide for them. Instead, they'll view their contribution to the insurance payments as a pay cut that you're pressuring them to take.

Despite these disadvantages, it still makes sense for some businesses to hire employees rather than contractors or agencies to manage their ads. It's the only way to lock down certain premium talent, and it gives you more direct control over your campaigns. And that's why I mostly used employees to manage my ad campaigns at my previous companies.

But it's important to know what you're getting into before you make the decision to hire employees.

I have very few employees for Social Response Marketing because of the disadvantages I laid out above. Instead, I get things done with a network of contractors, agencies, and partner companies.

I find this approach FAR less stressful than dealing with a lot of employees. And while you need employees to build a really huge company, many people are making millions in profit every year without them.

I still have a small number of W-2 employees on my payroll, and for certain very key people it still makes sense. But I carefully consider all of the disadvantages above before making any W-2 hire, and only move forward if it still makes sense despite the drawbacks.

How To Hire An In-House Advertising Team

To create an in-house YouTube marketing team, you'll need to hire the following employees to start with:

- A video editor who has a basic understanding of marketing (salary range of $30,000 - $60,000 in the US)

- A graphic designer with a basic understanding of marketing ($40,000 - $70,000)

- A copywriter with a track record of success with YouTube marketing ($100,000- $150,000)

- A Google Ads manager with a track record of success with YouTube marketing ($100,000 - $250,000)

If you're managing your own YouTube ads right now and you want to build a team to help you out, I recommend hiring people and handing off the work gradually.

For example, you could start by hiring a video editor, and spend the next few months gradually handing off all your editing work to them. A few months later you hire a designer, and you gradually transition your design work to them from your contract design. Then you hire your copywriter, then your ad manager last.

This gradual approach will enable you to spend enough time training each new hire before moving onto the next one. And this is key to making sure your team is successful.

Now, let's talk about the salaries...

Some business owners think these salaries seem high, and you could be tempted to start with lower paid employees. **I've found out from experience this is a huge mistake.**

If someone is managing your YouTube ad campaigns for less than $100,000 per year, you have to ask yourself why that is.

Why are they working so cheaply if they actually have the ability to generate hundreds of thousands in profits every month?

Anyone who can measurably bring profits to a business will be in demand, and will have constant job offers coming their way.

If someone is managing Google Ads on the cheap, it's because they have no track record of YouTube marketing profits to point to. You'll think you're saving money on their salary. But you'll end up spending more altogether when their campaigns inevitably lose you money.

So, don't cheap out when you're hiring employees. Hire the best and pay a premium, and your campaign profits will more than justify it.

If you don't have the budget for premium employees yet, work with contractors and agencies until you do. You'll get far better results working with partner companies and contractors than you will from working with bargain basement employees.

How To Hire Employees

The best system I've found for hiring star employees — and the system I personally use myself — is called Topgrading.

You can learn the Topgrading system from Brad Smart's *Topgrading* book. And I highly recommend you buy the book and use the system if you plan on hiring employees.

Here's a link to the book:

15StepsBonuses.com/Topgrading

While Topgrading is a great system, it is a very long and complex read. So, I'll give you a high level overview of how to hire employees to get you started...

First, post job ads clearly describing the positions you're looking for on multiple different job sites. If you don't get any quality responses to a job ad, re-write it with a different angle and try again.

Remember, your job ad is just that — an AD. If you don't get the response you're looking for, make another variation. Just like you do with your product ads.

If your ad copy is working well, you should have hundreds of resumes for each position to choose from. Review these resumes, and invite the top ten candidates for each position to a first round interview.

If you have an HR Director, have them do these first round interviews since they're incredibly time-consuming. Your HR Director's goal should be to identify the three candidates who have the strongest resumes, and who can demonstrate the most skills in YouTube marketing during the interview.

After this, you should personally do a second round of interviews with the most qualified candidates. These should be long, in-depth interviews. You should ask them many detailed questions about copywriting, video production, and Google Ads knowledge to gauge their skills. And you should also review their work history in exhaustive detail.

That's the idea — get a ton of resumes, conduct an ultra-thorough interview process to find the best candidate.

To learn how to write a great job ad, what to ask in the interviews, and all the other details you'll need to know to find someone great, make sure you check out the Topgrading book:

15StepsBonuses.com/Topgrading

How To Train And Manage Your Employees

For any W-2 employees you hire, I recommend that you personally spend 1-2 hours per day training them for their first 30 days on the job. This seems like a lot, but training them right will save you a lot of time correcting their mistakes later — not to mention the money you'll save from avoiding these errors.

If you've done a good job training your employees, you'll only have to meet with them once per week after this to manage them. In your meetings, you should review their work from the last week, give them feedback, and assign new tasks for the next week.

I also recommend doing performance reviews for your W-2 employees once every six months. Your employees all have goals of their own, and they will all want to receive raises or promotions over time. Performance reviews give you a chance to give raises and promotions to your best employees, and to give the others feedback on how they can earn raises and promotions in the future.

Make sure you compensate your star employees competitively, otherwise they'll eventually leave you for a higher paying company.

My personal management philosophy is based on the teachings of Jack Welch, the former CEO of General Electric and one of the greatest managers of all time. To learn more about Jack Welch's approach to managing people, I highly recommend checking out his book *Winning*.

15StepsBonuses.com/Winning

How To Know If You Should Hire An Agency

For some business owners, the advantages of employees will outweigh the disadvantages. But for many business owners, hiring an agency or contractor will make more sense than hiring an employee.

Hiring a YouTube marketing agency has a lot of advantages, but of course it has its drawbacks as well.

First of all, you will not have as much control over your campaigns as you would with an employee you train for an hour every day.

If your Core Strength is not YouTube marketing, then this isn't a big deal. You'll probably get better results by setting the big picture goals and letting a specialist handle the details. But if YouTube marketing is your Core Strength, this can be a significant disadvantage.

Second, most YouTube advertising agencies cannot handle all aspects of the YouTube advertising process.

You'll need to hire an agency to manage your ads, a copywriter to write your scripts, a video production company to produce your videos, and a graphic designer to create your thumbnails and other design assets.

This can lead to significant communication problems and confusion coordinating projects between many different outsourced companies. But this challenge can be overcome – and I'll show you some ways to do this later in this chapter.

Finally, the best agencies are very in demand and only want to work with the most qualified clients. But I'll show you some ways you can overcome this later in this chapter to make your company a more desirable client for top agencies, even if you don't have a huge advertising budget right now.

The "Common Sense" Method Of Finding The Best Agencies That Nobody Uses

By far the most important factor in deciding which advertising agency you should hire is **their track record of success specifically with YouTube marketing.**

This seems like simple common sense, but it's actually not. Many business owners make the mistake of hiring someone because of their success generally with online marketing. Or even worse, they'll hire someone to manage their YouTube ads based on their success with making TV ads in the past.

These inexperienced business owners think all marketing platforms are the same, and that a skilled marketer can dominate any platform. And I confess, I've made this mistake myself in the past.

What I've learned is that the skills that make you great at Facebook or Google Search or TV advertising are much different than the skills that make you great at YouTube advertising. There are some things they have in common, but many things that are different and specific to each platform.

Because of this, a track record of YouTube marketing success should be the primary thing you look for when hiring an agency.

Success with other online advertising platforms does count for something. But it should be a secondary factor in your decision, and should be considered far less than the agency's YouTube track record.

Very Important: Get To Know The Person Who Is Actually Managing Your Ads

I've had some agencies I've hired work out very well in the past, and I've also been burned and lost money with agencies many times.

When I lost money and had a bad experience with an agency, it usually went like this.

I (or an executive in my company) would meet the owner of an agency, or one of its sales reps. They're charismatic and seem incredibly knowledgeable. They tell us they want to personally work with us to run our campaigns, and they'll be there every step of the way!

We'd then sign a retainer contract. After that the agency owner or sales rep would no longer be involved, and they'd move on to selling other new clients. Instead, we got someone who we never met — and who we knew nothing about — managing our ads. Often, this would be a low-paid, poorly trained person.

In hindsight, it's not surprising that relationships with this type of agency usually didn't work out. If we had met the person actually managing our ads from the beginning, it would have been obvious that he was never going to make our campaigns a success.

So, don't repeat my mistakes. When you're hiring an agency, **make sure you meet the person who will be actually managing your ads — not just the agency owner or sales rep.**

This isn't to say the owner of the agency or the system the agency uses doesn't matter. It is important, and even junior ad managers can produce good profits if they're trained in a good system.

But the person implementing the system matters too. So, make sure to interview that person before hiring an agency. Otherwise, you'll think you're hiring a YouTube advertising savant to manage your campaigns, when your marketing is actually getting delegated to interns.

The Advantages Of Hiring An Agency

There are definitely some challenges that go with hiring an agency. But there are also some huge advantages to working with the right YouTube marketing agency, and it'll be important to maximize these advantages if you go the agency route.

- **You get access to specialists who work ONLY on YouTube ads all day.** If you're hiring a full-time employee, they'll probably need to split their time between many different advertising platforms. Since mastering each platform is very complex, this tends to produce marketers who are a jack of all trades and master of none.

  If you're running a small business, you can't justify a highly paid, full-time employee to manage your YouTube ads. But an agency with multiple clients can.

  By working with an agency, you can access these types of elite YouTube specialists that would otherwise be impossible for your business to hire.

- **You save a ton of money.** First of all, you'll have no fixed costs draining your profits. If your employee's campaigns lose you money, it can be difficult to fire them — especially if you're friends with them or if you work in person alongside them. But if an agency's campaigns aren't performing, it's much easier to cut your losses once it's clear it's not going to work out.

  You're dealing with another business owner who understands that you can only pay him if he performs.

  You'll also save a huge amount on taxes and benefits (usually about 30% of the employee's base salary in total.)

- **You save a ton of time.** Hiring, training, and managing a great employee takes a huge amount of time. If you want to be very personally involved in running your YouTube campaigns every day, this can still be a good option. If it's not practical for you to spend hours every day managing your team, an agency is probably the best solution.

- **You can align your agency's incentives with yours more closely than an employee.** Because most employees receive the bulk of their compensation from a salary, there isn't much incentive for them to push hard to make your campaigns better. While there are some exceptions, most employees are only motivated to work hard enough to avoid getting fired because of this lack of incentive.

  With an agency, you can create a much better incentive structure. The right deal will reward the agency handsomely if they knock it out of the park for you, which will be a huge incentive for them to go the extra mile on your campaigns. And by the same token, if their performance is mediocre, you can structure it so they make almost nothing — again, a big incentive to improve performance.

How To Create A Payment Structure That Aligns Your Agency's Incentives With Yours

Knowing how to do this is critically important, and can be the difference between success and failure when working with an agency.

There are a few different ways that you can structure contracts with agencies.

The most common way is a **flat fee** contract. This is when you simply pay a certain amount per month and the agency manages your ads.

The problem with this structure is that it provides little incentive for the agency to do a good job. Let's say you're paying an agency $10,000 a month to manage your ads. If they blow the doors off and drive a million dollars in profit in a month, they'll still only make ten grand. And if they do a mediocre job and don't make you any profit, they'll make exactly the same amount.

Similar to an employee's salary, a flat fee only structure incentivizes an agency to do the bare minimum to avoid getting fired. So, it's not in your best interests as the person hiring the agency.

But here's the problem...

Most in-demand agencies are not willing to work with a client if there is no flat monthly fee whatsoever. That's because even if agencies screen clients carefully, there will occasionally be some that drop the ball and don't do what's necessary on their side to get the campaigns to work.

But there's a difference in how top performing vs. low performing agencies look at flat fees...

An agency that does well for most of its clients will typically want a minimal flat fee. They'll see it as insurance against the unlikely worst case scenario of a client severely dropping the ball, and structure the bulk of their compensation as performance-based.

An agency that does poorly for its client will want the entire contract to be based on flat fees, or as much as they can possibly get. This is because they know from experience their campaigns usually lose money for clients, so performance based compensation is a no-go.

So, when hiring a YouTube marketing agency with a strong track record, it's OK to pay a minimal flat fee as part of the contract. The agency is taking risk and putting work into this as well, and a small amount to cover their costs if you totally drop the ball is reasonable.

But you should be looking for agencies that want to structure the bulk of their compensation as performance based, and you should avoid agencies who want to bulk of their compensation as a flat fee.

So, what performance based compensation options should you consider?

The most common form of performance based compensation with marketing agencies is the **percentage of ad spend model.** This is where you'll pay an agency a set percentage of your total advertising budget — usually 10-20%.

This model is better than the flat fee model, because it aligns your agency's incentives more with yours. Since you'll be setting the budget, the only way for them to get you to increase your ad spend is to get your campaigns to be profitable. They are then incentivized to drive as much volume as possible.

Under this model, the agency could make $20k, $30k, $50k or more per month if your campaigns are driving sufficient volume. And on the other hand, if your campaigns aren't converting and you restrict them to a small budget, they'll make almost nothing.

The percentage of ad spend model has many advantages. It's simple, and it incentivizes your agency to go the extra mile to drive as much revenue as possible. While you'll pay them very well if the campaigns kill it, it will be a win/win since you'll be making many times more in profit. And if their campaigns don't do well, you'll only owe a minimal agency fee — providing a big incentive for your agency to prevent this from happening.

But the percentage of ad spend model isn't perfect. Its main disadvantage is that it incentivizes your agency to maximize revenue and not necessarily profit.

Let's say that one agency spends $1 million on advertising and makes your back $1.1 million. Another agency spends $1 million, and makes your back $2 million. Under the percentage of ad spend model, both of these agencies will be paid the exact same amount.

But there is a third alternative, which provides even greater alignment between your goals and your agency's. And that is the **cost per lead model.**

Under the cost per lead model, you won't be paying for your advertising directly. Instead, your agency will pay for the ads.

And you'll pay them a fixed amount per lead that they drive for you.

For example, let's say you've calculated each lead is worth $10 to you on average. You could make a pay per lead deal with an agency to drive qualified leads for $3.

This model has a few huge advantages for you…

First of all, it incentivizes the agency to make you profit — not just revenue. If your agency is currently driving leads for $2, they'll massively increase their profits from your account by getting that lead cost down to $1. Under the percentage of ad spend or fixed fee models, the incentive to increase your ROI much weaker.

This structure is also the ONLY structure on which an agency is actually taking the risk of losing money on your account. If they are driving leads for $2 and they slack off and let the lead cost go to $4, that means they're losing $1 for every lead they're driving. Losing money will strongly motivate them to scale the campaigns down quickly, and then to quickly get the campaigns profitable again.

Second, it reduces your risk. You only pay for qualified leads, and once you have the lead it's a pretty good bet that you'll make cost to your average lead value from them.

If you've calculated your lead value correctly and are only driving qualified leads, then it is impossible for you to lose money with a cost per lead structure.

And finally, top performing agencies love the cost per lead structure. It's true that they are taking the risk, and funding all of the advertising. But if they get a campaign really dialed in, then a campaign can make more money from one cost per lead account than from ten flat fee accounts of the same size.

And if you're paying a CPL agency this much, that means you're making even bigger profits!

So why don't all business owners just hire agencies on a cost per lead model?

The biggest reason is that they're worried that an agency will drive low value leads that won't convert as well as their typical leads. This is an understandable fear. But by properly structuring your cost per lead agreement and making it clear you'll only pay for QUALIFIED leads, you can eliminate this risk.

For example, let's say you own a financial services company. You're killing it with YouTube leads who are older than 40 and who also live in the US.

In this case you should structure your contract so that you're only paying full price for leads that meet these criteria — over 40, American, and generated from YouTube. For leads outside your prime audience, you can either pay a much lower price or not pay for these leads at all.

You can easily make sure your agency is driving qualified leads by checking the settings in their Google Ads campaigns.

If you find that some campaigns are not driving qualified leads — say if one was running to teenagers in Vietnam — it would be fair to deem these leads not qualified, and to not accept or pay for these leads.

If you have a good definition of qualified leads, you don't need to worry about losing money on low value leads. But there's still another reason why the pay per lead model isn't common…

The biggest reason is that it requires a lot of trust between the agency and the client. This trust needs to be built over time, and agencies will usually not be willing to take a pay per lead with a client they don't have any working history with.

Look at it from the agency's point of view. If a flat fee or a percentage of ad spend client doesn't pay, then the agency just makes nothing. That sucks, but you can deal with it.

But if a pay per lead client skips out on their bill, the agency is looking at a massive loss — on top of working for nothing for months. Since they're fronting the money for the advertising, they are going to be seriously screwed if they don't get paid for the leads on the back end.

So, you can understand why few agencies are willing to accept the cost per lead model with clients they don't have a working history with.

Every structure has advantages and disadvantages. So how do you know which one is the best one for you to use with your agency?

The Structure I Personally Use To Work With Clients

I've hired many agencies to manage ads for my last company, and I've been hired to manage ads for many different clients as well. And using this experience I've developed a hybrid structure for working with clients that I think is better than any standard agency structure. It's fair to both the agency and the client, and it sets us up for a win/win working together.

I'll explain the details of which businesses qualify to work with me in the next chapter. Most businesses will not qualify to have my agency manage their ads, because we're looking for a very specific type of client.

If you have a smaller business that doesn't qualify yet, that's OK! You can request this same structure with a smaller agency, and it'll massively improve your results. And you can continue learning from me through my advanced video training courses.

So, here's how my agency's structure works…

When I first start working with a new client, I find the key is to keep things simple. The structure needs to incentivize my team and I to do a great job with the ads — and it needs to incentivize the client to do their part as well. I also recognize that hiring a new agency is a risk for the client.

So, I do everything possible to reduce the risk on their side so their campaigns, so they're making a profit before they're asked to pay me a significant amount.

I also recognize that once trust is built, it's almost always a win/win to eventually move to the cost per lead model. I make more, the client makes more, and everybody is happier. But it takes some time to build up to this level of trust.

To accomplish both goals, I use a **two-phase structure.**

For the first six months of a new ad management contract, the structure looks like this:

- A minimal monthly flat fee to cover my costs
- A percentage of the client's total ad spend (where most of my revenue comes from during this phase)

This structure aligns my incentives with the client's as much as possible when we've just started working together. Since I make almost all my revenue from a percentage of the client's ad spend, my goal is to grow their campaigns as large as I profitably can.

If the client totally drops the ball (say, if they never run the ads we make) then I'll have enough to break even on my costs and pay my team. But I won't make any money at all if this happens, so I'm very motivated to avoid this.

With six months of running ads under this structure, the client will be able to get an accurate gauge of how much the leads from their YouTube campaigns are worth. I'm also able to get a feel for how much it will cost to generate these leads.

So, after six months we move into the second phase — the pay per lead structure.

The client and I work out a fair commission for each lead I send them, and I'll transition to paying for their advertising myself. Not all clients choose to make the switch, but most do.

And it's been a win/win for me and for the client every time we've tried this.

When we transition to a pay per lead structure, the client and I will also set some guidelines for what they consider qualified leads. And my team and I will restrict the targeting to get the client only leads they consider qualified going forward.

How To Use This Structure With Another Agency

My business is now focused mostly on training others to run YouTube ads through video courses, books, and coaching programs. I'm very selective about the clients I'm taking on these days, and I'm taking on very few new ad management clients.

So, if you don't qualify to work with me, you can still use this structure to dramatically improve your results working another agency.

When an agency gives you a proposal, it will almost always be for a monthly flat fee, or a combination of a flat fee with a percentage of ad spend. And that's OK! This is the standard structure agencies work under. You'll just need to eventually convince them to transition to a cost per lead structure once trust has been built.

When they give you their initial proposal, counter-offer with a structure similar to what I described above. Offer them a minimal flat fee which just covers their costs from your account, and which they wouldn't make a profit on if the campaigns bomb. And structure the bulk of their compensation for the first six months as a percentage of your ad spend.

Tell them that you'd like to reassess after six months, and move to a pay per lead structure (where they pay for your advertising) if it's mutually agreed to. You don't need a definite deal up front, but just establish that this is the eventual goal for both of you.

If an agency is confident that they can do a good job with your account, they'll almost always agree to this deal. And when you're ready to move to a cost per lead structure, it'll be easy because you've set that expectation from the beginning.

If an agency loses money for most of its clients, they will insist on a pure flat fee structure (or a structure where most of their compensation comes from a flat fee.) If this happens, RUN!

There's a reason why they're not open to performance based compensation — they know their performance sucks!

Integrated Creative & Ad Management — The Final Important Thing To Look For When Hiring An Agency

So, the first two things you should look for in an agency are **a successful track record (specifically with YouTube advertising)** and **openness to performance-based compensation.**

We've covered these at length. But there is one more important factor you should consider before picking an agency.

And that is whether your agency has the ability to handle ALL aspects of YouTube marketing for you — not just management of Google Ads. Many agencies will only manage your Google Ads account, and will expect you to do all the copywriting, video production, YouTube setup, graphic design, etc. While this structure can work sometimes, I've learned from hiring dozens of agencies that it usually fails.

That's because to build a truly great YouTube campaign, your creative and Google Ads management need to be coordinated together. If you have an external agency managing your Google Ads, and you're making your creative in-house, this is a recipe for miscommunication and blown opportunities.

Most of my best ad ideas have come from analyzing data within Google Ads. For example, if I see that ads for women over 40 are converting very well, I'll design my next ad specifically for this demographic. This can be done with any other targeting method as well, and it produces FAR better ads than just writing blind with no data to inform you.

The agency managing your Google Ads also needs to be intimately familiar with your creative to know the best ads to use against their targeting. Because I personally write every ad script myself for my top clients, it's easy for me to decide which ad will work best to a certain demographic or audience.

But many agencies have the mentality that the creative is the client's responsibility. **In fact, I've hired agencies where the person running the ads DID NOT EVEN WATCH OUR COMMERCIALS! They had no idea what was in the videos they were advertising.** It's not surprising in hindsight that this led to disaster.

That's why it's a CRUCIAL advantage to have the same agency both making your creative and managing your campaigns. Use an agency like this if there is any way at all that you can.

Final Thoughts

Hiring the right employee, agency, or contractor to manage your ads isn't easy. But I promise you, it's worth learning how to do it.

The fact is, large Google Ads campaigns require work to run. You'll need to continually produce new ads to grow your campaigns, and this takes work as well.

If you continue doing everything yourself forever, you'll become a slave to your business. The only way to make more will be to work more. Chances are, you'll never grow a really big business with this approach, since there are only so many hours in a day.

But once you master the process of hiring employees or agencies to do the work for you, your life will become much easier.

You'll need to invest a lot of time up front to find the right person. But once you do, they can take hours of work off your plate — EVERY SINGLE DAY! And the right person or agency can keep your campaigns growing for years with minimal effort on your part once they're up and running.

This is how people are running businesses making a million dollars a year in profit — or more — while only working a few hours a week. They invested the time up front to find the right partner companies or employees, and as a result of that they can enjoy a great income and lifestyle for years.

Once you've got a great agency or a great time managing your ads, you'll really begin living the dream. You can work just a few hours a week if you want and still make a huge income. You'll have freedom, money, and a lifestyle most business owners will envy.

So, dedicate yourself to finding great people to manage your campaigns. You'll reap huge rewards from this dedication in the future!

Your Key Decision From This Chapter:

1) Decide whether you want to scale your campaigns up by hiring **in-house employees** or an **ad agency.** This will determine the rest of your action steps.

Your Action Steps If You Decide To Hire In-House Employees:

1. Write your job ad for your video editor if you don't yet have one, and post it on at least four job sites. I recommend **Craigslist, Indeed, LinkedIn, and Glassdoor.** If you already have a video editor, do these steps for the next lowest salary position I listed earlier in this chapter that you don't yet have in your company.

2. Once you have gotten at least fifty resumes, schedule first round interviews with your top ten candidates.

3. Perform your ten first round interviews, and schedule second round interviews with your top three candidates.

4. Perform your second round interviews, and make a job offer to your top candidate.

5. Spend at least one month on training, where you spend approximately one hour per day each workday with your new employee to show them how to manage your account.

6. Schedule a regular weekly meeting after this, to check in on results and to give feedback on how to improve.

7. When you are ready, repeat this hiring process for each of the other employees you'll need to build successful YouTube campaigns. Repeat this process until your YouTube marketing team is fully built out.

Your Action Steps If You Decide To Hire An Agency

1. Find three different ad agencies that have a track record of success with YouTube marketing to consider.

2. Schedule a call with each agency, and talk with the person who will be managing your ads.

3. Decide which agency you'll go with based on the factors in this chapter: **their YouTube marketing track record, the expertise of the person actually managing your ads, their openness to performance based compensation, and their ability to manage both video ad creation and Google Ads management.**

4. Negotiate the compensation structure with your agency using what you've learned in this chapter. Set the expectation that you'd like to transition to a pay per lead structure in six months once a solid working relationship has been established.

5. After three months, assess the results. Scale the campaigns up if you're profitable. If you are not profitable, adjust your approach or find a new agency.

6. After six months, negotiate a transition to a pay per lead model. This will reduce your risk, increase your agency's incentives to increase ROI, and overall be a win/win for everybody.

How We Can Work Together

Congratulations! You've finished the book, and you've made yourself more knowledgeable than 99% of YouTube advertisers by investing your time in learning the 15 Steps.

If you've been doing the action steps, you should be seeing some serious results with your YouTube channel and your business right now! And you might be wondering how you can take your success to the next level.

I'd love to help you with the next steps of your YouTube marketing journey. In this chapter, I'll show you how we can work together, and how to choose the right solution for your business.

Have Me Manage Your Ads For You

While my business is mostly focused on YouTube marketing training, I also work with a few select clients to manage their ads directly. If your business qualifies, I can work directly with you to write your scripts and manage your ads.

Because my time is limited, and I spend a significant amount of my personal time on each client account, I am very selective about the clients I manage ads for.

Most businesses will not qualify for ad management — and that's OK! There are many other options for us to work together that are less expensive, and more appropriate for smaller companies.

Here is what your business will need to qualify for ad management:

- A minimum of $100,000 per month in total online ad spend currently.

- A minimum budget of $10,000 per month for YouTube ads during our initial test phase, and agreement that we'll rapidly scale the budget up from there once the campaigns are profitable.

- A product that customers love, and a brand that's strong in my opinion. I'll assess this through looking at the product itself, online reviews, social media comments, BBB reviews, and other sources.

- An excellent sales funnel that I believe will work well when advertised on YouTube.

- A willingness to transition to a pay per lead model after six months, once a good working relationship has been established. If you know about how much a lead is worth to you and you can verbally commit to paying a high lead value, this will make me much more interested in working with you.

  I am also very interested in working with companies who are currently using the pay per lead model with other partner companies on a large scale.

I want to choose clients who are in the best position to succeed, and I know it's very important to select the highest potential clients I possibly can. Because of this, I prefer to work with businesses that have...

- A high customer value, and willingness to spend aggressively on advertising to acquire customers and leads.

- A previously existing YouTube presence, with a large, engaged subscriber base on your channel.

- Experience with Google Ads, and an existing Google Ads rep that I can work with to resolve any issues that come up.

- A product and business that I can get excited to create a marketing campaign around. I want to work on projects that are fun, and if your product has exciting possibilities and I enjoy working with you these will be a big factors in your favor.

If we work together on ad management, here's what you'll get:

- **I will script your YouTube ads.** After spending some time researching your business and your customers, I'll work with you to develop ten concepts for new ads that are drastically better than the videos you're using right now. I'll then personally script all of the initial ads myself, using my years of experience with YouTube marketing to guide me.

  Not only will I personally write your first ten ads, my CMO will write three new ads for you every month from my outlines as long as we're working together. Having a large amount of high-quality creative will give you a HUGE advantage over other advertisers, and it's the biggest reason why my clients prefer me over other YouTube agencies.

- **I will guide the editing process.** I will either work with your in-house editors, or I can hire a skilled editor for you to edit your ads. I'll give them initial instructions to edit the ads, and detailed feedback on their draft videos to ensure they come out perfect.

- **I will optimize your YouTube funnel or eCommerce store.** I'll make initial recommendations to increase the conversion of your YouTube funnel to start with. I'll then manage your YouTube funnel split testing process, deciding what the most impactful item would be to test and creating any necessary copy for your split test variations.

  If you have a funnel, this could include sales video variations, sales page variations, or variations of your shopping cart or upsell sequence. If you run an eCommerce store, I'll review your landing page, your overall store, and the Shopify apps you are using to enhance your store.

- **I will personally manage your ad campaigns.** I will personally decide how to organize your campaigns, how to target your ad groups, and which ads to use. I'll also oversee skilled ad managers who perform mechanical tasks in your account, such as setting bids according to my formula, or creating ad groups according to my directions.

If you're interested in this — and you meet all the criteria above — I encourage you to reach out! It could be a great opportunity for us to work together — especially since you've read this book and you're familiar with my advertising system.

To apply for ad management, just fill out the form here:

15StepsBonuses.com/BecomeAClient

Once you do, someone on my team will reach out to schedule a call. On the call, a member of my team will show you more about how we can help your business. We'll also get more details about your business to make sure it's a good fit.

We'll also walk you through the pricing structure on the call. It's based on the ideal structure that I laid out in this book: a minimal flat fee, a percentage of ad spend to start with, and the understood goal of transitioning to a CPL structure in six months.

For my new clients, my fees are usually between $150,000 - $300,000 for the first six months of our contract. Part of this cost will come from flat fees, and the bulk of it will come from a fixed percentage of ad spend.

After six months, my goal is to transition to a CPL deal. At this point you'll be making much more money, my agency will be making much more, and our incentives will be aligned for the long term.

Now, I know that these fees might be more than you can afford right now. You also may not be in a position to pay me as much per lead as other businesses can. **And because I put a significant amount of my personal time into each client's account, I can only take on 1-2 new clients per year.**

But don't worry — there are other less expensive ways that I can help you grow your YouTube campaigns.

Have Me To Personally Design A YouTube Marketing Plan For You, And Help You Implement It

The best option for most businesses to work with me is my **YouTube Strategic Coaching** program. It's ideal if you want a customized plan just for you, and you want to work directly with me to implement the plan.

When you sign up for YouTube Strategic Coaching, I'll first get some information about you, your business, and your customers. I'll then spend 5-10 hours doing research into your market, your competitors, and the YouTube environment for your industry. I'll then personally write up a detailed **YouTube Strategic Plan** that will show you exactly how to rapidly grow your YouTube profits over the next six months.

I do not outsource or delegate these plans — I write them all myself. I put a lot into these plans, and many clients have used them to add millions of dollars in YouTube profits to their business. It won't just be a generic plan — it'll be completely customized and designed from scratch for your business and your unique situation.

And when I say this plan will be detailed, I mean it! It'll lay out exactly what you and your team need to do to achieve success. No guesswork, and no vague recommendations.

Just straightforward directions for how to create your commercials, structure your campaigns, and optimize your website that you or anyone on your team can easily implement.

I'll also include **one coaching call per month for the next five months to help you implement the plan.** Each month, we'll focus on implementing one part of the plan — and on our call, you can ask me any questions that came up from last month's marketing.

If there are any issues or challenges that came up, I can recommend a solution for you based on my experience. These calls will also keep you motivated and on track to implement the plan, to make sure our vision for your YouTube campaigns becomes a reality.

There is no ad spend or business size requirement to work with me on YouTube Strategic Coaching. **However, you must commit to implementing the plan I give you and hitting our monthly goals in order to continue working with me as a coaching client, and you must fit a few other criteria as well.**

And I've got some good news if you're interested in having me coach you...

I prefer to coach clients who have read this book, since you're already familiar with my system and we won't have to spend so much time on the basics. So, because you've read this book, **I'm going to give you a 30% discount if you sign up for a coaching plan with me through the link below.**

To claim your discount — and to learn more about YouTube Strategic Coaching — go to:

15StepsBonuses.com/Coaching

YouTube Marketing Black Belt Video Course

The YouTube Marketing Black Belt Video Course is the best advanced YouTube marketing training program in the world. I **guarantee it will DOUBLE your profits from YouTube marketing, or you're entitled to a full refund.**

I can only afford to make a guarantee like this because I know what I teach you in the Black Belt course produces HUGE results for clients.

This book teaches you the high-level, overarching principles behind my YouTube marketing system. But the Black Belt course is where you'll learn the all-important details necessary to master the 15 steps.

The Black Belt course teaches you how to...

- **Write killer YouTube ad scripts** — You'll get a top tier education in copywriting specifically for YouTube ads and YouTube funnels. I'll go deeper into the details of how to write great ad scripts, and teach you techniques that were too advanced to go over in depth in this book.

- **Make jaw-droppingly impressive video** — You'll learn exactly how to film and edit a YouTube ad, straight from the video experts who make my own ads.

  These advanced techniques will WOW your viewers, and give you a huge edge over advertisers using basic video production.

- **Build an engaged community of raving fans** — You'll learn exactly how to make content videos that support your advertising, and which can be used in advanced advertising campaigns. You'll also learn advanced techniques to juice your subscriber count and engagement by strategically using advertising.

- **Create a shockingly profitable YouTube sales website** — I'll walk you through exactly how to create a great sales video, and how to optimize your sales funnel or eCommerce store. You'll also learn many sales page, shopping cart, and upsell techniques which have been proven to work specifically on YouTube traffic.

- **Manage your Google Ads account like a pro** — I'll show you exactly how I manage my own campaigns, and walk you through exactly what to do to get great results from yours. You'll learn advanced targeting strategies, advanced campaign types, advanced split testing strategies...and more.

I've bought every YouTube advertising course on the market, and I am confident that this course is far better than anything else available right now. **And I guarantee that you'll agree once you get access — or I'll refund every cent you paid.**

And I've got some more good news for you...

Since you've read this book, I want to offer you a discount on signing up for YouTube Marketing Black Belt. **Through the link below only, you can get a whopping 40% off the regular price of the course.**

To learn more about YouTube Marketing Black Belt — and to claim your discount — go to:

15StepsBonuses.com/YouTubeBlackBelt

Schedule An Introductory Call With A Team Member

If you're not sure which program is right for you, then you can talk with a YouTube Advertising Coach on my team who can help you decide.

On the call, you can tell your coach more about your business, your market, and your budget. They'll recommend a solution that they know has worked well for clients in your situation before.

From reading Step 15, you know that I put a lot into getting the best people on my team. The specialist you'll talk to will be highly paid and highly skilled.

Because their time is valuable, they won't be able to give you detailed free advice on how to improve your YouTube advertising on the call. But they can lay out in broad strokes what needs to be done to take your account to the next level — and they can show you which product is the best for your needs.

To schedule a free call with an advertising specialist, go to:

15StepsBonuses.com/FreeConsult

THE END?

This isn't the end. This is the beginning.

The beginning of you reaching new levels of success with YouTube marketing. And hopefully, the beginning of us working together in a bigger way to grow your campaigns.

I encourage you to check out the products and coaching programs I talked about before. But regardless of whether you decide to become a client right now, we should keep in touch!

Here are the best ways for us to stay connected:

First, my YouTube channel (obviously.) You can subscribe to the channel at:

15StepsBonuses.com/YouTubeChannel

You should also subscribe to my email list. You'll get free YouTube marketing tips a few times a week, and I'll also send you exclusive videos I don't post on my channel.

If you're not getting my emails already, get on my list here:

15StepsBonuses.com/Email

And finally, ...if this book helped you improve your YouTube marketing, I'd love to hear your success story! Helping entrepreneurs is the reason why I started this business. If my work made an impact on you, I'd really love to hear about it.

So, send me an email, or make me a video letting me know what you think about the book! I'd especially appreciate video testimonials since they'll help me spread the word to other entrepreneurs.

Send your success stories to me at
dan@socialresponsemarketing.com.

Thank you for reading this book. And cheers to your successful future!